NAKED BEFORE THE M

NAKED BEFORE THE MOUNTAIN

by

PIERRE MAZEAUD

With a Preface by Walter Bonatti

Translated by
GEOFFREY SUTTON

LONDON
VICTOR GOLLANCZ LTD
1974

First published in Germany under the title
Schritte himmelwärts © Heering-Verlag GmbH 1968
Published in France under the title
Montagne pour un homme nu © B. Arthaud 1971
English translation © Victor Gollancz Ltd 1974

ISBN 0 575 01651

Printed in Great Britain by
The Camelot Press Ltd, London and Southampton

*" To my friends who
died where they chose . . ."*

CONTENTS

LIST OF ILLUSTRATIONS

All unacknowledged photographs are from the author's
collection.

PREFACE

PIERRE MAZEAUD is my friend. Those who, like me, have shared with him both the glories and tragedies of mountaineering, and who can thus claim to know him truly, will find this book exactly what they would have expected, vivid and lucid as its author.

Mazeaud is one of the world's leading climbers, a Magistrate and a Deputy. He is also a man whose fine sensitivity and generous emotions win our liking. Few have his gift for describing grandeur in simple phrases. With his flowing, passionate, convincing style he shows us the way to the essential values of life.

These pages of personal narrative are a human document, a profile for a new generation of mountain climbers. I hope that the author will not mind my adding that they are also a healthy gust of fresh air in a world of weakness, of hearts sick with their own listlessness.

WALTER BONATTI

CHAPTER I

Which May Serve as an Introduction

MOST MEN ARE able to rationalize the course of their lives, to find some logic in their vocations. For my part, I must admit to having great difficulty in discovering the origin of my passions, and especially my passion for the mountains.

I suppose that the only plausible explanation lies in my character. I have always loved the combat, spending my energies violently, drawing on my resources to the maximum—sometimes even to a disturbing extent, because one may wonder how long it is possible to hold out at a certain rate.

My father may also have played a decisive role. When we lived at Grenoble, he made me spend my holidays ranging the Dauphiné not only so that I should acquire a love of nature, but also because it gave him an opportunity to make sure that I had learnt the passages from Virgil or Schiller which I would have to construe at school in due course. I hated learning and reciting my lessons so much that my mind must often have floated away towards some steep rock face or summit, the dialogue with which need not be in a dead or foreign language. Thus perhaps already as a child the spirit of revolt brought me into contact with the dizzy world of schist, gneiss, limestone, granite and other difficult geological names. When people tell me nowadays that I am like my father, I reply that I hope not for the sake of my own children.

Although he played the piano so that I should play it—how well I remember those evenings of duets, Ravel's "Mother Goose"—and although he took up Greek so that I should hear it, he introduced me to sport because he was a keen sportsman himself. This was his big mistake: I took to it only too enthusiastically, and he used to have to come and drag me back from the sportsground to my neglected books.

The years went by, and my father and I became friends. At weekends we would range over the surrounding peaks. In time this became a habit, and as the difficulties increased it even happened sometimes that we forgot the German exercises and Latin compositions. I was happy in myself discovering this world of silence which I came to love. In it I found the measure of my character.

The war parted us and I soon began to feel nostaglia for our weekly walks and climbs. My mother went off to be near her wounded husband, and I was left alone in the house, thus becoming my own master. I no longer visited the mountains with their scented paths, birdsong and the rough feel of rock, but lay in the sunshine at the municipal swimming pool or chatted idly with my schoolfriends Collignon and Chatain. In winter I went in for easy ski races. And all the time I was growing.

I was expelled from school for absenteeism, for idleness and even for lack of ability, so that when my father returned I was a perfect pretext for new manifestations of paternal authority. Sadly, I had to leave Grenoble without even saying goodbye to my friends. No doubt I supposed that I would come back; a childhood and all its memories cannot just be rubbed out like that. But I was sixteen years old, and the excitement of new horizons soon effaced my regrets.

CHAPTER II

Return to the Mountains

ALTHOUGH I WAS now living in Paris, my studies were there to keep my feet on the ground. After a short interlude in Normandy I got through my two baccalauréats* with some difficulty, and was proud to be admitted to the philosophy class at Louis-le-Grand. Quite soon I left my father and mother, a rebel as always, and began several wonderful years as a housemaster in a boarding school. My family still having some influence over me, however, my father induced me to go off to Chamonix for the summer. He took a poor view of my behaviour, of the way I had given up practising any sport, and considered it a sort of repudiation of my past.

I already knew the Mecca of the Alps quite well from having skied there on a number of occasions. I now really began to discover the mountains and to return to them as to a shrine to calm the successive crises of youth. A few weeks far from the capital had power to efface the impurities of humdrum city life, even the worst of them. This return to the past must have saved me; in the course of a few years some inner impulsion was to make it my very reason for living.

It was thus in 1947 that I began mountaineering seriously. The great climbers of that time, Terray, Lachenal, Rébuffat, who were later to become friends, were the object of my un-limited admiration. The sport was developing rapidly, and I wanted to throw myself into it body and soul. It came as a frustrating disappointment to learn that mountaineering was a craft which had to be learnt.

We did some long climbs in the region of the Argentière and Tour glaciers. I was impressed by the north faces of the surrounding mountains, and people told me that they were the most beautiful in the world. Meanwhile we trudged up

---

* Translator's note: the French school-leaving examinations. Louis-le-Grand is a famous lycée in Paris, to which it is a distinction to be admitted.

interminable glacier slopes to the foot of the easy rocks of the
Tour Noir or the Pointe des Améthystes.

In order to satisfy me, somebody agreed to take me up
Mont Blanc. I spent a sleepless night at the Grands Mulets
hut, and next morning climbed on up to the Vallot, feeling
rather as though it were a ceremonial. Led by René Payot,
who was to meet his death on the same mountain some years
later, we then sped on to the summit. I felt a somewhat ill-
founded satisfaction in having proved myself as good a man
as the older climbers who accompanied me, and also an
immense joy at looking out from such a height. I was happy
to be standing at over 4800 metres, and cared nothing for the
names of the lower summits around. My intention had been
to leave my childhood behind, and here I was reverting to a
child's delight in this discovery. Later, Mont Blanc was often
to seem to me a veritable Calvary; but what does it matter,
since I am happy there? Fulfilled as I was, the descent naturally
seemed both dull and endless. I wanted to tell people about it
all, to give free rein to my pride. No doubt mountaineers had
a right to my respect, but now I was one of them or at least
soon would be, and already I understood that mountaineering
was something more than the idealized version plains-dwellers
have of it as a school of bravery, purity and self-surpassment.
In fact it was difficult, and demanded passion.

After this experience, the next step was to climb a rock
mountain. The same season I was proud to lead a friend up
the Moine. On the traverse of the Nonne and the Evêque I
got lost and ended up on some slabs where only my agility
saved our lives. I had found a new world from which I desired
never to be separated. I also wanted to keep the secret of it to
myself, and felt a kind of repugnance at the idea of disclosing
it. Above all, I knew that I could return to this haven of peace
each summer. I was determined to become a mountaineer
and envious of those who were so already. Now that I had
returned to the mountains I would never abandon them again.
An annual rendezvous was made: I have never failed to
keep it!

In Paris I found a new way of life full of freedom, but above
all I was making friends, not childhood playmates any longer,
but men absorbed by the same ideas, sharing the same

anxieties, reacting in the same way, puzzling over the same problems of growing up. It was good to meet every evening and wander all night through St Germain from one jazz-cellar to another until, after a plate of soup at les Halles,* we would lie down to sleep somewhere on the quays until it was time for me to go and wake up my pupils at six o'clock. Among these friends were Alain with his romantic, childish face, who wanted to write; Pierre, whose drawings and paintings always seemed imbued with the instability of our lives; and Louis, the intellectual and wit; unforgotten faces.

However, I had not completely lost touch with the world of mountaineering. I still envied its great men and spent hours buried in the books of Welzenbach, Heckmair, Comici, Gervasatti, de Chatellus and Allain. These kept alive the flame whenever the round of daily existence threatened to extinguish it. And finally I was introduced to the rocks of Fontainebleau.

My uncle, another Pierre, was fanatically devoted to "Bleau". Together with Louis, who lodged at my uncle's house, I left the city each Sunday morning to spend the day in strange places with sacred names such as Cuvier, Remparts, Aspremont or Dame Jeanne, and it was there that I experienced my first real rock-climbing. If the leading Parisian mountaineers had not had this training ground on their doorstep at this time, I am sure that certain Alpine ascents would still remain unclimbed, not only on account of their difficulty but because the spirit of enterprise and competition developed on these exceptional outcrops only 50 kilometres from Paris was a decisive factor in their conquest.

Every weekend I practiced without much success on the rocks at Paillon or Prestat, or followed the yellow or red routes, still respectful of leading lights such as Poulet and Poincenot or of others like Lainé, Berardini and Paragot who were becoming members of the same select company. I hardly dared to speak to them, and gladly swallowed the sarcastic comments which I called on my own head. It was a sort of

*Translator's note: the old Paris markets, now destroyed, where it was fashionable for those enjoying a night out to take a bowl of onion soup among the night workers before returning home at dawn.

cult, but also an apprenticeship to manhood. For men they were, as they have many times proved.

Through them, at this period, I discovered the real meaning of mountaineering. In order to understand not only orders of difficulty but the meaning of certain conversations, I plunged headlong into every kind of Alpine literature, avid of knowledge. It was not long before I knew the lives of the great mountaineers in all their detail, and there was hardly a rock in the Alps or other ranges with which I was not familiar.

Fontainebleau, once known only to a privileged few, now widely publicized and almost an obligatory part of a climber's education, was for us a kind of club. The first few steps had something almost solemn about them; and then, quite quickly, one was received into the circle and became part of the scene. Although I have travelled far since then, I still return every year to Fontainebleau to try to revive those first feelings of exaltation.

Even Paris, that all-devouring monster, could not keep us away from our weekly ration of joy, or weaken our longing to escape to the mountains in summer. Already we could feel the difference between ourselves, full of the life of the capital, passing sleepless nights and spending our days in pursuit of objects no sooner attained than forgotten, and the others for whom Fontainebleau was a sort of sacred ritual to be kept up throughout the week. Well, we were quite happy about the difference, and at that age our resilience was such that we could stand anything.

Louis and I were already thinking seriously about the coming Alpine season, and on the strength of our results on these sandstone outcrops a few metres high we were looking forward to doing some of the big climbs. Respectful as we were of the aristocrats of the Parisian climbing world, we wanted to prove to ourselves and others that no climb could withstand our youthful impetuousness. Only our studies held us back at first, and then, one day in July 1949, we were free to go. Owing to the modesty of our means, earned by one as a housemaster and by the other as a litter collector, we started off hitch-hiking from the Porte d'Italie draped in a strange array of equipment purchased at great cost in the shop of "the master", Pierre Allain.

As to projects, our Vallot guidebooks were full of underlined passages, but the main thing was to get away at all. As an introduction to hitch-hiking, it was a fairly horrifying trip. Sometimes one of us would hide in the ditch so as not to perturb some well-intentioned driver. We travelled from Paris to Montargis seated on a load of porcelain bidets before discovering that we were heading the wrong way, and then began the efforts to persuade drivers to take us in the direction of Lyons. Altogether we took four days and five nights to reach Chamonix. We were overcome by lassitude, and even spoke of returning home. After all, did we really care so much about mountains?

However, our grumbling was not intended seriously. We found room at the Paradis des Praz and set up our climbing base camp at Pré du Rocher on the lower slopes of the Aiguilles de Chamonix. There followed wild races up the mountains and back down to our little tent perched high above the valley. Knowing nothing about the mountains, we were none the less determined. Our attempt on the south ridge of the Aiguille du Moine was not particularly reassuring, it is true; Terray and Lachenal had advised against it, and we went astray on pitches which were anything but enjoyable to a pair of beginners. In spite of this, we were convinced that we could do the Charmoz-Grépon traverse.

In the small hours of the morning on the Nantillons glacier memories of my first footsteps in the mountains came flooding back. Then, there had been nothing to do but follow where I was led. Now everything was different, even hostile. We were alone in this world of ice, looking for the way, ignorant of the dangers, disrespectfully confronting a historic traverse.

Leaving part of our equipment at the foot of the Charmoz-Grépon couloir*—rock-climbers like us were sure to be back soon—we tackled the first difficulties. But the finding of the route called for experience in which we were lacking. All we had to go on was the flat description in the guidebook with its tale of distinctive pinnacles, sloping slabs, cracked corners and unclimbable overhangs. Progress was slow, and the number of swear-words matched the increasing difficulties and our growing fatigue. On the summit ridge, instead of the feeling of

* Translator's note: a gully, but the French word is in very common usage among English-speaking climbers.

satisfaction we were expecting, we experienced a thunder-
storm, wind and snow. In a moment everything was changed.
Naturally we had foreseen the possibility of bad weather, but
not like this. It seemed nothing less than unfair to make us
lose our way, and both of us vowed that if we were lucky
enough to get back to camp we would never climb again but
return to Paris where there were pretty girls, jazz music and
the company of our friends.

There was no alternative to retreat. Starting from the
"Bâton Wicks"* we began a series of rappels† which got
shorter and shorter as we cut lengths off our new rope in order
to make slings. The situation became more and more serious
. . . about 60 feet away from the easy Charmoz-Grépon couloir,
the existence of which we did not suspect. At one point, for
lack of a good block to rappel from, I had to hammer in a
piton in an awkward position, only to see it twist over when
Louis' weight came on it. In positions of danger one becomes
simultaneously selfish and devout, and I was no exception.

Back on the glacier our fears melted away and we felt ready
to try again. It was all a big joke, and a couple of Bleausards‡
would always come through.

This first warning should have taught us a lesson, but the
difficulties soon paled in retrospect and already we felt able
to cope with any others we might meet. I thought Louis was
a great rock-climber, and he took me for an experienced
mountaineer. We had only one regret, and that was not to
have measured ourselves against the Grépon. Two days later,
however, matters became more complicated and we had to
change our ideas. The tragic story of 24th July 1949 deserves
to be told.

Hoping to avenge ourselves, we left our tent in its pleasant

* Translator's note: a well-known pinnacle on the ridge of the
Grands Charmoz, named after a member of the party that first
climbed it.

† A method of descent which consists of hooking the centre of
the rope over a piton or convenient piece of rock, then sliding down
the two strands to a ledge where the rope is pulled down and the
process repeated if necessary. Also known in English by the German
word "Abseil". Abseiling from a sling makes the rope less likely to
get stuck when pulled from below.

‡ Somebody who climbs regularly at Fontainebleau.

nook above the Blaitière alp, half way between Montenvers and Plan de l'Aiguille, and set out to do the ordinary route on the Aiguille du Peigne. On the path we overtook a lot of guided parties, and I recognised Clément Hugon. The gully in which the climb begins is noted for being complicated, and having gone slightly astray at one point we waited for one of the other parties to go by. Louis showed great skill in dealing with this maze, and we arrived feeling calm and confident at the fork in the couloir where the difficulties begin in the form of a corner which the Vallot guidebook describes as "the problem".

In order to give ourselves time to study the pitch, we let several parties go by, some of which branched off to climb the Aiguille des Pélerins by the Carmichael route. As some of these parties were climbing very slowly, Louis grew impatient and tried climbing up to the left. There was an anchor piton* which added to the confusion, and it looked as though it would be possible to traverse back to the proper route higher up.

Louis climbed over a small overhang and got to grips with a series of cracks, working his way upwards slowly but surely. The rope ran out through the mousqueton.† I heard him hesitate, looking for holds, and instinctively gripped the rope more tightly. He was trying to find a place to put a piton, and I remember thinking: "It's no good, there isn't anywhere". All around us it was like a sports ground, swarming with climbers using the same jargon and sometimes the same expletives. Louis was tiring and seemed to be trying to get back. He had gone silent. Suddenly I heard an oath and he went flying into space to crash heavily against the rock a few metres below me. I tried to speak to him; people were calling to him from all sides, but the only reply was a few groans. Seized with fear I scrambled down and bent over him. His face was covered in blood. He started slightly like a shocked child and seemed to recognize me. Time passed as I waited for help to arrive, and gradually he returned to consciousness, complaining of pain and blaming himself for having fallen

* A metal spike with a ring on the end, also known as a peg. They may be used either for protection or as an aid to progress.

† A metal link with a spring-loaded gate used for clipping the rope to a sling or a piton. More often called in English by its German name of "Karabiner", or "krab" for short.

off. The mountains had turned hostile, and in my desire to comfort him I did not notice that the weather was changing.

Jean Brunaud arrived with his party. Clearly it was necessary to get Louis off the mountain, and he courageously withstood this long and painful trial. The rope had burnt my arm and shoulder, but in the presence of my friend with his broken arm and leg I preferred not to mention it. As we got back to the fork in the couloir we heard the first crashes of thunder; soon the couloir was in the heart of the storm and everything became an inferno. Shocked by the discharges and jerking like puppets we tried to flee, carrying our companion who neither complained nor groaned.

Above our heads another drama was being played out. Rébuffat overtook us and told us that Welbacher had been killed by a stroke of lightning that had also badly burned Gurékian, leaving an open wound in the thigh, and wounded Pierrot Leroux in the legs. Hospitals, graveyards . . . we had to get out of this place. The first thing was to evacuate the living; another party could come back later for the dead. We owe our lives to Rébuffat who led us down out of that hellish gully with Louis on his back. As they descended the long slab where there is a fixed chain and which the storm had changed into a raging torrent, Louis was almost drowned. His courage impressed everybody. At the bottom of the rocks he was laid on the snow and given a push so that he would slide down the slope. Slide he did, but into the rimaye,* and we had to look for him and pull him out. Dazzled with lightning and deafened with thunder we finally got back to the cable-car station where Pierrot Leroux was waiting for us with Gurékian on his shoulders. The day ended at the hospital in Chamonix. On the way down they told me all about Welbacher, and I learnt that two other parties had met their deaths, one on the Grépon, the other on the Fou.

The mountain had struck. I still wonder what possessed me to go on after that fatal Sunday.

The following day, leaving Louis in hospital for a few days, I went back up to Montenvers on my own, a kind of confused dialogue taking place inside me. We were young and in-

* The rimaye, also known in English by its German name "Bergschrund", is the large crevasse formed around the head of a glacier where it detaches itself from the mountain.

experienced; maybe it would be better to give up. We had only avoided death thanks to the presence of others. It was an introduction to human solidarity; the others had helped us although we were strangers. That night alone at the foot of the Aiguilles was full of anxiety, yet to my uneasiness before that enormous silence my being replied with a message of hope. Because I had been able to suffer, I had been able to know this treacherous mountain world. Henceforward I would approach it differently, with care, realizing that mountaineering is a risky sport where lives may depend on a turn of the dice—a sport, also, which places a premium on human qualities.

Louis quickly recovered. I began to feel some pleasure in the mountains again and set out to improve my knowledge with new companions. I was finding my way back. Like a wounded soldier, I needed to fight again so as to forget my wounds. First came some snow routes like the traverse of Les Courtes and the Pointe Isabelle in the amazing Talèfre cirque, then some climbs in the Aiguilles Rouges to regain my confidence on rock. The Dent du Géant came reassuringly at the end of the season. If the mountains were taken seriously they no longer seemed hostile, and I could love them again.

At the end of September I got my revenge by leading the traverse of the Grépon. I had secretly been getting all the information I could about the pitches and preparing myself for them, thus overcoming the fear of the unknown. I had become fully aware of the mountain environment, and the dialogue which had begun on Mont Blanc could continue. I think it was at this point that I began to love the mountains passionately and could develop into a mountaineer.

Back in Paris, although I continued to climb at Fontainebleau on Sundays, the mountains soon faded from my mind. But Paris is Paris and brings its own kinds of satisfaction; I even discovered politics. Soon I was attending my first meetings at the Mutualité, exchanging closely argued letters with Camus, taking an interest in the Mouvement de la Liberté.*

* A political movement. The Mutualité is a hall in Paris much used for political meetings.

CHAPTER III

The Dialogue Sustained: My First Serious Attempts

THE FOLLOWING SUMMER I returned to the range of Mont Blanc. Louis was anxious to wipe out a disagreeable first impression, and I wanted henceforward to approach mountains in the way I had approached the Grépon, in other words the way which leads to success.

Our first climb was the Forbes ridge of the Aiguille du Chardonnet. We were too slow, and it was under a brazen sun that we reached the saddle before the final descent to the Glacier du Tour. For fear of avalanches we had to wait there, and our bodies bore the stamp of this forced halt for several weeks. Burnt and parched as we were, we were happy to have done this magnificent classic. The view out over the Argentière basin and the north face of the Aiguille Verte made me appreciate the quality of the climb, and when I repeated it six years later my pleasure was hardly abated.

For a long time I had been wanting to traverse the highest summit in Europe, and so it was that Louis and I got to know the dangerous ascent up to the Aiguille du Goûter. Next morning we climbed quickly up the summit ridge in cold, fine weather, and began the descent. Our badly laid course nearly cost us our lives, as we set out towards Mont Blanc de Courmayeur and the enormous precipices that flank the Brouillard ridge. Luckily we discovered our mistake in time and turned back towards the Col de la Brenva, sprinting over Mont Maudit and Mont Blanc de Tacul to the Vallée Blanche. In spite of our mistake in route-finding we had only taken four hours, and proud of our speed we proceeded to lose ourselves in the Géant icefall, so that we only just caught the last train from Montenvers.

Montenvers. It was always good to get back there after a climb, under the envious gaze of the tourists. It made little difference where you had come from; they devoured you with their eyes. The Dru and the Col du Géant produced the same effect on the tripper, who saw crampons, ice-axes, rucksacks and tired men, and jumped straight to a conclusion. For Louis, this was his best and last climb. A few days later he returned to Dakar, and the horrors of military life soon erased the joys of the high summits from his mind.

I was still at the stage of family mountaineering, not yet knowing the great climbers well enough to envisage climbing with them. My uncle and I therefore did a couple of interesting climbs rendered pleasanter by the company of Colette Prieur and Michèle Nallet. The first of these was the Aiguille du Requin by the Voie des Plaques, where I just avoided a first bivouac by arriving back at the hut at 10 o'clock at night, and the second was the traverse of the Aiguilles Dorées where the hand-jamming in the Javelle crack gave me a painful impression of the strenuous climbing offered by the typical Chamonix chimney.

This uncle, who, as I have already said, bore the same name as myself, was a man at once admirable and unbearable, so that I felt a kind of simultaneous rudeness and respect towards him. I spent innumerable Sundays with him at Fontainebleau and later at the Saussois, to which he introduced me as well. During the month of August we mountaineered together, and it gave me much pleasure on difficult pitches to hear him complaining and finally calling me names, older as he was and a friend into the bargain. Later I passed him on to Michel Bastien, who became his regular guide. I have never been able to forget the words he spoke when he knew himself to be dying: "Petit Pierre," he said—for among climbers he was always known as "Grand Pierre"—"at least I passed the finest day and night of my life in the mountains." He meant the south ridge of the Aiguille Noire de Peuteret, where he had been forced to bivouac.

I had been longing to get to grips with the Aiguille Verte, a summit much desired by all novice mountaineers. With Bernard Novel of Lyons I climbed the Moine ridge, a long series of towers and cornices. At that time it was my best climb and my finest four thousand metre summit. As I got out of the Montenvers train on the way back down, I ran into a friend and immediately went back with him to do the Blaitière. After that I felt justified in striking my little tent at Les Praz and returning to Paris and my job as supervisor at the holiday course at Sainte-Barbe—the month of September being paid at double the normal rate.

I felt pleased in a general way with this season, during which I had learnt a great deal by dint of patient work. I had done my climbs in an atmosphere of sufficient calm, and I was no longer completely unknown. Instead of following along behind others, I had become a leader. Nevertheless, I continued to visit Fontainebleau on Sundays, feeling less insignificant and less embarrassed now in the company of the great. Henceforward I could take part in mountain talk and knew my way around sufficiently not to make a fool of myself by mixing up the names of the party that made the first ascent of the Walker Spur with those who made the first ascent of the Pointe Walker.

CHAPTER IV

Living at Last ... for a Time

I DECIDED TO go and do a year's military service at the Ecole militaire de Haute Montagne. My heart was urging me on, and although I did not yet have a very long or impressive list of climbs to my credit, it was enough to get me selected. At last I could live as I wished, in the mountains. Moreover I had reached a stage in my life when I needed to think things over seriously and put an end to a period of carefree youth. I therefore relinquished my exemption and, one day in April 1952, set off to join the 27th Battalion, Chasseurs Alpins, at Annecy.

The first difficulty cropped up at once. They wanted to send me to officers' training school. I refused. A black mark the very first day! I was therefore posted to Bourg-Saint-Maurice, which was a little nearer Mont Blanc, and where I ran into Sennelier, an alumnus of Sainte-Barbe. Barrack life. I was meeting real men from every kind of background, among them Soubize, a voluble Pyrenean who had done a lot of mountaineering and who, at the drop of a hat, would show you hundreds of photos of his first ascents.

Those were halcyon days. We lived in a state of nature, without a care in the world. Sennelier and I would take long, lonely walks in the surrounding hills. Finally our basic military training was over, and we could leave for Chamonix. Dumont and some of the others remained behind; the wild Pyrenean came with us. On our arrival at the E.H.M. we were marched in before the commanding officer, de Thiersant, a leader of men. It was the beginning of an ideal life, in permanent contact with nature, thinking of the Alps and of the great climbs to come, or lazing around at les Pècles.

The army is a kind of melting pot. Into it are cast intellectuals like Giraud, solid Savoyard peasants like Creton and Balmat, rebels like myself, passive personalities like Bonlieu, legendary characters like Laffont to whom we shall have occasion to revert, all in a sort of ferment.

My reputation as a mountain-lover having preceded me,

I was immediately attached to the Ski Scouts, which in practice meant that all I had to do was to climb all summer and ski all winter. I was even detailed off to take a certain second lieutenant climbing on Sundays, a weighty matter indeed since the man had a university degree. Suffice it to relate the first and the last of the climbs which we did together.

We bivouacked near the Montenvers with a view to traversing the Grépon next day. Military discipline was maintained between the officer and his subordinate that quiet evening, though he was not reticent in retailing his mountain experience. I was almost impressed. The following morning I let him take precedence on the path, then on the glacier. At the rimaye we roped up, and gradually we reached the foot of the Mummery Crack. I climbed up and took in the rope. Our bold candidate then began to behave strangely. The past master of mountaineering, who had been boasting about his great deeds, did not seem to be doing so well. In the end he had to be pulled and even cursed. The formalities went by the board, and from then on he got plain speaking as used by other ranks. The rest of the climb was in the same style, and I had to haul him bodily up the final crack to the summit. On the way back down the glacier, however, he became as overweening as before. It was insufferable.

He next decided to redeem himself, and by swinging his rank while the section was on consignment he got authorization to climb the Grépon again, this time by the Mer de Glace face. As far as I was concerned all that mattered was to be up in the mountains, and if I had a sack to drag up behind me, what did I care? Not one word did I speak on the way up to the Tour Rouge hut; and the following day, amid the atmosphere of those astonishing slabs, I paid but scant attention to my second. From the Brèche Balfour I climbed the Knubel crack alone, having no great interest in renewing the hoisting operation, and himself no great interest in the summit. Our relations came to an end at this point, as I thought, but the man had a long memory and a few months later made me pay dearly for his adventures.

Climbing mad as I was, I was always looking for companions. Unfortunately many of my contemporaries saw their national service as the occasion for a rest cure, and once away from compulsory operations and forced marches they spent all their time in the National or the Choucas, two well-known Chamonix bistrots.

At this time I had a couple of scarcely believable adventures. The first was when, thinking I was on the Dru, I ended up at nightfall on the lower part of the Aiguille Sans Nom, completely lost. What is more, this comic incident was repeated a few years later, as though experience must be undergone more than once to be fully absorbed. On this second occasion, having set off for the Tour Verte, I found myself below the summit block of the Aiguille de Roc.

The second adventure was just as incredible. Tired of being on my own, I persuaded Soubize to accompany me. Somewhat calmer and more restrained than during our days at Bourg-Saint-Maurice, he consented not to be ill for once. As a training climb we therefore did a little first ascent, the traverse of the Clochetons de Planpraz in reverse. I still remember having some difficulty with the pegging on the central pinnacle. We also did the Ménégaux route on the Aiguille de l'M in quite a rapid time, but to the best of my knowledge these were the only two times when our southerner felt fit. Like many others of my friends, he was so subject to sudden fatigue when faced with the prospect of getting up to climb in the morning, as for example at the foot of the south ridge of the Fou and the Y couloir on the Aiguille Verte, that it made one envisage taking up solo climbing.

My father came up to see if military service left me any time for working on my doctoral thesis in law, but was not really surprised to find me wholly preoccupied with mountaineering. We spent several days together, and I took him up the NNE ridge of the Aiguille de l'M and the Doigt d'Etala. These were moments of subtle satisfaction in getting my own back at last. He came through the test with flying colours, cursing the war for the wound he had received in one knee in the Vosges in 1945, and rediscovering a pleasure which Paris had effaced from his mind. Since that time he has returned every year, and at sixty-five has done most of the classic climbs. Living at Fontainebleau, he goes out each morning to train for his week-end at Saussois or his summer holiday in Vésubie or at Chamonix. His usual guides, my friends Vaucher and Desmaison, are constantly surprised by his energy in the Dolomites and the western Alps. It is true that on one occasion

I had to threaten to unrope in order to induce him to follow me up a delicate pitch, but his unaccustomed gentleness prevented me from carrying out the threat. How many wonderful moments I owe him. To learn that at his age he is still thinking of routes like the north face of the Dru fills me with pride and hope.

Winter at the Ecole de Haute Montagne was wonderful, a real life consisting of a heady mixture of skiing and leaves in Paris. In January, however, the second lieutenant whom we left on the Grépon reared his head again. Running into him one day in Mégève, and no doubt slightly the worse for drink, I let him have the rough edge of my tongue. Although the commanding officer demurred he stuck to his guns, and I was led away by the military police to the disciplinary camp at Clermont-Ferrand and clapped under close arrest, a communist, an outlaw, and worst of all insolent to an aspiring officer. Not very long before, my friend Balmat had been sent off to a similar unit for almost helping the same gentleman to break some kind of speed record by simply giving him a push down the side of the Egralets. Our recollections of the next five months were remarkably similar, and Chardonnet knows full well that if ever the day comes when his fate depends on us we shall be of one mind.

In a world of good soldiers I must have merited disgrace, but since nothing lasts forever what does it matter? From garbage orderly, pulling my cart of rubbish out of town under the surveillance of two armed men, I graduated to master of prison ceremonies. It was something of a shock to exchange the good life under the shade of the Chamonix larches for the bare walls of a correction camp in the Vauban, and the arrangements of a friendly commanding officer for the orders of an impersonal colonel: such was the military career of one unimportant soldier who, all things considered, did not do too badly during his twelve months' service.

Finally it was all over. I was thinking of marriage, turning over a new leaf, settling down to work and founding a family. While writing my thesis I served a term at the bar, then another with a solicitor, before burying myself in the monotonous, meaningless life of an office. There was little time left for Chamonix, but with the ineffable Pipo Laffont I did succeed in making the second ascent of the Aiguille Pourrie,

the name of which speaks for itself,* and, thanks entirely to
my own fault, in suffering a resounding defeat on the north
ridge of the Aiguille de Peigne. It is written that I shall never
reach the summit of that mountain.

Simply to keep in training, according to my father, I passed
the examinations for the magistracy, a kind of obligation in
our family, and began to lecture on Roman and civil law at
the university. I became aware, also, that this contact with
my students would save me from growing old and set in my
ways.

One Sunday in 1953, at last, I came to know the Saussois.
Since that time few weekends have gone by without my being
there. I thirsted to know all the different routes, and thus I
developed into a rock-climber. There on the banks of the
Yonne I found real friends, Berardini, Couzy, Paragot, the
cream of the Parisian mountaineers. Thanks to their encouragement I stuck to this apprenticeship, and the majority of my
first ascents are primarily due to them. At that time they
were getting ready for the expedition to Aconcagua, and when
Berardini remarked one day during a visit to Bastien in hospital
that their glory would be measured by the number of amputa-
tions, he spoke no more than the truth. In the event, only one
person escaped without any.

* Translator's note: pourri = rotten.

CHAPTER V

The End of a Myth

AT THIS TIME I was absorbed in my daily round of work, but at weekends I went off to train in the Ardennes or, when there was time, at Chamonix. My regular companion was Robert Dubois. Our approach to climbing was the same, a kind of gambling. As the year went on, we began to think of more than merely classic climbs. Our successes in outcrop climbing and our habitual teamwork incited us to push our standard higher; we enjoyed both free and artificial climbing, and sometimes spent whole days hanging from pitons. We were of an age when one believes in one's possibilities, and took our training very seriously. In the spring we climbed les Ecrins and les Agneaux on skis.

During these years I managed some pleasant climbs at Chamonix, brands snatched from the fire between the claims of married life. Gradually I became more integrated in the life of the mountains, and by my persistence harder and more serious ascents became possible. In 1956 I climbed the north faces of the Aiguille du Plan and the Piz Badile, and the following year the Grand Capucin, the south ridge of the Aiguille Noire de Peuterey, and the traverse of the Aiguilles de Diable.

It was Philippe Dreux who really introduced me to ice-climbing, and I have vivid memories of the maze of ice-towers on the Plan. Even more impressed by the leader than by the difficulties, I finally took over the lead so as to move a bit faster. That day gave me my first real view of the Chamonix face of the Aiguille du Fou, awakening in me the desire to make the first ascent.

The Badile was quite a different story. We were a party of four, Cauderlier, Vidal, Robert Dubois and myself. From Chamonix we headed over the Forclaz and the Simplon past the Italian lakes with their innumerable customs posts, a route which I was to get to know. We slept out near Como. In the morning, after a cheerful start, we crossed the frontier yet again and drove up to Promontogno and Bondo, surely the

Pitons, karabiners, étriers—the bricabrac of artificial climbing

Climbing a roof overhang by artificial means

two most beautiful villages in the world with their shingled roofs. As we walked up towards the hut through the tall grass, the famous precipice unveiled itself. Here we met Vaucher, still quite a little boy, whose companion had recently been drowned in a mountain torrent. The Badile is a peak which casts a special spell of its own, woven of the dramatic story of the first ascent. We passed a restless night, thinking of Cassin and his companions. For all four of us it was our first really big climb, and we were in a state of some trepidation crossing the glacier next morning by torchlight.

The corner with which the climb begins seemed easy enough —five years later, in winter, it was to take me a whole day— and I carried on up the succeeding pitches. There were difficult horizontal traverses, and as our fatigue increased we slowed down. The pitch after the first Cassin bivouac seemed to me the most exposed on the entire face; I found myself battling in an awkward, overhanging chimney. Perhaps I was off the route, but more probably I had not tackled it the right way. Finally we came to the snow-patch in the middle of the face where we could take a rest. The view over the Piz Cengalo was magnificent, while that across the central gully was horrifying . . . yet it fascinated me.

It was typical Bregaglia climbing with good holds on sound rock. Robert and I led through. Before the roof overhang where Cassin showed his mettle I felt worried, but there were plenty of pitons and I got round it easily, without using étriers. Then came chimneys running with water and the second Rébuffat bivouac. The final traverse was so fine that I called out to Robert that it was like being at Saussois or la Rèche, delicate and altogether delectable. It is followed by a rappel, after which comes a sense of relief at having finished with the main difficulties. We found our way up the gully below the summit in darkness, and passed a chilly bivouac on the summit ridge. The night seemed unending, but we felt a peace that we may never again recapture, exchanging impressions and memories of particular pitches. We were all agreed on the beauty of the climb, and I still think that it is one of the finest faces in the Alps. The technical difficulties are not extreme, but the climbing is free and elegant.

For us it was a kind of confirmation. As we were the fifth French party to do the climb, it represented a graduation to

B

the ranks of the élite. Our methodical training had paid off, and we could hope for an outstanding end to the season.

It did not take us long to run down to the Gianetti hut, where Robert and I left Cauderlier and Vidal and set off, relaxed, calm and proud, to cross over the Passo di Bondo. After the glacier came the forest and the scent of pines. That evening, the adventure over, we were back beside the limpid waters of the lake of Como, thinking of Cassin and his epic battles on the Badile, the Cima Ovest di Lavaredo and the Walker spur of the Grandes Jorasses, which all climbers worthy of the name long to repeat. And indeed one repeats them rather like a pilgrimage, feeling deep respect for their author's super-human struggles.

The following year, as I have already stated, we did our first big artificial climb in the high Alps, the Bonatti route on the Grand Capucin. The party consisted of Robert, who was on great form, our Belgian friend Jean Alzetta, Pierre Courtet and myself. The climb was not fully pegged-up in those days, and we weighed all the equipment carefully before deciding what to take, a ceremonial occasion.

The evening passed quickly in the company of the likeable guardian at the cosmic laboratory near the Aiguille du Midi. We were late getting up in the morning, and it was midday before we started up the snowslopes leading to our climb. Sometimes it is best to forget about the time. With Robert leading, it did not take long to climb the initial grade VI slab. Pitch after splendid pitch followed, all artificial. It is truly an exceptional route, a masterpiece of design. Not a fault in the rock is neglected, and everywhere one feels the hand of the master. Two especially striking passages are the difficult mantelshelf on to the first bivouac ledge and the pitch of free climbing which follows it, exceptional on this climb. As dark-ness fell, I attacked the traverse leading to the foot of the 40 metre wall, banging at the pegs and feeling around for the horizontal crack like a blind man. Finally I got so tired that I dropped off to sleep, and it was two hours before the anguished cries of my companions woke me up.

It was a comfortable bivouac. Next morning the classic scene took place, everyone sleepy and stiff, cursing each other and the mountain, wishing they were at the seaside, etc. I pegged my way up the 40 metre wall, which certainly bears

Bonatti's trademark, then at two-thirds of the way up fell off.
I was held after a few metres, and climbed on to the comfortable ledge which was the site of Bonatti's second bivouac.
All we were missing was water. We paused for a few minutes
to speak to Trotskiar and Salson as they passed by a thousand
feet below on their way to the Grand Pilier d'Angle. How small
they looked! Then I set off into the long, twisting corner
which follows. After a few more pitches I reached the third
Bonatti bivouac. At this point we noticed that the sky was
clouding over rapidly. Our friends, who were still on the big
platform below, called up that they were going to retreat, and
began to prepare to abseil. The wind was rising. A storm of
hail struck the face of the mountain, then gave way to snow.
Alone on my stance, I unroped, cursing, and with some
difficulty succeeded in roping down to join Robert. Another
rappel and we were back on the edge of the north face, swinging
awkwardly to reach the stance. I was furious. We had to get
down the north face. After abseiling 60 metres in the raging
storm I looked around for the belay pitons left behind by
others who had suffered similar misfortunes. Finally I saw two
Simonds sprouting from a smooth, black, inhospitable slab in
the midst of the driving snow. Without any other form of protection I clipped an étrier to one of them and waited as the others
came by. The peg was beginning to twist from the weight of
four men, but we had to keep descending. Without knowing
where I should end up I launched out into another rappel,
and as though by a miracle arrived in the gully which runs
across the bottom of the face. The rimaye was below, and in
the total darkness I carried on down into it, having to make
desperate efforts to get out on the other side or remain in its
depths forever. We fled in extremis towards the Col du Géant,
and a few hours later I bumped into the ski-lift cabin which
had been carried away by the wind. Now that we knew where
we were, we were saved. We trudged on to the Torino hut.
Everything was locked and barred, so I broke down the door.
Next day we returned to Chamonix via the Aiguille di Midi,
cursing the Capucin as we passed by it.
    The weather improved, and with new plans in mind we set
out for Courmayeur, that astonishing village to which I was
to return so often, then the Val Veni with its fantastic view of
the Brenva face, and the Aiguille Noire de Peuterey which

evoked thoughts of the struggles of Welzenbach and his friends.

Up at the Aiguille Noire hut, Robert and I met up with two old acquaintances, Dreux and Soubize. The madder one is the more one laughs, but came the dawn. I took the eminent ice-climber on my rope, Robert the Pyrenean expert on his. Some people find this a wonderful climb, but I was annoyed by the lack of technical difficulty. It is true that I was on exceptional form, and poor Dreux was suffering the effects. The only parts that gave me anything to think about were the corner and traverse on the fifth tower. Soubize was blazing away with his camera like a machine gun. Slowed up by the size of the party, we bivouacked below the summit. Next morning the descent was a long-drawn-out torture of abseils over vertical earth and ice-pitons planted in tufts of grass. It took us ten hours to get back to the hut in the coomb known as the Fauteuil des Allemands. I blame it all on our friend Toni Gobbi, who had sketched out the route for us on a piece of paper!

At Aosta I met my wife and children, but refusing to make any sacrifice in the name of tourism I went straight back to Chamonix.

Now I had seen the Italian side of Mont Blanc I was hypno-tized by it. It seemed a world apart, and one that I must get to know at all costs. Henceforward the Innominata, Brouillard and Peuterey were to keep me awake at night, but happily I had no foreboding that one day I would have to fight for my life up there and to mourn four friends.

Still with the same party, I ended the season with the traverse of the Aiguilles de Diable. The Isolée stands apart from the other pinnacles of the group; one waits for it to appear in order to sum it up. Why has it not been named after Armand Charlet, who was the first to climb it? Robert climbed it like a set piece, disdaining all aid and security as he moved over the overhang. When I reached the same spot I launched out too and was soon on the summit. There was no need to say anything, just a look and a feeling of friendship. There in the background, the Capucin seemed to be sneering at us. The ascent up to the summit of Mont Blanc de Tacul was slow and heart-breaking, but down the other side it was a mad dash to get to the Aiguille du Midi in time to catch the cable-car and so down to Chamonix, flushed with enthusiasm.

From that time on I no longer saw the mountains in a

mythical light: we had come to terms. I had become aware of my own capabilities. Henceforth I could get to know the mountains, to look on them as great friends, but friends which I could judge. New difficulties were coming into reach, and that winter I had plenty to dream about.

CHAPTER VI

Reality at Last

ALTHOUGH MOUNTAINEERING had become an obsession, as these pages bear witness, I still had to earn a living. It is time for me to admit that I never stick long at anything which does not really interest me. I approach my work and my life in the same spirit as my weekends climbing. No doubt this is wearing, both to myself and to those I meet on my way, but one must try to do everything in order to have nothing to regret. This period of my life was full of troubles, which also impelled me to escape frequently into the mountains. I had made the most of Paris—one can only really enjoy it in freedom—and now I detested it. Though married, I was alone. Thus I spent much time dreaming of mountaineering, and as with all dreams a certain proportion came true.

Robert Dubois having also got married, we saw nothing more of each other. I passed my weekends at Saussois with Couzy, Desmaison, habitués such as the inexhaustible Berardini and Paragot who are still regulars even today, and newcomers such as Jacquemard and Mevel. To tell the truth I had no real projects, so I just set off quietly for Chamonix. There was a lot of rain that year, and after seventeen wet days in succession we tended to cluster more willingly in the Bar du Soleil than on the buttresses or north faces.

To make the most of a moment of relatively good weather, I climbed the old Brenva route on Mont Blanc with Guido Magnone, Ravier and Merle. Originally we had intended to try the Route Major, but once we got up to the Col de la Fourche hut Magnone for some reason proposed the Old Brenva. For us the main thing was just to be on this grandiose face, and nobody raised any objection. Everything here is on a different scale. The silence hangs heavily, only broken from time to time by the roar of falling ice, and the mountaineer feels dwarfed by so much grandeur and beauty.

Feeling on great form, I took over the lead when we reached the Col Moore. Rain had been falling at very high altitude, rendering the ice-slopes beyond the col extremely difficult, so we all tied together on one rope. For hours I had to hack steps in the rotten, dangerous surface. Each time I ran out the rope, I placed an ice-piton for security. On the delicate final traverse under the seracs I was at the limit of balance. It was from this point that my dear friends Marysette Agnel and Maurice Claret her husband fell twelve hundred metres to their deaths the following day. I now own their little chalet below the Brévant, where their son often comes to visit me.

Exhausted as we were on reaching the Col de la Brenva, we committed the folly of traversing the north face of Mont Blanc, despite the danger of windslabs, in order to reach the Vallot hut directly. There followed an equally exhausting descent to the Grands Mulets, ploughing through the snow up to our waists. It was particularly bad for the heavily built Guido. Back at the old hut Roger Merle got busy with cooking our supper; that feeling of relaxation after the climb is one of the pleasures of mountaineering. That night we slept comfortably, then returned to Chamonix next day.

Once again the rain and snow set in, and all the time the holidays were going by. René Desmaison and Jean Couzy, just back from their first ascent of the north ridge of the Aiguille Noire, suggested that I should join them and the well-known skier Collet on a trip to the Dolomites. To say that I was overjoyed would be an understatement. It was wonderful to be setting off together in my little black Renault. After Brescia came the city of Trento and the first limestone crags, then a short halt at the Sella pass to climb one of Tissi's routes, then the Pordoi range and at last Cortina, a pearl set in a ring of mountains. All was sunlight and joy. We drove on up to the foot of the Tre Cime and the Mazzorana hut, the palace of Lavaredo.

Jean and René had important plans, and although they did not succeed in putting them into practice, it meant that for the first few days Collet and I climbed together. We began with the Spigolo Giallo, and I confess to having been surprised. The initial corner gives magnificent climbing, but the pitches of grade IV which follow are unexpectedly fine. The climb bears the signature of its author, the great Comici. There were no pitons to belay to, and I was afraid in case Collet should get into difficulty. He is a great, powerful monster of

15 stone, which had enabled him to approach Toni Sailer's times at the Cortina Olympic Games. The final pitches are impressive in the extreme. At this point I caught up with a party led by Serge Coupé, and both of us were gripped by the view between our feet. A number of people had fallen 1000 feet from here without even touching the rock; indeed, it had happened only the previous day, and all the pitons in the final groove had been torn out. Nor was this the end of the horrors. Two Austrians had just been killed on the descent, and I launched out into the first rappel in a state of great nervous tension.

I wanted to efface all this death and fear from my mind. While René and Jean set off to climb the German direct route up the north face of the Cima Grande, a marvellous line which I shall have occasion to refer to again, Collet and I attacked the Comici route which begins a few yards to the right. On reaching the top of the first pitch, however, my solid second man declared that he was feeling tired, so we had to abseil off. Back at the hut, my head hanging low, and furious with Collet, I ran into Louis Durand, a friend from France. He had not done a lot of rock-climbing, but on the spur of the moment I suggested doing the climb to him.

It turned into a wonderful day. All the way up I relived the contest of Comici and the Dimai brothers with the rock on this fantastic face. Pitch followed difficult pitch, culminating in the exit from the overhanging part of the face, where I had been told that I would find a rope hanging down. Instead, the wind was blowing it out horizontally, and short of both holds and protection I threw myself desperately into a mantelshelf that finally landed me clear of the verticality and the difficulties. Higher up, near the crossing of the summit, I trod delicately again, thinking of the young German who had fallen at this point a few years previously. On this mountain every step has a story. We emerged from the final chimneys in pitch darkness and bivouacked on the spot, happy to have completed this great climb.

I am always happy to take my friends climbing, but I must record that Louis Durand's joy made me happier than I had ever been. He could not stop talking about it. He had dreamed of this climb, and now it had become a reality. He was fulfilled almost to the point of delirium.

Next evening, back at the hut, René and Jean reappeared after making the third ascent of the Brandler route. It was a great occasion. The television reporters were out in strength, and Couzy's judgement immediately went the rounds: "The hardest of the lot. More serious than the Cima Su Alto. Terrible, even when fully pegged."

René suggested to me that we might try the Cassin route on the Cima Ovest. He had done it already, but for me it was a dream coming true. René led. He was on astonishing form and used a minimum of pitons. I followed him like his shadow, depegging rapidly. Soon we came to the famous traverse where Pompanin had hung a railway compartment notice saying "It is dangerous to lean out", and indeed, climbing as second man with my pockets stuffed full of Prusik loops, I nearly fell off. The pitch is almost at the limit of possibility, and between one's legs is a vista of receding cliff on which, by contrast with the somehow more inviting Cima Grande, one feels lost and frightened. Just a few of Cassin's original pitons; the solitude is oppressive. A year later the two of us were to spend an entire week attached to this great face. Presently we came to the end of the overhanging section; ahead it was sounder and merely vertical, and the yellow rock gave way to grey-blue, and finally black. Seven hours from the time we had started we were on the summit, the fastest time up to then.

By about 2 p.m. we were back at the foot of the mountain, planning to repeat Toni Egger's feat of climbing the north face of the Cima Grande the same day. Unfortunately Couzy and Weber had borrowed our car, so we grumblingly gave up our project.

When Couzy got back he seemed slightly put out by our speed; he himself had had to bivouac on the climb. In effect, René had just demonstrated that he had now become the best French climber, and, I would add, the safest. He was to be my teacher for the next two years, and I owe him all that I have become.

Chamonix is like a magnet, drawing us back from wherever else we wander in the Alps. I wanted to end the season with a big first ascent. From the Col de la Fourche I had observed the magnificent pillar of rock which rises 600 metres from the Combe Maudite to the summit of the Isolée. On arrival, however, I now learnt that it had just been done by a Swiss party. I decided to try for the second ascent nevertheless, and made a rendezvous at the cosmic research laboratory on the Aiguille du Midi with my friend Nano Vernotte and two Belgians, Foquet and Duchesne, who were to be killed in Greenland soon afterwards with Alzetta and Nadine Simandl.

The night passed as nights do before a big climb. Having no description of the route, we were in a state of some tension, as before a first ascent. In the small hours of the morning we hurried down the glacier by the light of our head-torches, then round the Grand Capucin. As day broke I was already climbing the ice-slope that led to the first rocks.

I felt on form, and the pitches went by. I particularly remember a very delicate traverse from one line of cracks to another, where Nano and the Belgians left behind the pitons I had placed with so much difficulty. The early part of the pillar is in the shade, hostile and sombre, mostly free climbing. Towards noon we came to the much easier central section which robs the ascent of unity. Still, there were a few severe pitches, and then, late in the afternoon, we came to some splendid artificial climbing; I had never done artificial at such high altitude before. There was a magnificent cracked corner, not particularly exposed, where I stood in the top rungs of my étriers, placing the pitons as far apart as I could, while Nano watched me attentively. The ropes came tight or slack at just the right moment, as though we were practising on an outcrop. From every point of view, I had the perfect second. It was difficult to escape from the corner at the top, but this led to an ample ledge where we decided to bivouac when Duchesne had finished depegging. He was fifty-one years old at the time; we called him "Papa".

It was a pleasant bivouac. We chaffed each other as one usually does on these occasions when the next day seems unlikely to bring any particular difficulty. There was no problem about route-finding, as we were right on the crest of the ridge. We ate, chatted and slept under the icy stars. The moon shone on the Brenva face. Towards morning we saw lights heading towards Col Moore and knew that it must be time to get out of our sleeping bags. This is always the worst part, but one soon forgets about it.

I was expecting to find easy rock, but everything was covered in clear ice and I had to battle for hours in these unpleasant conditions. Across on the crest of the ridge the sunlight was beckoning to me, and finally, with extreme difficulty, I was able to traverse to the right. The wall was compact, over-hanging, and offered neither holds nor cracks for pegging. After some initial hesitation, I got across it on some tiny rugo-sities. The ropes were sticking, and I cursed Nano roundly although it was no fault of his that they ran through so many angles. At last I reached the ridge, and all was sunlight and joy again. Some grooves of medium difficulty led to the summit, where we lolled brewing tea and watching some Polish climbers making a belated ascent of the 700 metre Boccalate couloir that dropped away below our feet. Before us rose the Aiguilles de Diable. I thought of the various pitches, the traverses of the Pointes Carmen and Médiane. Two rappels then took us down to the little col which separates the Isolée from the main ridge. Once again we endured the slow, endless grind up to the summit of Mont Blanc de Tacul at over 4000 metres. Rotten snow, rotten rock, and time flying by; a real punish-ment. Once the difficulties are over the nerves are relaxed and fatigue increases. It is the sort of ascent on which one talks to oneself. It was impossible to hurry, but ultimately the joy of having won through again triumphed over all other feelings. At last we came to the summit. On the way down we sank deeply into the snow, but it didn't seem to matter. By evening we were back at the "Cosmiques". The circle had been closed; we could sleep.

During the month of January, Desmaison came to see me. We had been training seriously together on the Saussois for some time, and now he proposed that we should make a winter ascent of the east face of the Grand Capucin. I was caught up in the idea, and accepted at once; this would be the final initiation.

Heavily loaded, we drove through the night from Paris to Chamonix and caught the first cable-car up to the Aiguille du Midi. Taking leave of friends who were doing the Vallée Blanche, we skied slowly down. The face appeared to be in climbable condition, and at 5 o'clock we set up our bivouac at the foot. As night fell, the wind and snow began to whirl about the tent, and we constantly had to get up and shake the walls and roof clear of the encroaching mass. The condensation was awful, and we were soon soaked to the skin. The nights are long in the mountains in winter, and we whiled away the time by talking. We knew that the climb was out of the question; the problem was how to get down the Vallée Blanche.

In the morning the clouds were so thick that it was hard to see more than about a metre ahead. Battered by the wind and roped together, we left the Capucin behind, groping our way down to the icefall. The visibility was as bad as ever. It took us nine hours to reach Chapeau, where we encountered Gendre and Dubost who had been trying the Aiguille Verte.

A week later I saw René off at the airport on his way to Jannu in the Himalayas. That evening I had a lecture to give at the Faculty of Law. A student who was reading Le Monde announced that two Italians had made the first winter ascent of the east face of the Capucin. I cursed them and the student too!

The spring of 1958 remains for me the great moment of my life, for it was then that I met Pierre Kohlman, my best friend. From that time until his death we were inseparable, both in Paris and in the mountains. One day in the Ardennes, Alzetta was trying to do a climb called "La corde magique" without artificial aid. I tried in my turn, without success. At that moment Kohlman appeared and went calmly up, suppleness and harmony in every movement. It was quite clear that he was a better climber. We went on and did a few more climbs together, not speaking much because he was deaf and had to wear a hearing aid, but we understood each other. In his life as in his climbing, Pierre was balanced and exceptional. There was an element of eternity in his smile. By the time we left the Ardennes we had learnt to know one another and to appreciate our shared passion for rock climbing. I drove him back to Paris, and from then on we were never apart until a black destiny robbed me of my truest friend.

CHAPTER VII

The Pains and the Pleasures

THE YEAR 1959 was a kind of methodical preparation. Desmaison and I had a project to pay homage to the memory of the greatest of French mountaineers, Jean Couzy, who had been killed early in November by a falling stone on the Pic de Bure. The news reached us at the Saussois, where we had just completed the first ascent of the hardest route on the crag, symbolically called "l'Ovest". Though only 50 metres high, it had taken three days and called for seventeen expansion bolts in succession. Immediately, we set off for Jean's funeral at Montmaur. By a curious irony, when I had been climbing with Couzy only a week earlier, he had told me that we should clip in to all the pitons because he intended to go on living and climbing for a long time.

On our way back to Paris, we decided to try to carry out Couzy's project of putting a direct route up the north face of the Cima Ovest di Lavaredo. René went off on an expedition to the Himalayas but wrote to me regularly once a week, and I replied. Meanwhile, I went on training and assembled the equipment. The only problem was to find two more companions, as the climb would call for a party of at least four. Still by post, we agreed that Kohlman and Lagesse should be asked to join us. Secretly I revealed our plans to them, and thenceforward the three of us spent all our spare time making ready.

At this time, linked by our friendship, Pierre and I climbed an uncountable number of routes each weekend at the Saussois. On one occasion I remember that we soloed the Arête Jaune and the Echelle, one behind the other. Pegging away in turn, we engineered the Pilier de l'Echelle and a direct connexion between it and the Super-Echelle. The competitive spirit was germinating in us, encouraged by René's letters. We had one idea, to succeed. Our thoughts were fixed on June and the great unclimbed stretch of rock to the left of the Cassin route.

Our friends felt well enough that something was up, but we

kept our secret. I left my car in its garage and went everywhere on foot. As the winter went by, we sometimes bivouacked in Pierre's garden. Gradually the days and the months passed until René came back from Jannu. Two days later we were ready to go.

It was Saturday evening when our cars reached the rendezvous at the Porte d'Italie, my old black Dauphine and Bernard Lagesse's 2CV. We kissed our wives goodbye on the pavement. All four of us felt ready for the finest adventure of our lives; the harder the fight, the greater the satisfaction. Late that night we bivouacked on the verge of the road near Belfort. When we woke in the morning, we were thrown into consternation by hearing on the radio that an Italian party was attacking the north face of the Cima Ovest. After so many preparations, after keeping our secret so carefully . . . but we decided to go on anyway. After all, there were plenty of other things to do.

So on we drove through Bâle, Zürich, over the Arlberg pass, where we spent our second night, down the Tyrol, thinking of Hermann Buhl as we passed through Innsbruck, then over the Brenner to Dobbiaco. About 5 o'clock in the afternoon we stopped: there in the distance were the north walls. René and I knew them already, but Pierre and Bernard were shocked at first, then began to exult over the majesty of those prodigious faces.

We drove rapidly through Cortina so as not to be seen, then on up to the "Mazzorana palace" where we were immediately informed about the situation. The members of the Scoiattoli* were competing with two of our Swiss friends, Weber and Schelbert, for the first ascent of the direct route. It was a combat of giants. The Italians were fielding their full team, including Lacedelli, Franceschi, Zardini and, above all, Michielli, who was to become my friend.

Michielli's nickname was Strobel. Together with Stenico, Aste, Zeni, Maestri and Franceschini, he was in the top rank of Dolomite climbers of his time. One day, while climbing alone, he slipped. A year later to the day, also while climbing alone, Zeni joined him in the eternal silence. Their loss was felt by mountaineers the world over.

* Translator's note: Scoiattoli = squirrels, the name of a famous climbing group from Cortina.

We were now going to join battle with these titans by trying to open up a more elegant line to the left, where the overhanging zone was 300 metres high and the difficulties more sustained. Already that first night at the Auronzo hut the fever got into our blood. It began to snow, but who cared? We spent the evening getting our gear ready to carry up to the foot of the face. There were almost a hundred pitons, fifty karabiners, thirty or so wooden wedges, three 80 metre ropes, plus food, drink and stimulants for a week.

We set off very early, heavily loaded. It was still snowing. The wind buffeted us and suddenly the clouds parted, revealing the north face and its overhangs like a hallucination above us. It was a moment of realization. Both the Swiss and the Italians had retreated because of the weather. Overhead, ropes hung clear of the rock; at the foot of the wall was stacked a veritable armoury of equipment, hundreds of pitons and wedges, dozens of ropes. A hundred metres above us a sack was hanging from a piton, but in order to look at it we had to crane over backwards. Pierre and Bernard were overawed by the proportions of the overhang, and indeed it is difficult to conjure up. A sense of despair began to overcome me also. Only René retained his lucidity and wandered along the foot of the face to find what was to become the start of the French route.

Setting down the sacks, we began to study the face, but soon began to feel dizzy. The overhanging zone was fully 100 metres higher than where the Italians had attacked. The rock was all yellow* and the exit was barred by a roof overhang of ten metres. It was an effort to imagine climbing here at all, it all looked so impossible. Heart, muscles and mind all grew tense at the thought of spending a week in such a situation. Surely this represented the limit of human possibility; yet there to our right was the work of the Swiss and Italians to reassure us. We would have something to say in the matter too. One of the strangest, most horrifying chapters in the history of climbing was about to be written. The competition for the first ascents of the north faces of the Eiger and Grandes Jorasses was perhaps equally keen, but at least the competitors were not climbing side by side.

No doubt because we were overimpressed, we went back

* Translator's note: and therefore loose.

down to the hut. All day long we were jumpy, keeping our fear
to ourselves, making hearty jokes. Pierre looked serious, René
kept a tight control of himself, Bernard trembled, and I had
the air of someone on whom realization has just burst in.

Next morning dawned fine, and there was a crowd at the
foot of the face. The Italians got away early. Having learnt of
our project, they wanted to reach the top first. As far as we
were concerned, there was no doubt about this: they were
already 200 metres ahead of us, close to the Kasparek bivouac
and thus to the existing finish of the Cassin route. The only
competition we could offer was on the score of severity.
Lacedelli was sure that our line was impossible. Only Strobel
encouraged us before seizing the end of a rope that was hanging 30 metres out from the face and climbing it on Prusik
loops. It was horrifying to watch. Incidentally, I would remark
in passing that this method was not invented by American
climbers, as many believe. It had already been tried out in
1929 by Comici and others in Val Rosandra and the Julian Alps.

We left the Italians to their supporters, and slowly, feeling
somewhat overwhelmed, slunk across to the end of the ledge
where we had left our equipment, which now seemed rather
inadequate. Here we sat down for a pow-wow, and René
explained his plan of campaign. Hiding our fear, we listened
to him, dwarfed by the overhangs above. Our imaginations
were crowded with disquieting pictures. Would we be able to
forget them in the heat of action?

René and I were to set off first, placing the pitons and leaving
them behind us. Pierre and Bernard would supply us from
below with food, drink and equipment, by means of a cord as
slender as the thread of life in moments of despair. More than
anything else, these provisions would be supplies of hope in the
midst of an overhanging desert. Three days later, heavily
loaded, they would try to catch us up, leaving all the kit in situ
in case of a forced retreat. That final roof overhang looked
exceedingly problematical.

Over on our right, while we were slowly getting ready, the
Italians were already climbing. René and I methodically
donned our gear, feeling a kind of respect for the great wall
that hung over us, absorbing us body and soul. It was like
going through a rite.

Finally René left the ledge and climbed the first few metres, beginning the apparently endless struggle, weighed down with pegs, karabiners and the four ropes. Pierre, Bernard and I were astonished by our own silence as we stood there on the ledge while I paid out the ropes. The only noise came from René, who was already fighting. The rock was vertical; two ropes slid between my fingers and stirred the karabiners hanging from the pegs, that would not hold a fall. We developed our own jargon: "Tight. Now slack." These words were to form my bond with life for whole days and nights. Something about the repetition reminded me of Mazotti's account of his ascent of the south face of the Matterhorn, the way the climbers waited impatiently for the day, then for the night, and so on incessantly.

René had surmounted the first 40 metres. According to his custom he drove in some solid anchor pitons; then it was my turn to climb, trailing great masses of spare étriers, pegs, karabiners and the 300 metre line which linked us to the world of men. I was concentrating too hard to speak to my friends as I set off. There is something solemn about making the first movement; I was to feel the same emotion when I repeated the climb several years later. Gradually, taking care over every move, I rejoined my leader. It was important not to change anything in this routine which we had worked out together and were now putting into practice. The smallest mistake could become a disaster. The ropes had to be kept apart, the kit arranged, and then our sacks had to be pulled up on the rope which linked us to Pierre and Bernard. Below us, our friends were complaining of the cold, while we, trussed up in our harness like a pair of parachute jumpers, were practically choking with the heat.

Slowly I passed René the equipment I had recovered from the pitch. We said nothing, but his smile meant more than any number of words. Then he was off again. After a delicate traverse leftwards, he arrived at the foot of a yellow wall which ended in a roof overhang. As to this yellow rock, we simply had to get used to it; it was to stay with us all the way to the end of the difficulties. As René climbed, the ropes hung clear of the rock. The wall was already overhanging, and between his feet he could see Kohlman organizing the kit back on the first ledge. One by one he drove in the pegs heavily but calmly, with loving care. This great climb, artificial from end to end, was to be his work of art. With a craftsman's eye he scrutinized the rock, using no more aid than was necessary, holding his breath as he tested each new piton with the rope, never making a superfluous gesture. It was the repetition of a ritual which was to lead us to victory. Presently he was over the roof, then two others. Finally he stopped and took a belay. By the time I joined him again, I was already impressed with his artistry. Somehow, one felt safe with him.

This stance, like all those that were to follow, was on étriers. The long ascending line of pegs was the sole trace of human passage in this world of unfriendly overhangs.

By the time we had done three pitches it was getting late. Time had slipped by without our noticing it; for climbers concentrating on the smallest movements, what difference is there between a minute, an hour and an eternity? As the face ahead of us looked more difficult than ever, it seemed best to go down for the night and return to the battle in the morning. Slowly we reversed the pitches we had climbed, and as darkness fell we found ourselves back in the world of men. Bernard and Pierre were staggered. A whole day for three pitches! However, our faith in ultimate victory succeeded in convincing them.

After a quiet night at the hut, Pierre and Bernard took over the job of pegging the route. The plan was that they should then come down in their turn at nightfall, and the following day René and I would make our bid for the summit. We spent what seemed an interminable day watching our friends work their way upwards. As we watched we chatted amicably with Hugo Weber and Albin Schelbert, who had to sit there and observe the hordes of Italians climbing up the pegs which they had placed. Soon they would attack in their turn, and maybe we would see them again.

Pierre was battling it out 100 metres above our heads on a white wall of completely rotten rock. On the cord that hung direct from him to the ground we sent up a note of encouragement and a bunch of very small Cassin pegs, the only ones that would consent to go in and offer any security, however slight. It was impossible to speak to him: not only was he completely absorbed by the job in hand, but deaf into the bargain. We knew that our own chances depended on his success in forcing the pitch that was to lead us into the line of the great crack that wound its way through 150 metres of the face. His battle was taking its place beside former ones like Cassin's and the present struggle between the Swiss and the Italians. As though to distract our attention, we spoke of this and that, but our minds and hearts were really up on the face. This direct route up it had become a kind of vocation; it was intolerable to be sitting on the ground while the time dragged by.

By the evening Pierre and Bernard had only done two more pitches, but the white wall had been overcome and the crack reached. To save us time in the morning, Pierre left a long caving ladder hanging down to earth. All together again, we made our way back to the hut, ate, swallowed all our vitamin pills, and went to sleep. Later, Mazzorana was to tell us that we seemed a bit stunned that evening.

Like a repeated pattern in a dance, we left the hut next morning in heavily loaded cars, grinding our way up the steep, difficult road to the other hut opposite the Spigolo Giallo, then slowly on foot over the col. As we crossed it the stones were already whistling down from the Cima Grande. There were the Italians in their camp, the support party watching their friends above. On reaching the start of our own climb we felt very much alone. The Scoiattoli were there in force, and numbers help to damp down fear. We were only four, and the Swiss only two.

The start again. This time we must put everything into it in order to win through. René set off first, then it was my turn. Without any transition, we were back in the inferno. The caving ladder was playing tricks; as I climbed it, it swung clear of the wall, oscillating horribly. I cursed Pierre for his bright idea, while he, from the ground, stoutly maintained its advantages.

Gradually we got back our rhythm, climbing pitches, taking belays, working the ropes. Towards ten o'clock, René reached Pierre's last peg. As usual, he placed an extra peg, then brought me up and was on his way again. The crack was getting wider, and our smaller wooden wedges were coming in useful. The silence was punctuated by the sound of the hammer and human struggles.

Presently the crack petered out under a ten metre roof overhang. The spare rope for kit-hauling, which hung clear of the pitons and thus showed the line of the vertical, swung far out in empty space. A slight traverse to the right brought René to a small ledge which we christened "the balcony", where, for the first and last time we were able to take a stance standing on rock rather than sitting on our swing seats. I made use of a short rest to hoist up some more equipment. Pierre and Bernard were starting to look very small. Over to our right the Italians were singing: what could they find to be gay about in a place like this?

A few moves of free climbing to the right now brought René on to a vertical, unbroken wall, which just had to be climbed. Some metres higher, a horizontal fault led back to the continuation of the crack. Using all his craft, it took René several hours to place a number of expansion bolts. By the time I joined him again, it was late. Our faces betrayed our despair. What good was all our training, our faith and will to succeed? The traverse left looked impossible, yet it was the only line. I hauled up the rest of the kit; a quick survey showed its inadequacy. There were about thirty pitons left. We needed about 250.

Silence, fear, exhaustion: all further effort would be in vain. It was as though we were transfixed 200 metres above the foot of the crag and 150 below the final roof. Both of us understood. Nothing was impossible, but we would have to come back next year with more equipment, and already, by the mere fact of so thinking, the decision to retreat was tacitly taken. Well then, better to get on with it and accept our defeat. After a discussion with the others we lowered everything to them on the rope. We were pointlessly happy, like children who had come to a decision. The sacks whizzed down the rope and crashed into the ground, bursting our two bottles of Chianti and cutting Pierre, who was carefully supervising operations, with the broken glass. It was like being in a delirium compounded of the bitterness of defeat and the joy of being finished with the ordeal.

Over to our right, the Italians were also descending in a series of impressive rappels. We had not noticed that behind us the weather had changed, and a wall of rain and snow was now advancing. This had not been our motive for giving up, but it brought us balm by removing the last element of doubt. By 11 p.m. we were back on the ground, and before long at the hut. Next day we would be on the road to Paris.

In fact, nothing of the kind happened, and the next day turned out to be miraculous. Defeated and disillusioned, we were wandering about in the streets of Cortina, when we met a journalist, Giovanna Mariotti, who had been looking for us. It was out of the question, she said, for us to give up now that we had done half of the climb, and the harder half at that. In order to convince us she had organized a whole cast of folk to exhort us to finish the route before somebody else did so. It was the finest line on the face. We should return to it as soon as the weather improved. Paradox of paradoxes, they even drank to our health as though we were already the victors. It seemed that the eyes of mountaineers everywhere were turned on us. The competition had won the attention of the press all over the world. As for the kit, they would give it to us. Gartner picked us out 300 pitons, 60 wedges, 80 metres of new rope and a 300 metre cord. He even insisted on providing clothes. Borne on on this incredible flood of hope, how could we back out?

Seated before monstrous ice-creams, we took our decision. Next day we would return to the face and finish out by the top.

It seems essential to emphasize this great wave of fellow feeling. Even though the Scoiattoli were in the competition, the sporting instincts of the people of Cortina triumphed over local pride. In such an atmosphere of friendship and joy there could be no question of failure. That would be letting our supporters down. Somehow we felt clothed in the human warmth of their confidence in us all.

Giovanna and her friends were smiling. They had won. Now it was up to us to win too. Up at the hut that evening, the Mazzoranas showed the same fiery faith. For the first time we no longer felt alone but dropped off to sleep confident, glad to be alive and eager to fight and win.

Next day was Sunday. The weather was still bad, so we rested. As we carried our new equipment up to the foot of the face we stopped briefly at the little chapel, perhaps to pray, to leave our fears in the hands of God. Pierre was visibly happy.

When we looked up at the face with Mazzorana it no longer seemed hostile. If we tackled the long traverse left a couple of metres higher it would certainly be easier, and then we would be back in the crack, which led to a wall of compact rock and the final roof overhang. Through the binoculars we could scrutinize every detail. As we sat beside pools which reflected the last retreating storm clouds, we felt that the sun would be back in the morning. A great upwelling of life inside us enabled us to dominate the appalling north face. The miracle had happened.

Mazzorana and his attractive wife got up to see us off for the last time that Monday morning at the beginning of July. Calmly, in full awareness of the ordeal that was waiting for us above the balcony where our thoughts were already at work, we left the realm of men once and for all. Pierre and Bernard plodded slowly up to the col and we followed along behind. Lugubriously we passed under the moonlit north faces. As we reached the foot of the Cima Ovest we were astonished to find Weber and Schelbert just starting up again. Having heard that the Italians had come down, they had returned from Biel on their motorcycle. Combat or competition? Both at once, but contained in one generous impulse. In the event they quickly reached the Kasparek bivouac, but in an injured condition which obliged them to finish by the Cassin route. They returned in time to finish simultaneously with us—a week later!

We spoke to them as they started along the system of cracks leading left under the huge roof, happy at the trick they had played on the Scoiattoli. Ropes began to rain down: Hugo was dropping the lines which the Italians had left fixed so as to enable them to get back up quickly. A hard game was being played on the Cima Ovest. Cassin had had his rivals too. Now it was our turn.

Hurriedly we sorted out the gear. René and I chatted with the others as we got ready. They were to remain in support on the ground for three more days, then to follow us; they too were taking part in the first ascent.

For the third time I set off up the first pitch. It was 5 a.m. Soon we reached the ladder, and then, by 8 o'clock, the balcony. René decided on a few minutes' rest in the early sunlight, which was soon to vanish until the evening: this was a north face.

Presently we reached the farthest point attained three days earlier. Now the fight to the death was about to begin. Sitting in our étriers, taking our time, we hauled up more kit and got ready, letting Pierre know by a written message that all was

going well. The overhang was such that we were now a full
20 metres out from the foot of the face. I hardly dared look
down between my legs, where I could see Bernard in front of
me, but 200 metres below. Out to our right Weber and Schelbert were climbing up pegs placed by their adversaries, who
had just reached the point of attack and were gazing up in
stupefaction.

Armed with 60 pitons, 10 wedges, 10 étriers and nearly 70
karabiners, René moved off into the unknown. Sitting in my
swing seat I watched his every movement, ready to respond
instantly to his directions, working the ropes as he required.
Ritual gestures. In such places friendship has a more literal
meaning than elsewhere, materialized by the rope between us.

Gradually, with neat movements, René dealt with the smooth
three metre wall which had repulsed us before. It was an
impressive sight: he was above me, but the overhang was
such that I had to lean over backwards to see him. I took
several photos. Our nerves were so taut, our concentration so
great that we had no perception of time.

This was where the great traverse began. Through the binoculars it had looked quite reasonable; now it turned out to be
nothing but a blind crack, into which only our tiniest pitons
would penetrate. Bit by bit René made his way along it to the
left until the whole rope was run out and he had to take a
stance. Once again we shouted down to Pierre and Bernard
for more equipment which I hauled up before starting my
slow toil above and in empty space, like a circus acrobat
without a tightrope. I was operating in another medium, where
only the laws of equilibrium held sway. Each movement must
be considered, each piton treated with loving care. In spite of
all my deliberation some of them came out, so that the long
trail of pegs that marked our passage was sometimes sparse.
Calmly each étrier was recovered, the karabiners gingerly
retrieved. There were nearly ninety of them for this one pitch.
Everything here was on another scale and the climber himself
seemed a different man, transmuted into something illusive.
When I reached René, it was already 8 o'clock in the evening.

We decided to bivouac where we were, hanging clear of the
rock, two metres apart for the sake of greater security. We said
nothing to each other, but just hauled up the bivouac equipment from below while Bernard and Pierre, respecting our

privacy, quit their base camp and wandered away through the gathering darkness. First we ate, then slowly prepared for the night, pulling on our down-filled clothing, two blue and yellow splotches against the immensity of the wall. Well lashed to our belays, we sat on our swingseats and cracked jokes while waiting for sleep to come. With darkness, the ropes hanging in space began their insensate dance, twisting and crossing at the whim of the wind. We had to watch them, pull them, unkink them, drop them again, let them go slack. It served to pass away the time. Finally a last friendly word of confidence, and slowly, under the effect of the sleeping pills we had taken, our bodies relaxed and our heads, lacking a softer pillow, leant against the limestone as though in respect.

Anxiety and uncertainty persisted in dream, or, more literally, in a state of semiconsciousness. What would happen tomorrow? We shifted, changing position to avoid cramp in our aching backsides, dropped off to sleep, started awake again by the sound of Weber's hammer. Even at that time of the night he was still pegging away.

At dawn on the Tuesday we prepared to move house. The acrobats prepared for the new day with the same care that they had shown in rounding off the old one the evening before. Bernard and Pierre were there on time, and we inquired after each other's nights. They hung a sack on the line and we hauled it up. To our surprise, we found ourselves reading the morning newspapers from Cortina and Paris. When was somebody going to instal the telephone?

After a frugal breakfast and further methodical preparations, René set off again. We still had 40 metres of traversing left in order to reach the crack which we had been following on and off since leaving the bottom of the face, but which we had abandoned when it disappeared under the big roof. The ropes danced to the music of the pitons and étriers as René moved away from me. Lost in the immensity of the wall like mariners on an unfriendly sea of which the waves were overhangs, we still had certain reassurances. We had acquired the certainty that our willpower was the key to success. More important, there was the presence of our friends down below working away to see that we got the right equipment, watching our least gestures with almost paternal care. Over to our right there was the joy of Weber and Schelbert who had finally

reached the Kasparek bivouac, and the Italians who, frustrated
of the first ascent, were setting off to make a new direct finish
to the summit instead of finishing up the Cassin route like
their rivals.

Pierre and Bernard sent up a message telling us how impatient they were to get started and catch us up. I discussed
their proposal with René as he climbed, then scribbled our
reply on a piece of paper. For the time being they must go on
waiting; we needed their help where they were. Perhaps in a
couple of days they would be able to abandon their inglorious
role which was, however, vital to the success of the climb.
Without their aid what could we do? I slid the message down
the line on a karabiner, and presently they shouted up their
consent mingled with impatience and encouragement for the
day's climbing.

René, the craftsman, continued work on his masterpiece.
It should be clearly said that this great climb was entirely his
in its conception, its planning, the training for it, and above
all in the unconquerable will with which he carried it through.
Already the finest climber in France, with this achievement he
attained the very front rank of mountaineers anywhere in the
world. His faith and enthusiasm have appealed particularly
to the younger generation. At this time we were close friends.
Subsequently our friendship was troubled by certain clouds,
but in due course common sense got the upper hand and we
understood and valued each other again. His long list of
achievements elicits universal respect, yet in spite of it all he
remains humble, and no doubt this is what I particularly
appreciate about him.

For the moment, then, he was in play, communicating with
the inert yet warm world of rock he loves. Scrutinizing it for
the smallest cracks, he placed the pitons with delicate artistry,
a veritable dance-like rhythm. Judging the possibilities, working out the solution, then finally imposing it, he performed a
kind of Indian rope trick as he moved slowly but surely from
étrier to étrier. Space is his estate. I watched admiringly, kill-
ing time by observing his movements, manœuvring the ropes
as best I could. Simultaneously, with a little splinter of limestone, I scratched the words "mardi, 2ème jour" on the rock.

Repeated hammering, deliberate gestures, the running of
the rope. From time to time a momentary pause to light a

cigarette, and the often-repeated words, as though recorded:
"Hold it there", or "Tension". Sometimes there would be a
slightly longer instruction such as: "Pierre, watch out, this is
a bad peg." And indeed, some of them fell out simply as a
result of the rope running through them. Thus René left his
indelible trademark on this face that he wanted for his own.
As I watched I was aware that I owed this experience entirely
to him.

Below us, the face was reflected in the blue pools, so clear
that we could see right to the bottom of them. The sight
reminded us of our thirst. By the following day these thoughts
had become an obsession and our bodies so dehydrated that
our minds almost lost their clarity. We shouted and sang as
though to exacerbate this desire which seemed on the point of
provoking hallucinations. Also the echoes comforted us, making
us feel less alone, as a child might talk and make a noise to
keep away fear as it walked through a forest in the dark.

At last René came to the end of the traverse, tired but happy
to be back in the crack where it was easier to see how to place
the pegs, and where we could start moving upwards again.
Once he was solidly installed I passed him the sacks, which
swung into space like great birds. Without neglecting security,
I tried to climb across to him as fast as I could, but time still
slid by inexorably, and by the time I reached him it was
4 o'clock. We had taken 12 hours over one pitch. It was
frightening to think of how much was to come.

The crack at this point was a regular gash in the rock, less
hospitable than it had looked at first, yellow and vertical—the
hanging ropes showed that quite clearly. Only our biggest
wooden wedges gave us any security at all, however doubtful.
First came a few moves of free climbing in this maze of artificial.
The rock was white and dissolved into powder at the touch.
Disdainfully, René made the maximum use of what seemed
likely to hold. Nevertheless, the next 30 metres called for
nearly thirty wedges and ten pegs. A short pitch of ten metres
with a very delicate move in the middle of it then led us leftwards to a platform about one metre square, a sort of balcony
in the centre of the face. We equipped it with so many belay
pegs and wedges that you might have thought we were going
to retire there for the rest of our lives, but in fact we were only
getting ready for the night.

Next we hoisted up the equipment on the 200 metres of line, especially the water that Pierre and Bernard had obtained for us; we were dying of thirst. It took us nearly half an hour to lower and pull back the sacks each time, bellowing "heave-ho" at the top of our voices. Each time it seemed as though we were hoisting a ton, and it was a cruel disappointment to find a mere twenty pitons or so. Pierre also hauled from below, and as the pulley peg was not very safe we were terrified of being catapulted into space. We saw him backing 300 metres down the screes in order to give us the maximum help, his position revealed in the darkness by his head-torch. In the same way, to him we were two points of light in the centre of the north wall.

Above all we wanted to sleep, seated in our strange position. For a while we sang to distract our attention from our growing cramp, then chatted about this and that, about the climb which obsessed us, about our friendship. A storm broke, but it made no difference, as the rain fell 20 metres outside our ledge. At last each of us became involved in his private coil of thought, already a kind of half slumber.

I saw my children, whose names I had carved in the rock at one of the stances. I thought of my father and mother and their fears, of my wife, of my friends. The disquieting silence had the curious effect of making me think of the contrast of Paris, that killer city where all is tumult and disproportion, yet where one wills to live totally. Then my thoughts were drawn back to the obsession of this climb. What would happen tomorrow, up on the great roof overhang that capped the face?

We were writing a new page in the history of artificial climbing, living through moments of exaltation. Why climb, why suffer, why overcome? We would know the answer when this nightmare was over, and it would be the same our forerunners had given. Techniques, methods, means evolved, but always the men and their will were the same. Think only of the present. For us, to look into the future was like staring into a black hole. This north face was strangely like life: it was best to live each moment, and the consequences of looking further were regret, bitterness, sometimes discouragement. To think of the future was to contrast it with today, so that yesterday no longer seemed what it had been. Yesterday, my evenings of sadness and solitude that I had lived through serenely. Today I weighed them up, thinking that tomorrow would be better. No, follow the film for the film, listen to the music for its own sake, live and often repeat this same speech, never hope that tomorrow may be better. Thus wipe out every trace of despair, and so of apprehension.

No doubt René was conducting some such internal dialogue at the same time. No doubt, also, his essential sanity saved him from a number of problems. I wished I was like him.

Throughout this great competition we had the feeling that, like the athlete winning a point for his team at the stadium, we were striking a blow for our country, and that our climb would restore it to a leading position in the mountaineering world. Only here there were no crowds to applaud the struggle, and this is certainly the big difference between our sport and some others where the presence of spectators creates a spirit of chauvinism. We were living through the same adventure as the Italians and Swiss. There would be no victors, no vanquished and no prize but the respect of those who understood the meaning of the word "mountaineering".

On the morning of Wednesday, the third day, we were woken by the sun and by a man calling to us from the Demüt ridge. The sunlight was a sign that we had overslept. The man was Gino Soldà, who had come to film us with his 16 mm camera. We were a curious pair of film-stars: without a director and worn out by our efforts and lack of sleep, acting out a script called "the direct route". Gino spoke to us from his stance on the edge of the face about 100 metres away. It was comforting to have the famous conqueror of the southwest face of the Marmolada so close to us. He remained by us the whole day and returned the following morning.

Having made contact with our support party on the ground we got ready in a sort of dream. René donned a pair of leather gloves to protect his hands, all bruised and cut from the constant pegging. The climbing began with a short, delicate traverse to the left, after which he climbed over a roof and I could see him no longer. Only his voice recalled his existence as he directed me how to work the ropes. He was hoping to finish before the evening; in the event, he climbed one pitch that day. The pegging was excessively difficult, and increasing fatigue contributed to slowing him down. For him the day was one long fight on an overhanging wall, consisting mainly of a leftward traverse to avoid a large roof overhang, so that by the end of it he had climbed 30 metres but had gained no more than seven or eight metres in height. For me it was a day of anxiety; if René could not climb any farther, we should have to get back down.

I do not know if I thought about anything very much during those interminable hours, but I do know that René's courage aroused my unbounded admiration. Towards 7 o'clock in the evening he was back at my side, having left the equipment in situ. He was exhausted and gloomy. We had to find a way out, but how? What ordeal lay in store for us?

I had done nothing all day but watch over the ropes, yet I felt nervously and physically exhausted. How must he be feeling? The loneliness was beginning to oppress us also, and we began to annoy each other. The sound I made chewing gum to alleviate my thirst got on his nerves. When I fell silent, this upset him too. Finally we decided to sing and the atmosphere improved. We smiled, happy to have recovered our self-control. René admitted he had been slow. After a night's rest he would feel better, and we would finish the climb tomorrow. I believed him.

We decided to notify Bernard and Pierre that they could start next morning with the remainder of the kit. Since the pegs had all been left in place, they would soon catch us up and we would reach the summit at the same time. It was important that the whole team should finish together. We could hear their shouts of joy down below, and the pulley began to move. Their message said how pleased they were, and that they would set off with a hundred pitons, food, ten litres of water, and their own personal climbing and bivouacking gear. René and I then pulled up one more heavy load, and nightfall found us singing again as we watched the moon rise, its light reflected in the pools that had so obsessed us during the heat of the day. As though the happiness of our friends had communicated itself to us, for the first time we sat there cracking jokes, thinking of finishing the climb, Cortina, beer, and the rewards of success.

We were woken early on Thursday morning by Pierre and Bernard swinging into action. Pierre being deaf, Bernard had to yell at him during the rope manœuvres, and we could hear them as though they were already beside us. We shouted down that we would see them this evening at the end of the difficulties.

We were in a hurry to get it over with, so our preparations were hasty. We wanted to get away from this unpleasant spot on which we had now spent two nights. Quickly the infernal round of acrobatics began again, and before long René was back at the end of yesterday's traverse. Many of the pegs were none too sound, so I took a stance while there were still ten of them between us. At this point, seated under a great roof, René took a number of impressive photos looking down, while I did the same. Six years later at the Tissi hut below the Civetta I was to have the surprise of seeing that one of them had become the frontispiece of the Alpine Club's guide to the Dolomites.

The wind now began to make the rope manoeuvres difficult, twisting and swinging the ropes into tangles that sometimes took almost an hour to undo. The wall above René was not only vertical, but so smooth and compact that for several metres he had to drill holes and place expansion bolts. The rock was hard and difficult to pierce. It gave a feeling of unreality to see him sitting there in his étriers. We had been dangling in acrobatic positions under interminable overhangs for so long, surrounded on all sides by empty space, that we had lost all notion of the vertical.

While René was toiling away, I straddled my legs so as to peer down between them at Bernard and Pierre. It was an impressive sight. Pierre was leading, but progress was slow and he seemed to be having trouble. When I called to him he complained of a shortage of karabiners—he had a mere 40, whereas we had 90—and also of rope drag. I could see him making desperate efforts to haul in slack and hold it between his teeth while he clipped into the next peg, as one might do on an outcrop problem.

As they reached the beginning of the long traverse where we had passed our first bivouac, an incident occurred which was to entail heavy consequences for all of us. They were hauling up a container of ten litres of water when, for some unknown reason, the line broke and the precious freight was lost. This was the beginning of our torture by thirst. Moreover, Hugo Weber had been going to attach the remainder of the kit to this same line. Now all he could do was to call up words of encouragement.

René and I had two litres of water and two litres of grappa left, and we now sent the others half of this on the line which linked us, and on which we were to continue to receive the equipment we needed. I now watched helplessly as Pierre, for some reason I shall never understand—perhaps he had unroped in order to alter his belay—let the end of it escape. Slowly it swung out until it hung a good 30 metres behind him. I hauled it up, hung a weighted sack on the end of it and tried to swing it in to him, but it was no good, the overhang was too great. Since the line was no more use to us, I let it fall the 300 metres to the ground. It described a few horrifying arabesques, whistling as it fell.

René and I were appalled: we were going to have to finish out the climb with the small amount of remaining kit. As for Pierre and Bernard, they had only forty karabiners and nothing to drink. For the rest of the day I could hear Pierre suffering, and when he leant back from the rock to look at me his face was a picture of pain and despair. Our own dry throats soon called us back to reality also. Our bodies ached and violent cramps racked our legs from days of sitting in étriers. From the start we had been living mainly on vitamins, so that our stomachs were all knotted up. Our nerves were very nearly worn out. In our increasingly desperate situation only Soldà, who reappeared on the ridge towards the end of the afternoon, brought us any crumb of comfort.

As afternoon shaded into evening we began to be obsessed again with the pools below the face. It was like a hallucination. We longed to dive into their cool depths naked, without this heavy burden of ropes and harnesses, and drink until we were drunk on their water.

Three hundred metres below, friends from the Locatelli and Auronzo huts had wandered up to see how we were getting on. How good it was to hear the encouragements of these Italian climbers, even when we could not understand their words. It made us realize that, as four young Frenchmen attacking the greatest problem of the time on practically their first visit to the Dolomites, we bore a heavy responsibility not to let down all the hopes that had been placed in us. This international mountaineering solidarity went far beyond all competition, however legitimate. We were soon to learn that among our visitors had been our rivals Michielli, Zardini, Franceschi, Weber and Schelbert.

So night came down and caught us all in different places, as though fate were making a game of it. René was blocked 15 metres above me on loose pitons in friable, overhanging rock. Two hundred metres below, Pierre was half way across the first big traverse, while Bernard was at its beginning. Each of us sat alone with his thoughts. There was nothing to eat or drink. I sat there on my swing seat, my feet in étriers swinging clear of the rock like the ropes which twisted around below me so that I had to disentangle them several times in the course of the night.

It was a night of acute anxiety, passed in the shadow of the final roof overhang. We could think of nothing else. Could we get over it? It stuck out a good five metres, and so far we had not been able to see a crack in it anywhere. Of all the uncertainties we might feel in the face of the unknown in mountaineering, this was the worst. We slept little, disturbed by the worries which we wanted to share with each other. In effect, the night was one long complaint by four fighters who had come to the end of their strength. René and I conversed in low, despairing tones, and Pierre and Bernard, who were expecting to catch us up, did the same between themselves; but when we called down to them it was with cheerful voices, and they always replied with words of encouragement.

This was the hardest night of all for us, the fourth we had spent on the face. For our companions it was a long first night, but they had worse to come.

I do not know what made me think of the Code Civil, but late in the night I found myself reciting its articles to myself. As I was later to tell my students, this is the sort of thing that a university education can lead you to.

With the first glimmers of light, René began to move. It was now Friday; surely it must be the last day of torture. The rock was bad, so that he had to use a lot of pitons and wedges. As we got closer to the roof, the rock became damp. Our lips tried to suck the humid limestone, on which we could see tiny spiders scuttling around, a curious phenomenon there between heaven and earth.

Glancing down between my feet while safeguarding René,

The Chamonix Aiguilles

Mont Blanc and the east face of the Grand Capucin

who was trying to place pegs behind a flake that kept widening at each blow of the hammer, I saw a strange sight. Having reached the end of the long traverse, Pierre gave some instructions to Bernard which I did not catch. Suddenly a dark shape went swinging out across the face, and for a moment I thought that it was Bernard falling, pulling out all the pegs as he went, and that they would both be torn off into space. My emotion lasted only a moment before I realized that the dark shape was just the leader's navy-blue sack that he was hauling up after him.

I climbed up towards René, but it seemed better to stop while there were still a number of pitons between us for the sake of security. There was never any sort of stance. When I got close enough, René would be off again on the infernal round of pegs, karabiners, ropes, étriers, moving up, while I took in tight, let out slack, and then again pegs, karabiners . . . and so the hours went by. Presently a rising traverse to the right, rendered excessively awkward by the state of the rock, led René up under the great roof. It was the moment of truth. The answer to all our doubts and speculations was about to be given.

Under that oppressive overhang René began to traverse delicately to the right, warning me as he went that every single one of the pitons was unsound. I concentrated all my attention on handling the ropes, my hands sore from so many days of the work. Moving horizontally now, he eased his weight from peg to peg and stirrup to stirrup, controlling his fear. Suddenly a peg came out and he swung backwards, but the previous peg held firm. Immediately he was on his way again. From my swing-seat 15 metres lower I could hear his unquiet breathing, I suffered his suffering, I shared his adventure, ready at any moment to play my part, while all the time the flake behind which my belay pegs were driven was little by little canting away from the face. . . .

René stopped and announced that he had found a crack in the roof which might be peggable. It was so fine that from my stance I was unable to see it. There then followed the most amazing sight which it will be given to me to see in my life-time. Parallel to the horizontal line of the roof, René drove in an expansion bolt. He cursed because the ropes would not run, but I was letting them go completely slack and it was just that with 40 pitons between us they were going through so many angles that he had to make superhuman efforts to haul them in. Completely exhausted, he let them go, and then had to begin all over again. Now he was three metres out from the face, outlined against the sky, lying back on his étriers, his hands groping for the smallest weakness in the rock, trembling with fatigue and nervous tension; a struggle for survival by a man nearing the end of his strength.

Another piton and then another. Gingerly, hedging the risk with as many precautions as possible, he clipped on an étrier and tested it, then moved out on to it. Now his body was curved around the end of the roof. At such a moment and in such a place there could be no question of taking photos, but they would have been dramatic. Both our hearts skipped a beat as the mere rope friction pulled out first one of the expansion bolts, then a big channel piton. The position became more horrifying than ever. Below us, Pierre and Bernard had stopped moving and were watching. I was too busy concentrating on René to speak to them. Slowly he moved up on to the top rung of his étriers, and in this position was able to reach a place where he could put another piton, disappearing above the overhang on to the face above. Now I could only hear him, but his panting told of continuing effort.

Suddenly he called out that we were at Saussois. It was all over, he had sound enough pegs to make a stance, and the face was leaning back. In point of fact, after five days spent among overhangs, he was unable to recognize the simple vertical. But he had won. I shouted with joy, and below me Pierre and Bernard cheered René, lord of the Cima Ovest. There was general delirium. They must have been able to hear us down in Cortina. While René was settling himself, sorting out ropes and hauling up the sacks, I inwardly thanked and acknowledged him as the master climber that he was and is. The fear and uncertainty were over, the time of joy and pride had begun.

I set off in my turn, but without anxiety. Nothing awful was going to happen. There remained the struggle with the roof and the ropes, but now that I was certain of the outcome I felt refreshed and keen as on the first day. For the benefit of Pierre and Bernard I replaced the pegs that had fallen out, and before long found myself up under the roof. Carefully, moving gently so as not to put more strain than necessary on the pitons, I leant out backwards. As I reached the lip of the overhang I looked through my legs at Pierre and Bernard 150 metres below and called out "See you soon". A further 200 metres beyond them I could see the ledge at the foot of the face with some of our gear still lying on it. But the sight was too appalling, and I turned back quickly to escape from it, leaving behind as I did so the whole hostile environment where we had lived and suffered for five days. Perhaps there was a twinge of regret that the fight and all its pains were over, and last of all a thought for Pierre and Bernard.

Even before I reached the stance, René passed me a bag of equipment we no longer needed. I let it fall into space, following it with my eyes until it crashed into the scree, where we could look for it later.

Like René, I thought that the face now leant back, but it was an illusion. Two hundred metres of verticality remained, and once we had the ropes arranged René set off quickly, climbing freely. At dusk he reached a wide ledge. By the time it was my turn I could see nothing in the darkness and was literally hoisted up.

Our head-torches revealed an enormous terrace. For the first time we could sleep lying down. Out of excitement or the winding down of tension which our bodies had been enduring too long, we talked as we attended to our wounds, mainly on the hands. We still had a few vitamin pills to suck, and the fiery grappa with which to assuage our thirst. At the first mouthful it gave a sensation of coolness, but it had to be spat out quickly before it started to burn. Finally we dropped contentedly off to sleep.

It was a fine night, untroubled by nightmares. Our minds and bodies were calm. Victory was ours, and on our ledge everything was still. Next morning, which was Saturday, we were woken by the sun. Life seemed very good. For the first time for nearly a week we were able to get ready without any cares. Slowly we pulled off our down-filled clothing and sorted out the gear without thinking of our thirst or hunger, and indeed we had almost forgotten the taste of food during the last few days. We also left a note for Pierre and Bernard, who would have passed a less pleasant night than we.

After following the ledge to the left for 30 metres or so, we attacked. The rock was vertical, grey and honest. Unknown to us, the ledge led on round to the Demüt ridge, and all parties since the third ascent have followed it. I think this is a pity, as the last 200 metres give beautiful free climbing. In our case we would not have followed the ledge even if we had known about it; we were too keen on our direct.

In the grade IV and V climbing that followed, René excelled himself. Several fine pitches brought us to the foot of a very delicate little corner where, cursing our luck—for we were very tired—we had to use several pitons. Having to carry the heavy sack, which for reasons of speed we had decided not to haul, I suffered particularly. René gave me all the help he could with the rope, but I began to feel increasingly weak as the pitches succeeded one another, until in the middle of a compact wall I found myself actually crying with the pain. It was the first time this had happened on the climb, and I hated myself for it. But my mind could no longer control my body; the muscles just refused to work, and I was unable to move up. René had to pull me out of my predicament before climbing on.

It was nearly 5 o'clock when we reached the circular ledge. I was dead beat, and could only crawl across the stones to embrace René. Determined to carry the route right to the summit, he climbed one last pitch. I belayed him from a sitting position, unable to get to my feet with 30 kilos on my back.

Two days earlier, Weber and Schelbert had set out to finish their own direct route, and were now climbing alongside us in friendly rivalry. Our ravaged faces inspired their pity.

Stepping on to the summit, René called me to come. That last pitch was at once the finest and the most painful of the whole climb. With tears in my eyes I summoned up my last resources, unable to find any words. My movements were those of a beginner, an invalid. There seemed to be no holds. Finally, at 6 o'clock, it was all over. We hugged each other with emotion: the greatest adventure of our lives had come to a happy end, and the French direct, the Jean Couzy route, was a reality.

Hugo and Albin were there, together with our friends Valerio Quinz and Giovanna, who had brought us food and drink. It was as though we were intoxicated with space and the nightmare that was over. Hugs, photos, tears, smiles, rest and the end of tension; all was accomplished. Hugo and Albin were feeling the same emotions, and despite a torrent of questions from Giovanna and Valerio we could not find time to speak. At 7 o'clock we started down behind Valerio, who helped and guided us like children. René and I took a last look at the summit and embraced each other once again. The only word I could find to say to him was "merci".

The seriousness and solemnity of the ascent had not entirely left us as we hurried down. Our thoughts were still on the face, now friendly to us, but where Pierre and Bernard were still fighting it out.

Hugo and Albin parted company with us at the col. It was as though they wished the celebrations to be for us alone. In their eyes their own route was only a partial success on account of the competition with the Italians, overshadowed by our great direct. Respectful of their feelings, we left them where they turned off to bivouac again under the north face.

Back on the scree I found myself running like an idiot towards the Auronzo hut in spite of the pain in my ankles, while René looked like a 100 metre sprinter. Abandoning ourselves to our instincts, our minds empty, we just ran and ran, a state of affairs made easier by the fact that it was impossible to stop without twisting an ankle on the limestone scree. Giovanna and Valerio were already waiting for us on the path. A hundred metres away was the hut, swarming with people, and suddenly we felt a sense of reticence, a desire to be left alone with our first ascent, our memories compounded of suffering and joy.

For the first time I was making direct contact with a world of journalists and tourists, hungry for heroes. In the midst of all this nonsense our friend Mazzorana came forward to greet us and we exchanged the sort of light banter usual on these occasions. But what did it matter? The essential thing was the joy that pervaded our whole being.

Photographers, television reporters, radio reporters, the whole tribe of journalists was there, more stringent than a board of examiners. It was touching to see how nicely René answered their questions. As for me, visibly bothered by so much sympathy, I replied as best I could. It went on and on, but that did not prevent me from drinking 17 beers in a row.

My dehydrated body was like a filled-up goatskin. Next came the autographing session, then the postcards on which to trace the line of our route and add a word or two . . . and yet how charming they were, all these Italians, Germans and Austrians. It was more than just a spectacle, it was their love of the mountains, of the Dolomites in particular, and how well I understood them. It was their pleasure and recognition that for the first time a French party had carried off the greatest prize in the area at that period, and at the first attempt. It was their way of thanking us, and I began to understand Giovanna's insistence eight days earlier in Cortina. As their joy became more and more unconfined, René and I felt proud not to have betrayed their confidence.

Over the evening meal our hosts plied us with every attention. Such was their kindness that I began to feel that Italy was my second home—and indeed I have never changed my mind. I have proved it over and over again in the course of my climbing career.

That night the reporters pursued us right into our bedroom. One of them, whom Giovanna could not get rid of, even wanted to see the marks and scars on our naked bodies.

When at last alone, we were unable to sleep, but lay there smoking cigarette after cigarette. Excitement had been piled on excitement. We almost regretted no longer being on "our" face, towards which we felt a bond of love. The very pitches held a fascination for us as we talked them over. We spoke of the face as of a woman we could both love without rivalry, recalling the beginning, the bivouacs, especially the one but last, and our fears. René confessed that he had been afraid that he might not succeed in finding a way through. And then the last night and yesterday.

Gradually we dozed off, only to start awake. The softness and warmth of the sheets unsettled us, and finally I lay down on the floor so as to be more comfortable. Then, at last, I could drift peacefully away.

We were already awake, thinking of Pierre and Bernard, as the light began to filter through our window at 4 o'clock. Despite the pain in our hands and legs we got up immediately to pay them a visit. It was a kind of pilgrimage.

An hour later we were plodding slowly up the accustomed track. Happy that our names would not be inscribed in it, we stopped a moment by the little shrine. Quietly, calmly, we climbed the hillside to the col and the fantastic vision of the north faces which had once so terrified and now delighted us, a kind of sadism or intellectual pleasure, above all a reassurance, an involvement with the memory.

From the col we strode through flowers in the early sunlight towards the Locatelli hut, savouring the sweetness of the Dolomites after their severity, encountering people of all ages (kept young by some miracle of the mountains) who recognized and greeted us. Our pictures were everywhere, even in people's minds. At the hut we met Rieder, the kindly guardian, for the first of many times. It was also our first visit to the hut itself. The view from the Locatelli on to the north faces of Lavaredo is one of the finest I know in the mountains. Once again it was a round of congratulations and a general hubbub in a dozen languages, among which German predominated this time.

With the help of field-glasses we picked out our friends, who were already above the final roof. Later we were to learn that they had gone on climbing all through the hours of darkness, and that the ropes had become so entangled that Pierre had finally had to cut them. Now they must be happy, we thought, watching and interpreting their gestures. The first ascent had been a team job, and now it was fully accomplished. We tried to shout up to them to finish by the Demüt, but like us they attacked direct, desiring an entire victory. We smiled at their success, our success, success in general. Tonight we would all be together again.

We returned to the foot of the face to recover our equipment, a rich and solemn moment. As we wandered down the scree to pick up the sack I had let drop from above the final overhang, suddenly a hail of stones burst about us, a full 40 metres out from the foot of the face. By a miracle neither of us was touched, but it was the most dangerous moment of the whole undertaking. Fear returned. The stones must have been knocked off the summit ledge by Pierre and Bernard, as though to signal their own moment of triumph.

As we hurried back to Auronzo, we saw our friends reaching the top of the scree-shoots just as we attained the road. In a few minutes they were with us and the four of us were throwing our arms around each other. The adventure and all our pains were over at last, and we expressed our emotion and mutual affection. It was the best moment of all, a kind of intoxication of generous feelings, of uncomplicated humanity. We were a family of four brothers as we tramped back towards Auronzo with nothing to tell each other but our joy.

That evening there was a great feast for the Scoiattoli, the Swiss and ourselves. It was an evening of fraternity, all the rivalry forgotten in a wave of profound friendship. We were together, the same men with the same thoughts and love of life. I can still see the smiles around me, especially those of our hosts and, most marvellous of all, of Giovanna. She who was the presiding spirit of this historic passage of arms was happy because everybody had won and was now united in the same open-hearted joy. It was her miracle, and all of us were grateful to her for this demonstration of her love for the mountains and the men who face their challenge.

There was a great chocolate cake in the form of the north face of the Cima Ovest, with the three direct routes picked out on it with cream. How good it was to be there, raising our glasses of grappa. Mountaineering is a world on its own, bringing us simplicity and love. Later, after the Swiss and Italians had gone down to Cortina, Strobel came back to visit us in our room. He, the greatest Italian rock-climber of his time, wanted to express his admiration. That night we could go to sleep truly happy. Pierre relived his ordeal in dreams, but this time his body would not bear any marks.

Next morning, after saying goodbye to our hosts, we descended to Cortina and passed a grand day getting drunker and drunker with the Scoiattoli, first at the Cristallo, then at the Padovena. These are the moments when victory can be savoured without a care in the world, a round of photos and autographs. We also had the pleasure of meeting Carlesso. At last came the moment to say goodbye, but happily not for long. And two little cars set off from Cortina to Paris by the way they had come.

We slept in a haystack near Innsbruck and then, unable to restrain our impatience any longer, René and I left the 2CV behind. As I drove, René slept beside me. I thought of all I owed to him, reliving the film of the climb in my imagination, all due to his tenacity, his willpower, his courage. We reached Paris and our wives and children at 2 a.m. As I drifted to sleep I was happy to be alive.

The east face of the Grand Capucin

Above: The French route on the north face of the Cima Ovest di Lavaredo

Below: Left to right: Kohlmann, Mazeaud, Signora Mazzorana, Signor Mazzorana the hut warden, Desmaison, Lagesse

René was on the telephone at 6 a.m. He was back off to Chamonix, where he had been appointed an instructor at the national school of mountaineering. Jean Franco, the director, was waiting for him. We would see each other next at Chamonix and plan new climbs together. And indeed it was not long before we were doing just that. The wheel had come full circle.

Yet life is not always quite so easy, and the other side of the coin of happiness is suffering. Henceforward the faces of René, Pierre and Bernard bore the stamp of a certain nobility acquired by their ordeal on the Cima Ovest, the sign of those who love the mountains passionately and give all to the battle.

Later, when I wrote these lines, I had just learned of the death of Lionel Terray, my friend. I thought of all he had meant to me, of all that he stood for, of his conception of climbing. Mountaineering is different from other sports. There are no onlookers, no applause. Our achievement is essentially lonely, nevertheless we are human like the others. Lionel is an example of those who outlive their death. His name is a symbol and a message; he has become something more than a man. Struck down in the thick of the fight, it is really now that he carries out his mission, conveying his message of total dedication, communicating the faith that he preserved so jealously throughout his life.

After Prélenfrey, Chamonix. There in the graveyard, among so many friends, Lionel was laid to rest. The whole climbing world was there to pay its last respects. Frison-Roche and above all Eggeler spoke from their hearts. Lucien Devies spoke of Terray's message. The only answer to the perplexing problem of mountaineering was those who practised it, the conquistadors of the useless. Around me all faces were serious, among them the young Chamoniard friends of Martinetti, Lionel's youthful companion in death. Knowing that I was thinking of Pierre and Antoine, Pierre Macaigne embraced me. The dead were our dead, and I wished to be of them, to fall as they had fallen, to die among these mountains that we love.

CHAPTER VIII

Among the Great—Perhaps

PARIS WAS SUFFOCATING me. I hated the place. The days seemed unending, life dehumanized, the city a heartless and headless monster consisting of nothing but tentacles. Even friendship had gone astray.

On the credit side there was the joy of seeing my daughters Chantal and Christine growing bigger. Looking at them in our little apartment in the rue Charles-Tellier, I thought of my own youth in Grenoble. My wife was at a loss to understand my maladjustment to our life, but how could it be otherwise for a mountaineer? The office was dead, the work sterile. Practical law was the discovery of the inapplicability of interesting theories. Only the students had any human warmth. The inescapable, compulsive loneliness of Paris is utterly different from the solitude we desire and seek in the mountains. Constantly I thought of bivouacs, the struggles of the day, the incomparable joy of the summit.

Naturally, Pierre and I had been hatching plans, though neither of us could take very long holidays. But what really mattered was to know that henceforward we could tackle the hardest climbs on granite. Our adventure on the Cima Ovest had given us absolute confidence in our powers. After a few days shaking off the fatigue of our trip to the Dolomites we had started training again at Saussois. The sight of the familiar rocks above the Yonne gave us a strange feeling. Compared with the limestone faces we had just returned from, these 50 metre crags seemed like child's play. Yet, without them, would we ever have climbed the Cima Ovest?

At the end of July, then, Kohlman and my whole family were packed into my small Dauphine, and we set off for Chamonix. We knew every bend of the road from having driven along it weekend after weekend, 630 kilometres there and 630 back. If somebody remarked that Parisian climbers were crazy, it would be difficult to disagree with them. We envy our fellow-climbers from Lyon and Grenoble, and still more those from Geneva, Milan, Innsbruck and Munich. On we drove past Sens, Auxerre, leaving Saussois away to our right, then Avallon, and a stop for coffee at La Rochepot. Towards 4 a.m. we reached the first foot-hills of the Alps after Tournus, one of the finest old collegial towns in France, then Bourg, Nantua and Bellegarde, where we drank yet another coffee according to the invariable ritual. Next came Annemasse and at last Chamonix and the Hotel de Paris, our sanctum sanctorum.

Above us was the splendour of the Aiguilles, the sun picking out the summits blanched by a recent snowfall. Each time we arrive under the Sainte-Marie viaduct we are seized by the same violent desire to climb the fantastic faces overhead, and above all the west face of the Dru, at that time certainly the finest pure rock-climb in the whole of the Alps, bearing the stamp of the personality of Lucien Berardini, aided by Marcel Lainé in particular. For French climbers the face is like a symbol. In those days the north and west faces made it "our" peak. Before long Bonatti, and later Harlin, were to restore an international character to this dizzy pinnacle.

Pierre and I were in a hurry to climb the Dru. Leaving our families in the chalet I had rented at Argentière, therefore, we set off to buy provisions in the shops of Chamonix. A bivouac was on the program, and maybe two, but we wanted them to be pleasant ones. We had had enough of spending our nights on swing seats as on the Cima Ovest. The pills we had swallowed for nourishment were definitely relegated to the order of accessories, and from now on we were sticking to bacon, cheese, sugared almonds and nougat.

At la Potinière we ran into friends from Paris either just back from or just about to set out for various climbs. Conditions, it seemed, were good. The west face of the Dru was apparently well pegged-up, so that we need only carry a few wedges and a dozen or so pegs. Two Belgian climbers, Foquet and Duchesne, wanted to come along with us, and although we knew that this would slow us down we agreed. The more idiots there are together, the gayer one is, and the weather seemed settled enough to permit a certain amount of laziness. They were wonderful friends. We had often climbed with them in the Ardennes, and a year previously we had made the second ascent of the Isolée together. Duchesne was fifty-one, so we called him "papa"; Foquet was younger, but an affair of the heart was preventing him from reaching perfect form. By a tragic stroke of destiny, Pierre and the two Belgians were to die on the same day in July 1961, 10,000 kilometres apart.

The Montenvers rack-railway was packed out with the usual frenzied crowd going into raptures without understanding anything. We felt like specimens offered up to their lack-lustre gaze. To obtain a little peace and quiet, Pierre unplugged his hearing aid, as he often did in the Paris metro. Instantly he was alone in the midst of bedlam. From Montenvers we looked up at the west face of the Dru towering 700 metres high like the prow of a gigantic ship, then descended to the Mer de Glace behind the lines of city-dwellers come to touch the ice and eternal snow they had heard about at school. Quickly we crossed over and climbed up the other side amid the scent of flowers and resin. A leaden sun burned down. Slowly we toiled up the crest of the moraine, leaving the greenery behind and entering into a barren world below the foot of the face, which was now so close that it seemed as though we could reach out and touch it.

We set down our sacks and prepared to bivouac in a hollow, well known to climbers, where I had already spent several nights hoping to do the north face of the Dru and the Nant Blanc face of the Aiguille Verte only to wake up in the morning to the sound of rain. Our primuses purred, then fell silent as we drifted off to sleep, the same thoughts of the face in all our minds. Fever, then calmness and repose until our awakening, which we knew would be like so many others, rough and disagreeable because of the earliness of the hour.

In the event, thanks to our laziness, it was late when we started up the Couloir des Drus in two parties. There are always stonefalls in this horrifying gully, by night and by day, and we could hear their peculiar thrumming whistle and smack against the rock around us. Pierre and I scrambled upwards as fast as we could, and before long we were poised to dash across the gully between two avalanches of stones to the shelter of the ledges on the other side. First, however, we had to wait for our Belgian companions, who were having trouble on this disagreeable terrain where the rocks were covered in a thin film of ice.

Once on easier ground, we wandered up the terraces, rather

surprised not to have encountered the strenuous corner which is the key to this first part of the climb. In fact, our form was such that we had climbed it without even noticing.

Towards 11 o'clock we reached the foot of the Vignes crack, the first major difficulty. It was 1 p.m. before we attacked it. Already I was disturbed by this extreme slowness, but again we had to wait for our companions who were far behind us among the maze of blocks left on the terraces by the massive rockfall of 1956, leaving an open wound in the compact wall. The view was splendid. Far down in the gulf below our feet we could see the little red trains at Montenvers and the seething crowd of insects on the Mer de Glace. The tiny black points seemed lost and frenzied on the great ribbon of pale ice. Warmed by the sun, we dozed peacefully.

At about 1 o'clock, then, we joined battle. We should have to work fast if, as we hoped, we were to bivouac after the big corner and the pendulum abseil which follows.

Pierre led off, and at once we were in a very different world. The west face of the Dru was not going to fall to the first comer. The wide crack was not only holdless, but there were no subsidiary cracks for placing pitons. After climbing up to Pierre, I continued. It was not my kind of pitch; I much prefer open climbing on granite slabs or limestone. Here it was all jamming, pulling and fighting, and our breathing translated our slow progress. On top of everything else, the crack is sensationally exposed. We thought of Vignes and Duplat who were the first to overcome this lower part of the face and who had since died on Nanda Devi. Soon it was Pierre's turn again. What a wonderful climbing machine, friend and brother-in-arms! He spoke little, just the minimum for the efficient conduct of affairs, but was always smiling. I am completely different, and make a lot of noise. It is true that in general I like to make myself clearly understood, and sometimes I used to wonder if Pierre was not playing games with his deafness. "Slack," I would shout, "give me some slack", and when the rope did not come free at once I would curse my partner and best friend with all the vocabulary at my command.

At grips with the narrowest part of the crack, Pierre took off his sack and left it. To get it clear, put it on and climb with it cost me a superhuman effort, but finally I reached him.

Above, a magnificent curving pitch brought us to the foot of
the 40 metre wall. At this point I had to lower a top-rope to
Foquet, who was getting exhausted on the last part of the
Vigne crack, then we had to wait again until they reached us.
We were seriously concerned by the time they were taking; at
this rate we should have to bivouac on the jammed block. But
Duchesne's smile somehow made up for everything.

The 40 metre wall is all artificial climbing, and I started up
it with feelings of high respect for those who had done the first
ascent, tapping the old pitons to make sure they were firm,
replacing the waterlogged yellowing wedges as I moved up
metre by metre on my étriers. It was splendid climbing,
bathed in sunlight. Pierre came up quickly to join me at the
stance, leaving the top-rope attached to the others in order to
save time. We had reached a gully full of snow and ice below
the jammed block, and the day was far gone. In this cold and
hostile place we should have to bivouac, and while Pierre
brought up the others, who were now climbing by the light of
their head-torches, I cast about to make things a little more
comfortable, heaving down blocks which stuck out too much.
All four of us had to pass the night standing in uncomfortable
positions, only Foquet's snoring troubling the silence. Finally
Duchesne subsided into sleep also, and huddled against each
other for maximum warmth Pierre and I thought of the need to
climb fast the next day.

In the middle of the night occurred one of the most signifi-
cant moments of my life, which enabled me to understand
Pierre's nobility, the depth of his feelings, the meaning of our
friendship. Foquet began to complain of the cold. Pierre, who
was shivering at my side equally paralysed by the bitter cold
in the snow runnel, immediately gave him his down jacket,
warmed him up and made a place for him to sit down, then
spent the rest of the night upright, one leg jammed in a crack,
controlling his shivering so as to disturb nobody. That was
Pierre's life in a nutshell; he lived not for himself but for others.

As the light returned, while my companions were still
huddled in the half-sleep which had overcome them in spite
of everything, I hacked my way up the ice gully with frozen
muscles while Pierre belayed me. My hands and feet were
hurting and the rope ran out slowly. Climbing over the
jammed block was a veritable torture which lasted for hours.

Even the pitons were coated in ice, and every hold had to be hacked clear with the hammer. The supposedly beautiful final mantelshelf called for my last resources, and I arrived on top of the block, at the foot of the magnificent 90 metre corner barred by impressive overhangs, more dead than alive. What feelings they must have had on the first ascent as they arrived on this austere balcony in the midst of overhanging walls, looking up only to see all hope of progress barred by a line of black, blank roofs.

The wind was icy, raising whirls of fresh snow that had fallen on the block, and at first I was unable to take in the rope. As Pierre climbed, unclipping the rope from the pegs, it began to come more easily; then, when he had arrived, the same thing happened to the rope which linked us to the Belgians. Two hours later we were all together again, Papa Duchesne bringing up the rear.

After a cup of hot bouillon, I set off up the first pitch of the famous corner, a great gash in the otherwise featureless wall. Both the pegs and the wedges seemed firm enough. When the overhang is as great as this, there is almost no weathering, as water falls clear of the rock. The rope behind me also swung clear. Certainly it was not like an overhang in the Dolomites, but it was quite enough to produce a quickening of the pulse. The climbing is magnificent, neither too difficult nor too dangerous. There are plenty of pegs, and our four-rung étriers were proving a great success. I had never before encountered such overhanging granite; when I stopped to belay, I could see my companions between my feet. They were sitting there chatting, paying no attention to what I was doing, but I knew that Pierre's apparent carelessness was not real, and that I could trust him with my life. Once when I had fallen off at Saussois, pulling out all the pitons, he had let go everything to grab me and hold me against the rock. It had looked more like rugby than climbing.

Soon he was up to my stance. Just time for a smile, to say that the climbing was fantastic and that he was happy to be with me on this route which we had dreamt of for so long, and he was off again. In effect, we were accomplishing a dream. As he led on, Duchesne was starting up the rock below me, a veritable prodigy to be leading the dièdre of the west face of the Dru at the age of fifty-one.

It did not take Pierre long to reach the beginning of the pendulum rappel. Trusting in the tight rope he gave me I rushed up the pitch, gathering karabiners and étriers as I went. This was our usual tactic: the leader took all the étriers and left them in situ, the second recovered them and then led through to repeat the same operation.

Quickly I slid down the pendulum abseil, perforce helping myself with the old fixed rope, blanched by the weather, very much against my will. I have an acute dislike of such practices. Fortunately it was all over in a few minutes. There was barely time to think that if the rope broke I should swing back under an enormous roof and would have to perform some daring manoeuvres with prusik loops. Then it was Pierre's turn to slide down. Together again, we admired the Lainé traverse, the line of which was shown by the remaining expansion bolts. What daring! He had spent a whole day traversing a few metres from the north to the west face at the point where Berardini's first attempt had failed. From there the latter had found this terrifyingly exposed pendulum.

Glancing back down the corner into the abyss, we could see our Belgian friends advancing slowly. We were rather horrified to observe that they had not yet reached the first stance, and decided that we had better wait for them even though it would mean another bivouac. Pierre took in their top-rope, which was passed through a few karabiners, while I sat there with a dry throat admiring the magnificent blades of rock over to my left which were eventually to be climbed by my friend John Harlin. Below my feet the Chamonix valley was bathed in sunlight, the swimming pool a tiny blue point which I was to gaze at nostalgically from many a point in the aiguilles. Down there, other friends would be looking up at the face and thinking of us, wondering why men climb. Troubled by the slowness of our companions, I dozed off. It was good to be with Pierre. The mountains were his kingdom. At this moment his thoughts were like mine. We shared the same passion for the great faces, the same respect for those who had climbed them first, the same deep joy of victory, and above all our friendship.

I had been sleeping for eight hours when our Belgian friends finally caught up with us. It was 7 p.m., and Pierre was preparing the bivouac. I did not like the look of the grey clouds on the Rochers des Fis, but there could be no question of going on for the moment. Foquet and Duchesne were tired out. Tomorrow we should have to climb as one party. Our throats were dry and burning as we got ready for the night. Pierre gave Foquet a piece of his mind for having drunk the last of the water when we had no more gas left for melting snow. He also reproached him for having hidden in his rucksack certain pitons which we had needed. To Pierre, who was always sacrificing himself for others, such selfishness was incomprehensible. Duchesne succeeded in calming him: tomorrow the climb would be over and we would forget everything, even our passing quarrels, as always, in the joy of victory.

We were woken by a storm over Mont Blanc, but it drifted off in the direction of Italy and we dozed off again. For our friends, however, it must have been worrying. Two bivouacs and we were still in the midst of the difficulties. Tomorrow would come the free climbing.

Very early in the morning we clambered out of our blue bivouac sacks, the same colour that Buhl mentioned in his account of the north face of the Eiger. Before long I was finding my way through the labyrinth of pitches turning the enormous overhangs which Lucien Berardini had called "the door-bolt". The line of faults nonetheless contained some pitches calling for a good deal of skill. I was feeling on great form, and Pierre belayed me while bringing up Duchesne at the same time. An ice-cloaked chimney demanded a major effort and led to a pudding-shaped grotto which had been used as bivouac site on the first ascent. Here, by some paradox, everything was rotten. It was as though the rock had been wounded. The granite and red porphyry had crystallized, and nothing was solid. Taking extreme precautions I continued on my way, and towards 8 a.m. pulled over on to the north face, where I was greeted by an icy wind.

At this point I had thought that the climb would be virtually over. In fact it was covered in ice and snow, and on ground which would otherwise have been easy I had to muster all my energy and skill. It was mixed climbing of the most awkward kind, and I had to use a considerable number of rock and ice pitons, especially on one overhang covered in dripping ice. Pierre slipped off and came on the rope while seconding it, and I had a moment of awful fear on account of my poor belay. I just had to hold on, or all four of us would go cascading down the north face. So I held and hoisted my companion, who by some miraculous manoeuvre managed to pull up and stand on an ice-bulge without crampons. The weather was changing, and already sleet was blanching the summit rocks. Finally I reached the comfort of the natural tunnel which links the north face with the ordinary route on the other side of the mountain. At this point the weather afforded us some respite, and the four of us sat down to enjoy a snack, and of course, now that the climb was over, a few jokes.

Before long we started down and, like many before us, lost the way. We were caught out by darkness while abseiling down to a comfortable ledge, and there we had to bivouac again, but this time in calm and security. Whatever happened, we knew that by the following evening we would be celebrating in "the Bivouac", a night club owned by our friend Janin. Duchesne looked after me like a father, while Pierre roped up again to go and look for water, his head-torch shining into the dark gulf like a searchlight.

Next morning, four tired climbers descended to the Charpoua Glacier. It was no easy matter to cross, but finally we reached the hut and nothing remained but to descend the moraine, cross the Mer de Glace to Montenvers, and stride down to Chamonix.

Our friends were relieved to see us. We had taken so long that they decided that we must have taken out all the pegs; I did not dare to tell them that all the pegs were in place. That evening in "the Bivouac", among our friends and girl-friends, one had only to look at Pierre's and Duchesne's faces, and no doubt mine too, to appreciate our joy.

The holidays were drawing to a close. Pierre and I had one more day in which to make a quick ascent of the Contamine route on the Aiguille du Midi, leaving the bistrots of Chamonix behind us with the first rays of the sun to live our real life in the mountains, to forget our cares in the combat with the yellow granite, a vertical world where we could be utterly ourselves, rid of all play-acting.

We led through, climbing rapidly. Once we had passed the overhang which the climb shares with the Rébuffat route it was a fine piece of artificial interspersed with bits of free

climbing. Everything seemed simple and logical; this time
there were no worries. It went so well that in some places we
climbed together without taking belays. The last corner on
the north-east face was choked with a thick layer of ice, but it
made no difference. We had decided that for that day nothing
was going to make any difference. By 10 o'clock we were on
the summit. One quick rappel, and we were among the crowd
on the observation platforms of the cable-car station. The
afternoon found us back in the bistrots, then it was time to go.

Before setting off for Paris, leaving my family at Chamonix,
I dropped Pierre at Les Contamines, where for the next fortnight he was to guide a group of blind mountaineers. Thus it
was that soon afterwards a party of twelve apparently drunk
persons was seen to traverse the Dômes de Miage via the
Aiguille de la Bérangère. After Pierre's death, several of his
blind friends told me how as they tramped over the high
snows they had felt so full of the joy of living that it was as
though they could see. That was Pierre.

Life in Paris is bearable in August. There is time for everything, including having fun in the evening, and even a little
work. Every Thursday there is the solemn ritual of the rendezvous at the Café l'Aurore in the rue la Boëtie, the real headquarters of the Club Alpin. There the only subject of
conversation is climbing. I always leave early in order to find
friends with other interests. These city mountaineers who go
to bed at 9 p.m. so as to keep up their form, how could they
understand that I never get to sleep before 4 o'clock in the
morning?

For me, Paris at this period of my life was essentially a
nocturnal city, compounded of everything one loves, a poem
of contrasts. I encountered old schoolfriends such as Louis and
Pierre, and learned of the death of Alain, my friend in the
philosophy class at Louis-le-Grand. It took me back to the
world of my first loves.

But however great the careless joy one feels in Paris in
August, the mountains are like a mistress for whom one would
sacrifice everything. Whenever the mind is empty of other
thoughts the Chamonix Aiguilles rise up in front of it, the
warmth of the granite, the chill of the ice. The sleepless nights
at Saint-Germain create a kind of paradox: inevitably one
begins to think of bivouacs, those marvellous hours of peace

or apprehension according to whether the difficulties of the climb are over or not, but always under the sky, in our natural element. Nothing else is so strong or so sweet as this ecstasy, this passion to conquer. Paris has its charms, there are moments when climbing conversation is inappropriate; in a word, everyday life has its own imperatives. There are bewildering and cloudy joys, an integral part of the being that gives itself up to them, abandoning all constraint, but the return to first principles is there in the background like a refuge. The mountaineer loves life in all its aspects and each moment is lived fully as in any combat, even that of love, but he only truly reveals himself in the mountains, like the sailor at sea, the painter on his canvas. There is nothing far-fetched about such comparisons; the exaltation is the same.

Slowly there began to be born in me a kind of desire to escape, or more precisely to appear as what I truly wished to become, to find a formula which would give meaning to my life. For the time being I could think of nothing but the mountains. Young people meant a lot to me, and I did all I could to keep the contact alive through my lectures at the Faculty of Law. Unfortunately I had to earn a living, and for the sake of my children I applied myself to the humdrum life of the office, so opposed to the forces that were boiling up in me. It would be necessary to wait a few more years yet before I could burst the chains that held me and free myself. For now, I had nothing but mountaineering and my mountaineering friends.

One Thursday evening Philippe Laffont suggested a week-end climb at Chamonix. It was a chance to see the Alps again, and also my children, since the family had remained at Chamonix. Having picked up Lucien Berardini, we set off at about 9 o'clock on Friday evening in Pipo's open Simca. With three of us in a two-seater it was an uncomfortable journey: tucked in behind the seats Lucien was unable to move despite his cramps. I sat in front with all the sacks on my knees, and Pipo the proprietor drove.

It was a typical Chamonix Saturday. From the Potinière to the National, we picked up the gossip, which climbs were in a fit state to be done, what had been done, and especially the first ascents. During the course of the evening we fell in with Magnone, and the four of us decided to do the Contamine route on the Aiguille du Peigne next day. We were expecting an easy time, but alas, between us and the Peigne lay another sleepless night. The Bivouac (the night club of the Hotel de Paris) was full of pretty girls, and our reputations required that we should be there. Naturally, since we were there, we had to drink. By 5 o'clock in the morning we were all blind drunk except for Guido, who had got a good night's sleep, and packed our sacks in a state of semiconsciousness, forgetting practically everything. We met him at the foot of the cable-car; he was most concerned at the state we were in. It was, it seemed, a serious climb, and there were we hardly able to stand up.

Ah well, maybe a little fresh air and altitude would wake us up. After all, how often had I reached the first cable-car at 6 o'clock in the morning, sometimes having to borrow kit left and right from my friends? And how often had I learned that fresh air makes no difference at all and that the first few pitches were wild, proving nothing but the remarkable feats of balance that climbers are capable of in such circumstances?

Following our master, we literally staggered after the great Guido up the path towards the Aiguille du Peigne. On the snowslopes Lucien and Pipo seemed to get back a little bit of form, but everything was swimming in front of my eyes. The slope got steeper and I groped my way upwards cursing women, whiskey and sleepless nights, trying to hold on to the glistening ice with my bare hands and risking falling off with every step. Presently I caught up the others and tied on with Pipo while Guido roped up with Lucien, who was coughing and vomiting in a corner as though about to render up his soul, though without losing his smile. It takes more than that to stop an elemental force like Lucien, who had been through it all before.

It all seemed too much of an effort. At the rate we were going, it was going to take a month to reach the summit. My faithful second, the ineffable Pipo, became sick in his turn, getting rid of litres of alcohol and whole packets of cigarettes in the process. It was quite a sight. Naturally, Guido tried to recall us to reason in tones at once paternal and commanding. And on we went, finding grade IV like grade VI. What was to become of us?

Presently Guido went astray, and finding that it was difficult to climb in such circumstances announced that we had better go down. I protested, and finally we made up one long wavy serpentine, myself at the sharp end, Guido bringing up the rear. Up in front, I soon began to feel better, and although I still got dizzy spells from time to time I began to enjoy the climbing. Only the strenuous moves recalled me to reality, and I remember a chimney barred by a large chockstone where I gave up the last drops of whiskey that remained in me. Next, a rightward traverse led me to the only artificial pitch, which wound through three fine little corners to a wide ledge. By this time I was going so happily that I forgot to use any étriers, which was just as well since I had left them behind in Chamonix, and even used a minimum of karabiners for the same excellent reason. As for climbing in these circumstances, well, after all, it is good to undergo every kind of experience. Behind me Pipo and Lucien were still complaining of feeling ill, but willpower or desire propelled them upward. Behind them again Guido was still grumbling, but nobody took any notice.

Things now became more difficult, at least for me, because the next four pitches consisted of grooves, a rock formation of which I have always had a holy horror. I have no major objection to cracks, chimneys, corners, free or artificial climbing, whatever the degree of difficulty, but I go through hell in grooves. It seems difficult to believe that some climbers like them. I set off in a state of nervous tension and climb fast, because there is never anywhere to rest. On this occasion I seemed to be on a pitch of VI sup. Fumbling desperately for a piton, although I knew that it would not go in properly, I realized with horror that these too had been left behind in Chamonix. Below me the others were happily chatting and vomiting, unaware that anything was wrong. When I had fought my way out of this desperate situation, they came up without a word of gratitude. I spoke with some emphasis of the beauty and extreme difficulty of these pitches. Pipo replied briefly that I must be a moron, because they were easy.

Presently, via a series of slabs, we reached the summit. Reassuming his paternal manner, Guido informed us that he would take care of operations. And indeed, we should have to hurry: it was already 5 o'clock, and the last cable-car went down at 6. He promptly led us off into a zone of shattered rock which threatened to peel off with us on it at any moment.

Personally, I preferred to climb back up and then descend the ordinary route. The others followed, and Guido resumed his dejected air. We caught the last cable-car just as it was leaving, and then minutes later were back in the Hotel de Paris, drinking and laughing at our escapade, at our friends who did not believe us, at ourselves and at the Peigne, the mountain whose summit I was destined never to reach.

But that was just the beginning. Once again it was a round of whiskeys, quantities of red wine with dinner, and then back to our regular port of call, the Bivouac, where we danced the hours away until midnight struck and it was time to go.

It was our third sleepless night in a row. Pipo drove, while Lucien and I bellowed our repertoire of dubious songs across the sleeping countryside. From time to time I dozed off, but fortunately Pipo continued to hold out. Towards 4 o'clock we stopped for coffee at La Rochepot, then hastened on past Morvan, Saussois and Auxerre. By 9 a.m. I was at my desk in my chambers, once more a serious company-law counsel, where, to tell all, I slept between cups of black coffee, disturbed only by the telephone.

Our first ascent on the Cima Ovest had caused a certain amount of stir. My relationship with René Desmaison was less cordial than it had been. By nature I am faithful in friendship, and I was as grateful as ever to René for having thought out and then led this exceptional climb. Thus I was keen to see him again and to show the world that we were still excellent friends. During the course of a weekend towards the end of August 1959, he came to see me while I was having lunch at my father's chalet in Argentière. One smile was enough to blow away the suspicions that some people had tried to create between us. We decided to try a fine first ascent, the north-west pillar of the Grands Charmoz, but according to custom kept our project secret. Back in Paris, I waited for René's telephone call.

The only person I took into my confidence was Pierre Kohlman, with whom I drove down to Saussois to train at weekends, and even to Fontainebleau after the office in the evening, where we sometimes finished in the dark.

It was during the last week of September that I received the long-awaited telephone call. Everything was ready. My family had just returned to Paris, and leaving them, I set off for

Chamonix after notifying Kohlman of my intentions. On arrival I went straight to the Ecole Nationale d'Alpinisme to pick up René, where we were soundly lectured on the virtue of prudence by the director, Jean Franco, who knew perfectly well that we would stop at nothing. For us it was not merely a question of doing a first ascent, but above all of demonstrating that Desmaison and Mazeaud had finished the Cima Ovest with only one feeling, namely friendship.

So there we were back on the cable-car to Plan de l'Aiguille. Our weighty sacks and the lateness of the hour—it was the last trip of the day—attracted a certain amount of attention. As though they were conspirators, the cable-car operators wished us good luck. What a fine bunch they are, always with a smile and a cheery word.

At the hut we were alone with the warden. With men of his stamp you can have genuine contact, a kind of poetry. I thought of Blaise Cendrars who had stayed there to write his book "Le Plan de l'Aiguille", and of Abel Gance who had shot part of his great film "La Roue" in the same place.

Getting up at 2 a.m. is no doubt the truly heroic side of mountaineering, more inhuman even than leaving a bivouac, because a hut is warmer. Noticing that he had forgotten his down jacket, René borrowed a blanket. By the light of our head-torches we packed our sacks, and after a hot breakfast set out at 3 o'clock, finding our way by starlight. The frost was painful, and slowly, to the rhythm of our footsteps scrunching over ice and stones and sometimes the sound of an ice-fall on the north face of the Plan, we made our way along underneath the Aiguilles. However often you follow this track it reserves a few surprises, and however well you think you know it you can still get lost. Towards 5 o'clock we came to the tongue of the Nantillons Glacier, and dawn was already lighting up the pillar, overpowering in its majesty.

The way up the glacier is short but awkward. A single piton at the base of a high, icy corner was the sole evidence of earlier attempts. No sooner was René tied on than he attacked as though he was going to give the pillar no chance. It seemed to make no difference that the cracks were choked with ice and the holds covered in verglas all the way up the difficult first pitch. Presently he reached a stance, hammered in a piton, and it was my turn. I was freezing, and, as always when the

On the Direttissima of the north face of the Cima Grande di
Lavaredo

Six days on the north face of the Cima Ovest

On the French route on the Cima Ovest most of the stances have to be taken in étriers or swing seats

going is disagreeable, I thought of Paris or of the pleasures of being at the seaside, which must be innumerable even though I have never tasted them.

It was now full daylight, and between my feet I could see our tracks up the snowfield, with Chamonix in the background. I led on up the next pitch, placing a few pitons on account of the cold which René, as usual, considered unnecessary. We were in an immense open corner some 120 metres high, full of snow and ice. The sun only warmed it for a while in the afternoon, and I could imagine the resulting waterfall, just like in the Dolomites. I was following a V-shaped crack, which for no obvious reason suddenly came to an end. Clearly, we should have to traverse to another which by some miracle of nature was not far away, as though they had had a rendezvous which both had decided not to keep at the last moment. The traverse was exposed and I began to peg, my right foot placed precariously on a tiny rugosity. Suddenly it shot away, and I found myself hanging stupidly from the piton. With no feeling left in my fingers I set off again, trying to keep my balance, but the equipment which I had slung around my waist was dragging me backwards, and once more I sensed that my feet might slip at any moment. Cautiously I began to make a long stride to the right. I was on the point of falling, and this time the consequences would be more serious. At maximum stretch, with René giving me tension on the rope, I seized the crack with my right hand. My left groped for a piton, which I then tried to hammer in, only to realize that it was no good. It always seems to happen in particularly desperate places, when the climber is on the verge of peeling off. More gropings. This time it was a Cassin piton which went in, ringing healthily. I clipped in a karabiner, took firm hold of it, and shot into space . . . the peg and karabiner went tinkling down the face into the bergschrund, while I swung back to the beginning of the traverse in a great arc. There seemed to be no harm done, so I started the business all over again. This time I reached the crack, and when René's turn came he used a sling to get the necessary tension for the long stride. I did my best to explain to him that as the greatest of contemporary French guides he ought not to leave the sling behind, but for the time being he seemed unwilling to listen to me.

René led the last part of the corner. As the day grew warmer, the water was beginning to run under the ice, and it was mid-day as we pulled out on to a magnificent terrace. Over on the Nantillons glacier, Julien was leading down the members of the current course at the Ecole Nationale. He shouted across to us that we were crazy, that the ordinary route was much farther to the right, that one paid dearly for such foolhardiness, that we need not expect any guides to come and rescue us. We said nothing, having no interest in telling him what we were up to. For us, it was a private joke.

From there on we had splendid climbing up hospitable sun-browned boiler-plates. A deep curving crack did its best to oppose us, but as usual René was on amazing form and merely played with the difficulties. The pillar was steep but not overhanging, and the free climbing among the wild granite slabs was of surpassing beauty. It was pure pleasure, heightened by the fact of being a first ascent. Presently an enormous fracture broke the pillar, at the level where the Grands Char-moz are cracked across. Here we had to tramp up screes and snowslopes to the wide ledge below the awkward-looking cracks which awaited us next day.

The sun went down behind the Rochers des Fis as we got ready to bivouac. The nights are cold at the end of September. As the little gas-cooker began to warm us, René pulled out his blanket that we should be happy to leave behind next morning. Without a thought for the future, we prepared dishes worthy of Oliver, the chef of the Grand Véfour. Then came the ritual of the pills, sacrosanct where René is concerned. All this passed the time away, and after we had chatted for a while of this and that we dropped off to sleep. Then came the cold, the stars, the occasional thunder of ice-falls on the Nantillons, and thoughts of those we loved. So each one passed his own night.

We needed hot drinks to help us through the painful business of waking up. We got ready all our kit before taking off our down jackets and facing the brutal shock of the cold. Every-thing was covered in ice. First of all there were some awkward blocks to climb over with numb fingers and toes. The slow monotony of the climb re-established itself, the rope running out, and from time to time a few directions emanated from the leader who remained unanswered, because the second was asleep. Sometimes the rope would get jammed, and then the leader's voice would rise a tone or two. Since he seemed to be responsible for his own safety, there was no shortage of hammering. Although we had lightened the sacks as much as possible they still seemed too heavy. The first few pitches were a matter of pure endurance, black, cold, inhospitable. The minutes passed like hours, accentuating an impression of mournful solitude.

Gradually, as the hours went by, this impression faded and was followed by the pleasure of climbing in the sun. This in turn gave way to fatigue, and then we felt lonely again and anxious to be done. Discouragement is only brought by the elements, when the human mechanism has to battle with wind, cold, rain or snow.

It may be asked whether the mountaineer is not therefore a kind of monster, a masochist, accepting and even welcoming hardship for no profit but a few moments of joy. However, this would be phrasing the question badly. We shall return to it in due course, but the essence of the matter is in passion, solitude and friendship. In order to satisfy the need for these, in order to know extreme ecstasy, one must accept extreme difficulty.

Presently we reached the foot of a wide chimney of frightening aspect. Overhanging and without minor cracks for pegging, it was barred higher up by a black overhang which added to our feelings of apathy. René tackled it while I belayed him, watching his movements, interpreting his breathing, tensed to the maximum. For lack of anywhere to plant a piton he was unable to rest, but nevertheless succeeded in making progress. It was astonishing to observe his endurance and co-ordination, but in me his obvious nervous tension was translated into fear. How would he succeed in finishing the pitch? Then he announced that he was stuck. My belay was merely psychological. It was one of the most trying moments I have known, but I helped guide his feet on to the holds, expecting at any moment to be torn off into space and land on the still-shadowed ledge where we had bivouacked. Choughs were flapping around us like vultures, birds of ill-omen. Despite my unlimited confidence in René I was possessed by fear . . . and yet somehow, slowly, he succeeded in retreating, arriving at my side exhausted. It had been one of those moments when the self shrinks to nothingness, closer to death and the emptiness

of eternity than to life. Most climbers would prefer a sudden
death; when the probability of it grows inexorably, it is
infinitely more terrible. René's features betrayed all this; he
was pale and trembling, and could speak only with difficulty.

I took over the lead. Abandoning the chimney as a well of
horror, I turned a corner to the right, thus losing verbal
contact with my partner. Now I felt alone. There was an
ascending crack which I filled with pitons as though our lives
depended on it. It did not take long to reach the end of the
pitch and shout down to René to come on. When he turned
the corner and saw the crack he smiled just as I had done.
The horror of the last few minutes was forgotten already. That
too is a part of mountaineering; experiences change to
memories.

Somewhat with the manner of a high diver having a second
try after a poor effort, René led on through, but before long
the crack thinned out into a compact, holdless slab. Seated
calmly in my étriers, I waited for my leader to find a solution.
It was impossible to go any farther in a direct line, but there
was no question of admitting defeat. How many such struggles
have ended in improbable victories over the apparently
unclimbable! Three specialists in this line were Cassin, Buhl and
Bonatti, but their feats in no way cancel out those of Welzenbach and other great mountaineers.

Making sure that the last peg was well in, René hung a
couple of étriers on it. He was now slightly above me, but well
out to my right on a slab of magnificently red granite. Then,
while I held the rope tight, he left the étriers and began a big
pendulum rappel towards a wider crack well over to the right.
After a good deal of coming and going he succeeded in getting
his left foot into the crack, jammed it, and then, as I carefully
paid out the rope, swung his weight across until he was face
to face with the next obstacle, the leaning crack itself. This was
a crux pitch where a few years later, on the occasion of the
second ascent, the ace climber Batkin was to break his leg,
requiring massive resources for his rescue.

Slowly, adhering to the face like a fly, making maximum
use of the smallest faults in the rock, René battled his way
upwards. The crack was too wide for pitons or wedges, yet too
narrow to jam the body in so as to get a rest. After a desperate
struggle, grinding his fists and left foot into the crack and

gaining friction for his right foot from mainly imaginary holds, he made a violent mantelshelf movement onto a wide ledge where the crack ended. Completely exhausted, he lay there for a few moments panting as though suffering from a heart attack. When he spoke again, it was to tell me that the climb was over and to come quickly. It was, he said, a difficult pitch, but as I liked this kind of climbing (he knew very well that I hated it) I should find it easy.

Leaving my comfortable étriers, I climbed the curving crack to the past piton and found myself face to face with the problem. My leader was above me and far to the right. It was not difficult to imagine the swing that would result if I let go. I stood there hesitating while René's exhortations flowed over me. I should have to unclip the karabiner; only the piton would remain behind as a sign of our having passed. At present it seemed to be mocking me. First of all I unclipped the rope, and then, at arm's length, the karabiner. Immediately I swung away, trying but failing to catch the edge of the crack at the end of my arc. Before I succeeded I had to have several tries, and finally, with René pulling as hard as he could, I managed to jam my left foot and climb the crack, arriving on the terrace exhausted but conscious that the difficulties were over.

Climbing together it did not take long to reach the summit, after which we took a short rest on the pinnacle known as Wicks' Stick. There is no moment like the end of a first ascent when at last one can relax in safety, friendship and joy.

We trotted quickly down the Charmoz-Grépon couloir, full of traces of those who had traversed Mummery's mountain. As it was September we found the Nantillons Glacier a slope of ice which had a few surprises in store for climbers without crampons. René slipped, I was unable to hold him, and away we went, faster and faster. It looked as though we were going to shoot over the "salle à manger" and go tumbling down the slabs beyond. By some reflex I threw myself with all my force to the left, René slid straight down the right-hand gully, and we were held by the rope stretched over the ice-ridge between. A short rest to get over the excitement seemed called for, and we were able to grin at each other in spite of our fatigue. By 6 o'clock, once again, we were on the last cable-car down to Chamonix.

For me the season was over, and it was a case of returning

to Paris. As I drove I thought of René and even felt quite pleased with myself. Our climb had all the effect we had hoped. On Monday morning the newspapers carried accounts of how Desmaison and Mazeaud had relapsed into making first ascents, and into friendship.

CHAPTER IX

When the Time is Ripe

AT THE BEGINNING of the winter of 1960 the weekends
which Kohlman and I spent skiing brought us into contact
with the mountains in a cold, hostile, inhuman guise. This was
the new attraction; we had decided to attempt the ultimate
combat, winter mountaineering. On 1st January, heavily
loaded, we left Paris for Berne and then Grindelwald. Ignoring
all the rules of decency, we were committing the vulgarity of
going straight for the north face of the Eiger.

On our arrival the sun was shining, the grass was bare of
snow, and already at this season there were flowers in the
meadows. Above us bulked the Ogre. Even in the valley it
inspired us with fear, but by the time we had taken the train
up to Kleine Scheidegg and seen the avalanches thundering
down the face, the fear became so paralyzing that we hurried
off towards Chamonix without a backward glance. The Eiger
is a sorceror who casts very different spells on his visitors.

We were now short of time. A long journey and a night's
bivouac in the streets of Annemasse led us back to the less
hostile climate of Chamonix. The weather was not good, but
with an eye to what seemed most reasonable in the circumstances, the first winter ascent of the west face of the Dru, we
plodded up to the bivouac. It was hard going and a long way,
but at Pierre's side everything seemed safe. The thick layer of
snow made it impossible to find the bivouac. It continued to
snow all night long, and in the morning there was nothing
left for it but to go down.

In mid-June, as soon as my lectures were over, I set off for
Chamonix with Alzetta. It was a trying journey; his driving
aroused more insistent fear than an exposed pitch of grade VI.
As we were interested in nothing but first ascents, we left some
of our kit at the Hotel de Paris and continued on to Courmayeur.

The grind up to the Gervasutti hut at the foot of the
Fréboudze glacier went slowly. The scenery is wild and

grandiose, no doubt the most striking in the whole range. The hut had been carried away by an avalanche in the course of the winter, which meant yet another bivouac under a starry sky.

Early in the morning we attacked the east face of the Petites Jorasses. Right from the outset it provided difficult artificial climbing up a magnificent 150 metre corner which took us a whole day to overcome. That night we bivouacked uncomfortably on an outward-sloping ledge, setting off again in the morning rather silently into a zone of roof overhangs where the difficulties increased. As the day went on our throats became more and more parched. Finally the weather deteriorated and forced us into retreat via a series of abseils and pendulums. We reached the remains of the hut more dead than alive, returning to Courmayeur in the rain. That walk back is now a nostalgic memory, but at the time I was not to know that Alzetta and three of his Belgian friends were to be killed in Greenland and that it was to be with Bonatti that I would finish the climb two years later.

Back at Chamonix, we decided to make the pleasant ascent of the Pointe Lachenal as a training climb. The route takes a line of astonishing purity amid magnificent surroundings, at its foot the crevasse in which the famous climber met his death. Around us were the pillars of Tacul, framing two impressive couloirs named after the great Italian climbers Boccalate and Gervasutti, both also killed in the mountains. In the foreground, skiers were gliding down the Vallée Blanche.

It did not take me long to get on to peak form, and I awaited Pierre Kohlman's arrival with impatience. He turned up one evening in July accompanied by Danièle Badier, a friend of mine and an excellent mountaineer. All that was missing was the fine weather. There followed a round of monotonous days wandering from cinema to cinema in the rain, and of idle evenings in the Bivouac, which had become a kind of headquarters. When we remembered, we made plans. As soon as the weather improved, we would do some climbing in the Aiguilles Rouges. Higher up, there was too much snow.

One morning it stopped raining, and, although the sky was still overcast, Pierre and I set out to do the first ascent of the south face direct on the Aiguille du Pouce with an Austrian friend, Leo Schlommer. This striking bastion had been

Piz Badile from the north. The Cengalo couloir is on the left

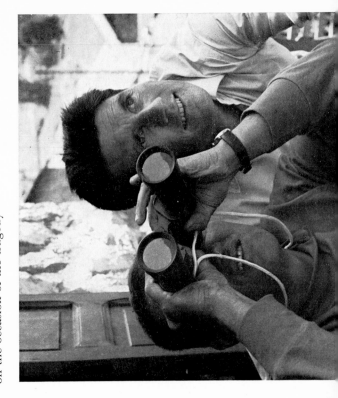

Left:
The Fresnay face of Mont Blanc: (1) the direct finish to the Innominata Ridge, (2) the central pillar, (3) the right-hand or Gervasutti pillar, (4) the Bonatti route, (5) the Peuterey ridge. The small circle on the central pillar marks the point reached on the occasion of the tragedy

Right:
Mazeaud (left) with Walter Bonatti

fascinating us for a long time, and we knew that we were not the only ones. It took us a whole day to wade through the fresh snow from the Brévent to the foot of the face, high up in a ring of mountains so calm and quiet that it seemed as though no one had ever been there before. The face itself was oppressive, heavy with menace. Nevertheless we had a pleasant bivouac.

Advancing to the attack in the morning, we were surprised by the difficulties right from the outset. The climbing was free, and there came a moment when I was right at the limit, like a bird about to take flight. In the whole day we climbed no more than 100 metres. Leo kept us amused, and I tried to dredge up fragments of my school German. Our bivouac that evening was overshadowed in more than one sense by the overhangs above us. These were the key to the next day's progress, and we could not get them off our minds. However, it did not take the weather long to give us something else to think about. We were treated to rain, snow, storm and, towards 3 o'clock in the morning, the yells of our Tyrolean friend, whose anchor piton had come out. Luckily the ropes held, and from 20 metres lower down he shouted up to us in picturesque French that he was all right apart from having had the fright of his life. Since there was nothing the matter and we wanted to finish the night under our plastic sheeting, we left him where he was. Clearly, we should have to go down to Chamonix next day in any case. There was no question of tackling the overhangs in these conditions, all too frequent in this region. We squelched back to Planpraz in the rain, but with the firm intention of returning.

That summer of 1960, Chamonix was in despair. There was fresh snow right down to Montenvers, and below, in the valley, there was day after day of icy rain. Morale sank to zero. Pierre returned to Paris to get on with some work, intending to come back should I telephone that conditions had improved. Other climbers wandered off to the Dolomites, but the weather there was no better. From utter boredom Dany and I took to tourism, occasionally driving over to Geneva to join our friends of the Androsace on the Salève. The first fine day we did the Rébuffat route on the Aiguille du Midi, a short but very pleasant climb on splendid rock, with fine slabs and cracks. On the less steep parts the snow held us up, but when we reached the top we were happy. Towards the end of July the weather improved slightly, inspiring hope. I wired Pierre, and next day there he was, smile and all, climbing down from the train.

As conditions high up were still bad, we returned to the Pouce with Philippe de Saint-Amand, a charming companion who had been hoping to join us on a first ascent for some time. Dany also thought of joining us, but to our regret changed her mind when we spoke of the overhangs, the thought of which was filling us with joy down in Chamonix; problems are always delightful when far away. As Leo was nowhere to be found, we finally set off as a party of three again.

From Planpraz it did not take us long this time to reach the foot of the face, where we duly found the equipment we had dumped on the last occasion. Not without difficulty, we reached our previous bivouac site at the end of the day. It was cold that night, and the starry sky reassured us as to the weather and our success, although the black overhangs bulging above our heads looked anything but protecting. Sleeping pills helped us to forget them, and at last we slept.

As dawn broke, Pierre led off in the style of a truly great climber, for whom victory was inevitable. Two pitches of extreme severity gave him something to think about, but, as usual, he used hardly any pitons. Climbing up to join him, one particularly exposed move on rotten rock frightened me even as second. Then it was my turn to lead again, and I moved up to the overhangs. It was going to be necessary to turn these by a long traverse to the left, so we brought up Philippe and drew up our order of battle. Belayed to a deeply driven channel peg, I watched Pierre as he started the traverse, climbing free with incredible ease and purity of movement. Back on the stance, which had little in common with the Place de la Concorde, the two of us hung uncomfortably from the peg. Thirty metres to the left, Pierre found a miraculous line of weakness through the roofs, which elsewhere projected for up to 15 metres. Here he hammered in a belay piton, and I sent Philippe across to him.

As I started to take out the piton, its head broke off at the first blow of the hammer. Stupefied, I gazed down at the small snow patch far below at the foot of the face, where the three of us might so easily have landed. Then it was my turn for the traverse. Frequently I found myself out of balance, particularly when I had to take out the blade pitons which we would need for our further progress.

The artificial pitch which followed up through the narrows was my lead, and brought me to the foot of a fine dièdre which Pierre climbed while I simultaneously safeguarded him and brought up Philippe. The daylight was going; we should have to hurry. Two more easy pitches were climbed in total darkness, then the slope gave back and we groped our way to a new bivouac just below the summit. The tension was over, so we could afford to shout, sing and drop off to sleep happy at having finished the job and added another first ascent to our list, a first ascent with the prodigious Kohlman; a memory that will not fade. And indeed we often had occasion to relive it together, as Géry, the Paris-Match photographer, had recorded our progress up the face.

Next morning, with the joy of victory in our faces, we got back to the téléphérique at La Flegère in a few hours. Down in Chamonix we ran into my father, highly amused, who was plotting the second ascent not for himself but for our friends Habib and La Fouine, who were not exactly pleased about the publicity we were getting in the local press. Before long we were to be informed that the second ascent was harder than the first!

For some time Pierre and I had been thinking of trying the first ascent of the entire north face of the Peigne, and Pierre had already made one attempt two years earlier. A famous French party, Berardini and Paragot, had envisaged the problem, and this was enough to incite us. On our way down from the Pouce we had seen that conditions at high altitude were still very bad, and we therefore decided to try for the Peigne. As Pierre already had an idea of the difficulties, he opted for a party of four, the second pair helping us with the equipment. In effect, the free climbing on the lower portion of the face would be followed by many artificial pitches, and a bivouac was to be expected.

Five o'clock in the morning at the foot of the cable-car to Plan de l'Aiguille. The sight of the four of us heavily loaded aroused some curiosity, but the onlookers were not totally in the dark about our intentions; knowing us, it could only be a new route. Taking leave of our friends of the cable-car team, Pierre and I hurried up to the foot of the face. Our companions were in less of a hurry. The plan was that they would recover the kit we left in place and catch up with us at the bivouac.

Plodding up through the rhododendron bushes, Pierre had trouble with his hearing aid but managed to repair it with a piton, a true work of art. It had rained so much during July and August that the slopes were bare of snow right up to the foot of the climb. Our eyes were irresistibly drawn to the south face of the Pouce, which seemed to smile at us across the valley from among the Aiguilles Rouges.

Pierre having already done the first part, I repeated it mainly free. It was fantastic climbing, difficult but beautiful, on vertical, sound rock, smooth slabs and strenuous cracks succeeding each other in turn. I was on form and enjoyed the effort. One chimney called not only for maximum climbing power, but for maximum lung power as well. They probably heard me in Chamonix. Pierre's hearing aid was out of order again, and as he could hear nothing he did the opposite of my instructions. When I called for slack the rope went tight, and when a heaven-sent piton enabled me to shout for tension it went slack. Each time I looked down, there was Pierre beaming as though everything was fine, although he said that he had been quicker on the occasion of his attempt. I shouted down that he could keep his nonsense to himself, but as he could not hear a word it made no difference, so I just went on fighting. As one pitch succeeded another and time went by, we saw our heavily loaded companions setting out in their turn.

Presently we reached the ultimate point attained in the course of previous attempts, a smooth, holdless slab in which I had to drill a hole for an expansion bolt. Pierre came up and joined me in my precarious stance on étriers. This was where the real problems began: we had to make an almost horizontal tension traverse to the right in order to reach a zone of over-hanging cracks. The roofs seemed to bar our way like blades. Clearly, we were in for some serious artificial climbing. Over to the right, parties on the easy ridge of the Peigne had stopped to stare at us, intrigued. As for me, I belayed as best I could, but only one peg stood between us and disaster. Was it tenacity or foolhardiness, uncertainty or risk?

Pierre launched out on the impressive tension traverse while I did my best to handle the ropes. After two hours of exhausting effort he succeeded in wedging himself in a crack 15 metres to the right, where he drove in a piton. For me the traverse was easier, as the rope was held in tension at both ends, but I was not sorry to end up in a healthier spot, thinking of those who would have to repeat the manoeuvre.

As evening fell we began preparations for an uncomfortable bivouac, shouting to the others that they would do better to stay where they were. We ate and smoked, or at least I smoked; Pierre was to smoke the one and only cigarette of his life when we reached the summit. As we emptied out the sacks I found a swing-seat which I selfishly wanted to keep for myself, and as Pierre refused it I was able to have my wish. Instead, he cocooned himself in one of the ropes, and presently I saw him a metre above me as through a net darkly, out of which he presently informed me that he was going to sleep well. Silence enveloped us, broken only by the strange sounds which mountains make at night, as though they were shifting, and the anxious voices of our friends calling up from two pitches below to ask how things looked for the following day. Ritual words. There seemed no point in replying, so we left them to their own imagination.

Suddenly, towards 3 o'clock, thunder, lightning and rain broke over our heads, recalling the sudden storm over the Peigne in July 1949. Pierre began to groan and complain as the hemp rope he had wound around him began to shrink in the downpour. Before long he seemed to be suffocating and would have cut the rope except that, in the total darkness it was impossible to tell which was which, and if he cut the wrong one it would be the final terrible drop into the night. His torture lasted until dawn. As for me, I sat there blessing the swing seat.

At first light, wishing to have done with this liquid hell, I brought up the others, safeguarding them across the traverse. They emerged soaked as from a river. The prospects were not encouraging. There were so many roofs and overhanging flakes above our heads that we hardly dared look up.

Delivered from his bonds, Pierre hurriedly made his preparations. The fight was fierce but effective; evidently, he intended to show the face who was master, and there was the extra incentive that the traverse-rope had been let slip and all retreat was now cut off. We led through pitch by pitch, while the water flowing down the face grew to the proportions of a river in flood. The cracked overhangs called for superhuman efforts, plus a lot of artificial aid. Sometimes pegs and wedges had to be cunningly coupled, and the fact that they stayed in proved the existence of a kindly providence. Our light haulage line was in constant use between the last man and the second in order to keep the leader well supplied with equipment. The streaming overhangs isolated us from each other increasingly, and the rope hung ever farther from the rock. In the course of one traverse to the left we had to climb through a sort of narrows where the water falling down through our sleeves came boiling out of our boots. It was quite a sight to see it happening to the others, but not so good when one's own turn came.

And yet we were making progress. Pierre climbed on, and I watched his every gesture, thinking that when my turn came to lead I would peg liberally. At last Pierre called down that he was almost there, to give him slack, and then that he was on top and that I could come. I did not bother to answer; the rain had finished off what remained of his batteries and he could hear nothing anyway.

As though to salute the grand master of this first ascent, the clouds parted, giving way to warming sunshine. On the summit we embraced. Now that we had come through, we were happy that the weather had made the climb harder still. I reached him a cigarette and he smoked it, as he had promised.

It did not seem long before four radiantly happy climbers got back to the cable-car station. There, to our stupefaction, we were shown a copy of the previous day's "Dauphiné Libéré", where the news of our success had been announced 24 hours in advance. And to think that the rain during the night had almost made us give up!

At the end of August Pierre went off to guide his blind scouts around the mountains in the rain. Dany, Michel Vaucher and I drove off to climb in the Calanques, a wonderful three-day trip in an open Peugeot 203. After Grenoble, we met my father at the Hotel de l'Europe in Uriage, recalling memories of my boyhood and early friendships. The night was spent under some straw bales in a field near La Grave, and when we woke in the morning there was an enchanted view of the Meije and the fascinating north face of the Rateau. After the Col du Lauteret we began to encounter a real southern sun as we rolled on towards Nice, and that evening we reached St Tropez, where we were stared at like wild beasts in a menagerie. We slept in a vineyard and woke up with indigestion. Early in the morning the port was utterly deserted, filling us with a sense of beauty and deeper reality.

Next evening was passed in Marseilles at the house of our friend Livanos, popularly known as "the Greek". He had just got back from a first ascent in the Engadine, and his non-stop stream of "fantastic, extreme, VI superior, just like the Dolomites" went on until 3 o'clock in the morning, by which time we were all asleep in our armchairs, including his wife Sonia. Nobody ever found out if he had stopped talking.

At Les Goudes and En Vau Michel and I broke all the speed records, completing the whole range of climbs in two days. The bivouac with a wood fire was marvellous, and the morning bathe was followed by the joy of more climbing. Dany showed remarkable talent as a rock-climber, and wished that she could sample the Dolomites.

No sooner said than done. Once again it was a remarkable trip, during the course of which Michel treated us to his repertoire of Leo Ferré and Georges Brassens for two whole days. Aix, Lyons, a stop in Geneva to pick up more kit and tell Michel's mother that he was going on with his holiday, then the Simplon and the Italian lakes, night and day, a meal chez Carlos at Trento, Cortina, the Auronzo hut and finally, at evening, the Locatelli.

As a result of our exploit on the Cima Ovest I was greeted like a veritable king. Rieder, the warden, showed me the entries in the hut book recording the repetitions. The route had just been done by the Spanish ace Anglada, who had written: "A ladder of pitons". Two years later at the Trento festival I was to pardon him over several bottles of Chianti.

Next day we had a quick climb up the Cassin route on the Cima Picolissima. Our progress had been closely watched from the Mazetta hut, and when we got down there the German climbers plied me with enough alcohol to last for a year. I drove back to Auronzo almost literally blind drunk, nearly going over the edge more than once.

The arrival of Hélène Dassonville now made our number up to four. Together we climbed the Preuss route, the rain on the descent making us wonder whether we were swimming or climbing. Next we teamed up with a group of French climbers, including Cauderlier, to make a long serpentine up a difficult route in the Paterno. Here I met Jacques Le Menestrel, and we decided to attempt the Brandler-Hasse direct route on the north face of the Cima Grande.

Despite the encouragements of Michel, who was heading for the Weber-Schelbert route on the Cima Ovest, it was an apprehensive pair that stepped up to the foot of the climb. Several parties wished us "Grüss Gott" as they passed by on their way to do the Comici route. We made ready in fear and trembling. Even to reach the first peg the leader had to get involved in serious difficulties while the second, who could do nothing for him in any case, was able to watch him with detached amusement from the path. When my turn came, however, with the heavy sack on my back I could get no farther than three metres before I had to climb down. It was no good, we should just have to haul the sack. I started off again.

With the regularity of a metronome we led through pitch after pitch, though not without incident when I got too far to the left or Jacques opined that we had been very late in setting out. And indeed, it had been nearly 10 o'clock.

The climbing was continuously extreme, and as I had never encountered anything quite like it before I kept up our morale by talking about the Cima Ovest. Every pitch was splendid, containing a minimum of pegs, filling us with admiration for those who had done the first ascent. The emotions were intense. The climbing was sustained, the holds far apart, the climber constantly at the limit, and only the solidity of the rock inspired any confidence. At the second stance one could not help thinking of Walter Philipp who had fallen 80 metres, happily without any ill effects. Late in the evening we came to the crux, the famous grade VI traverse. Jacques led it with only three pitons, whereas Vaucher had mentioned seven, and four years later I was to find 11. As darkness fell, Jacques warned me that he was faced with a problem as hard as at Fontainebleau. Nerves stretched to the maximum, I watched the rope and his movements. Suddenly he fell off, and my horrified eyes switched to the belay piton. It held. No harm was done, but I was sweating and feverish. He started again and this time succeeded, calling back: "O.K., come on". My feet slid, groping for invisible holds, and I traversed in a series of bounds, seeing nothing, arriving at his side in utter darkness, literally towed by the rope. We were happy to be together again on this wonderful bivouac site, a fine ledge in the middle of the inhuman, overhanging face.

We were too tired to chat, but dropped off to sleep in our down-filled clothing, waking in broad daylight, astonished to find that it had snowed a good ten centimetres in the night. The overhangs above us were already spewing cascades of icicles.

The artificial pitches which followed gave me a lot of hard work. The belays were too shaky to lead through, so it was up to me to battle with the roofs which one by one led us out over space. There were plenty of pitons, although I sometimes had to chop the ice away from them before I could clip in. Yet it was a rapturous feeling to be alone and lost on the great face; the Comici route was deserted, and only the distant refuge was there to remind us of the existence of other men.

I forged my way ahead slowly, sometimes fighting the rope-drag with the energy of despair. Occasionally a peg would come out, but by giving everything to the struggle I advanced metre by metre. As though to make up for lost time I literally hauled Jacques up after me. He was highly impressed by the difficulties and full of admiration for the German climbers who had found the route. The cold was so biting that my fingers sometimes stuck to the karabiners, and the strenuousness of the climbing was exhausting, but in spite of the suffering involved there could be no question of retreat. The very idea was unthinkable. We just had to persevere, concentrating mind and body to the uttermost on the need to climb on and on.

It did not seem long before the daylight began to ebb. We were obliged to bivouac at the end of the overhangs. The cold bit deeper and deeper as we sat huddled on the little box holding the book containing the names of those who had passed this way. Among them were several for whom we felt real veneration. Some of them have been killed since.

So many of the best leave us. Another loss to mountaineering since that time has been my friend John Harlin, killed on the first ascent of the direct route on the north face of the Eiger, a fantastic month-long siege in midwinter by ten exceptional climbers. As I read the news I could not restrain my tears thinking of my climbs with him, notably a first ascent on the Blaitière. Memories returned of holidays in my little chalet at Chamonix, his manly character, his kindness, the rope fixed on the Col de l'Innominata on the occasion of the Fresney disaster. Pictures of my dead friends came flooding back, so many of them, Kohlman, Guillaume, Vieille, Oggioni, Couzy, Terray, Alzetta, Kinshoffer, Michielli, Von Allmen, brothers-in-arms who have our undying admiration, to whom these lines are dedicated. Why should that climb on the Eiger have aroused so much controversy? What courage and strength was shown during that month of struggle, dedicated afterwards to the outstanding American climber John Harlin, the real driving force behind the exploit on which he met his death in the thick of the fight and, as seems noblest in retrospect, alone. I shall always be grateful to him for his example, his friendship, and, above all, for teaching me that there are no frontiers in mountaineering.

That night we did not sleep. It was still snowing, and our anxiety was too great for sleep to come. Would we succeed next day? Would we remain prisoners without bars, our only recourse this appalling emptiness around us? At daybreak, Jacques wasted no time. He could feel neither his hands nor his feet, but our burning desire to escape gave us confidence. A mass of ice at the jammed block led me to try going round on the outside, a pitch of VI without any pitons that I had to redescend when I discovered my mistake. Presently, however, we came to the final chimneys, and as we reached the circular ledges the sun came out. A pleasant surprise was waiting for us on the summit, where we found Michel Vaucher with a couple of his clients. Worried by the weather, he had come up to see if he could help. At last we could eat, drink and enjoy the company of our fellow men. In the course of the long descent our iron-hard features relaxed again into a semblance of humanity.

CHAPTER X

The Cengalo

DURING THE WINTER of 1960–61 Pierre Kohlman and I
slowly and methodically trained with a view to some winter
mountaineering. We now felt ourselves sufficiently mature in
technique and in ourselves to carry out some major feat, and
our minds were constantly bent on achievement. Our reading,
our conversation, our friendships, all that was essential in our
life, were invested in this capital, the interest on which was still
greater enthusiasm, which we kept up by frenzied training
sessions on the surrounding outcrops at weekends. We were
ready to choose the most difficult winter ascent that had yet
been done.

One evening in February we set out after a gargantuan
dinner at Léon's cooked for us by "maman" herself, who has
often wept for lost climbers. Having known most of them, she
considers herself an adoptive mother. The weight of equipment
in our hired 2 CV made ground clearance practically nil. I
sat in the driver's seat with Pierre beside me and the famous
Habib and no less renowned La Fouine, the heroes of the
Pouce, behind.

It was a journey full of fun and charm and laughter. At
Basel the Swiss wanted to lock up Habib, who is Algerian,
because it was the height of the crisis and Bourguiba was
having important meetings at Arosa. At a maximum of 80
kilometres per hour we took three days and nights to cover
the 1000 kilometres to the Julier pass, St Moritz, Bondo and a
snow-covered Promontogno where I was happy to arrive again.
I had never known Pierre quite so hilarious as on that journey,
and have never laughed quite so much. What was more, we
never once talked mountaineering. Nevertheless, we were not
to be allowed to forget it for long.

After a quiet night at Promontogno we set off on our skis,
bowed under enormous rucksacks, for the north face of the Piz
Badile, which we could see between two ranks of pines. What
riveted our attention, alas, was the whiteness of its icy armour.

The path was utterly different from what it had been in summer, it too all white. The only thing that seemed unchanged was the quietness. Late that evening we were still far from the intended bivouac site, and slept in a little wooden barn full of hay, covered with a layer of this natural down. In the morning we came out into an apocalyptic landscape, a desert not of sand but of snow. As we plodded up through the inhuman landscape the spell of the north face became more and more powerful. Towards evening, utterly exhausted, La Fouine set down his load and skied away down. The three of us went on.

After we had set up our camp in that ocean of white it was difficult to sleep on account of fatigue and fear. Without knowing it, we were beginning a long week. The next day was spent organizing everything for our siege of the Cassin route on the north face, of which we were hoping to make the first winter ascent. I made a solo reconnaissance, but returned demoralized. The Rébuffat dièdre was covered with ice, and success seemed not so much improbable as out of the question. The weather was magnificent, but the intense February cold and absence of sunlight made the problem one of the most difficult imaginable. The very fact that the face was neither particularly steep nor at high altitude meant that the snow did not slide off it but turned into a thick layer of hard ice.

I began to doubt our success, and my friends felt sceptical also. Nevertheless, we agreed to set out next morning and fix ropes as high as we could get, returning to camp in the evening. Each morning after that we would climb back up the ropes using prusik knots until we reached the central snow patch, after which we would go for the summit. It was all very nice in theory.

And so we duly followed my tracks the following morning up the snowslope that covered the first few pitches of the summer route. Even as we prepared to attack, the gleaming ice above robbed us of conviction.

We are taught as children that there is no such word as "impossible" in the French language. On this occasion it turned out that there was. It took us a whole day to reach the top of the first corner. When I came back down Pierre and Habib understood that I was giving up. Sometimes the mountain's defences are too much even for the most desperate efforts; sometimes they kill.

However, we were unwilling for our adventure to end in

total defeat, so we decided to try the easier north ridge. This time the attempt lasted two days before we were beaten back. Pierre and I climbed several pitches, but each time we were invaded by a feeling of hopelessness. In the course of one delicate traverse on snow-plastered slabs I was belaying him without any anchor when suddenly the snow broke away, carrying him with it. I began to slide also, but by some miracle managed to hold him until he stopped. This time it seemed as though we were going to drag each other off in turn until we hurtled to the bottom of the mountain, but a second miracle occurred and I felt the shock of the rope holding me. Pierre had had the presence of mind to get up and catch hold of it. Exhausted, we decided to give in, and rappelled back to the foot of the climb. Habib looked after us like a mother. It was to be five years before friends from Lecco succeeded in making the first winter ascent of this ridge after overcoming innumerable difficulties.

Next day, however, the marvellous weather encouraged us to remain. We dozed, but from time to time also began to cast glances at the north gully of the Piz Cengalo, the only portion of the entire vista that seemed to offer any hope at all. Pierre set off to reconnoitre, and the sight of his tracks in the snow began to provoke a desire to do this first winter ascent, not to return empty-handed, but in some degree to revenge ourselves on the mountain.

On his return, Pierre was optimistic for the first time since our arrival. The gully was steep, but if we climbed fast it would be all right. The hours of daylight are short at this time of the year, and a bivouac on our feet would be terrible. I decided to sleep outside the tent, and fell asleep feeling reassured. I wanted to live through those marvellous hours with the stars shining above my head. Somehow I felt alone in an accursed place, yet full of good hope. As my eyes closed I heard Pierre talking in his sleep and Habib telling him to shut up. Then I sank into unconsciousness.

In the morning we made our way across to the foot of the gully, passing underneath the north-east face of the Piz Badile which had repulsed us. The gully described a sort of vertical S shape down the mountain, seeming steeper as we got closer to it. Below the bergschrund we roped up and I set off, ploughing a track as deep as my stomach in the fresh snow. A yawning blue hole made me picture the interior of the crevasse. Presently I was able to belay and bring up my friends. For the next 15 hours Pierre and I were to lead through without stopping. We were really set on climbing this couloir. It was our test-piece, our proof that we had not come for nothing.

As soon as we were over the bergschrund, we entered into a world of verticality. The Cengalo was on our left, while to our right lay the terrible north-east face of the Badile, plated with bare ice. In order to safeguard ourselves carefully, and also because we were a party of three, we moved slowly. Each of us paid attention to his own work; we did not speak much. I would plough ahead through the deep snow, sometimes butting up against angles as high as 60 degrees, while Habib belayed me and Pierre climbed up to him. Then I would belay in my turn while Pierre came past and into the lead, followed by Habib. So we changed places again and again, but without any monotony, making our way calmly forward. As we rose higher relative to the north face of the Badile it became more and more horrifying. The weather was cold, and our limbs became frozen by the wind and the contact with the new snow, particularly during the long halts while the leader made his way forward.

At about mid-height things became dramatic. The slope was now at its maximum, and under the fresh snow the ice was so hard that the crampons would not bite into it. Between my legs I could look down 800 metres of couloir; the smallest mistake would mean falling down it, and I could imagine our bodies following the S-bend, bouncing off its rocky banks and smashing down to their deaths below. I did not want to look down, and yet, in order to explain various manoeuvres to my friends, I had to. Lost in the white immensity, two small black points were following me anxiously with their eyes. I took a few photographs and Pierre did the same.

Slowly the light began to ebb away, much as we wished somehow to hold it back. Pierre began to force the pace, and at times I found it frightening to watch him. In this couloir where the lack of sunlight meant that the new snow never altered and coalesced it was necessary to be doubly careful. Metre by metre we advanced, each of us tensely surveying not only his own progress but that of the others, because the least slip would be fatal to all three.

At last night thickened around us, and like children we were afraid of the dark, recommending each other to take care. Only the light of our head-torches seemed to link us with the world of the living. Far, far away the lights of Promontogno reminded us that other men were sitting enjoying the pleasures of their warm homes, while three lonely madmen gazed down from this soulless, lifeless couloir.

Slowly I climbed on, the small circle of light cast by my head-torch seeming to play with the wall of snow as my feet sought points of support. Underneath there was still nothing but ice. I could not rely on the support of my ice-axe, which found no hold in this floury mass. Below me the dark gulf yawned; above, in the leaden sky, twinkled a few stars. I was determined to avoid a bivouac in these circumstances and made my way upwards with many precautions, gripped with fear.

Presently the slope became so steep that my head bumped against it, and my torch suddenly went out. It seemed that the worst must happen, and yet at such moments my whole being is pervaded with stillness, as though my nerves would deny their own fright. I concentrated my mind on finding a solution, picked out in the pale light of my friends' torches. For a few moments I was as though paralysed, then slowly, slowly, set about changing the battery and broken bulb. I knew that one clumsy gesture would cost all our lives. The manoeuvre took an hour. My body was parallel with the slope, my forehead and arms touching the snow. Everything depended on my feet, which however had no firm hold, and I was afraid that they would skid away down the smooth, holdless ice-chute. It was at this juncture that Habib contributed to my morale with the shameless lie that he could hold me, and Pierre by reciting the "Our father . . ."

Then, as though by a miracle, my lamp shone again, and I could see an enormous cornice a short way above me. Between me and it, however, lay several metres of verticality. Having no illusions about our belay, I asked for all the slack and struggled on, my face frozen by repeated contact with the snow. At last I could touch the cornice, which overhung nearly two metres. It was real navvy's work tunnelling through it, and by the time I had hacked my way through the upper layer of ice I was panting and at the end of my strength. A last mantelshelf took me out on to the summit, whence I could shout joyfully to my friends, who were thus enabled to terminate their prayers and call back.

Like a madman I staggered around in the wind on the plateau, looking for a rock where I could plant a piton. Presently the search was rewarded, and I could return happily to the hole in the cornice to bring up my friends, who were also glad to know that the ordeal was almost over. As they arrived, we embraced. Our relief was all the greater for the fact that we had been frightened for fully fifteen hours. Now we were delirious with joy over our long first winter ascent and its successful conclusion. Our first action was to eat, chattering of the climb as we did so. We could think of nothing but those terrible hours during which we had reduced our complexes to simplicity again. I had the rather childish feeling of having surpassed myself, and when I confided in my companions I discovered that they felt the same. Danger and toil had brought forth joy. Presently we rolled ourselves into our sleeping-bags and slept. It was an ecstatic bivouac.

The following morning it was snowing. Hurriedly we descended in the direction of the Gianetti hut, only the roof of which was showing through the grey waste of snow. Then we turned the bastions of the south face of the Cengalo and with increasing weariness climbed up to the Passo di Bondo. I knew the route already, and felt buoyed up by my friends' trust in me. On the col we were struck by a veritable tempest of wind and snow; if we were to avoid another bivouac we should have to move fast, which on account of our fatigue might prove fatal. The fear of losing ourselves in this white whirling immensity gave us renewed strength, and I cleared the trail through an inextricable chaos of yawning crevasses, the largest I have ever seen. Carelessly we blundered down slopes which were ready to avalanche. When I think about them today, it makes me shiver: this is how so many disasters occur on descents.

Presently Habib left us to continue on down to Promontogno. Pierre and I toiled our way back up to the camp below the north face of the Badile. Torture as it was, there was the couloir in front of us with our steps smack up the middle of it.

Quickly we packed the equipment into our sacks and began the descent. More torture. The close weather had rendered the snow soft and heavy, and Pierre, who had never skied before, was constantly overbalanced by the weight of his sack. I did what I could to help, presently attaching him to the rope and towing, but this only made him fall the more often and painfully. All my life I shall remember that climb, with its terrible uphill and downhill ordeals.

As darkness fell we reached the little barn where we had slept on the way up, burst in the door, and fell fast asleep on the hay fully clothed and with our skis on our feet. It was quite a surprise to wake up in the morning and find ourselves already fully equipped for the descent. Even our rucksacks had not spoiled our slumbers.

It did not take long to run down, and on the way we met La Fouine waiting for us anxiously and impatiently. It was not a pleasant moment, as he informed us that the couloir had already been climbed in winter. I cursed him as a harbinger of evil. However, this was only his revenge for not having taken part. Ours was indeed the first winter ascent, as my great friend Riccardo Cassin was later to confirm.

As we read the newspaper that morning, Pierre and I learned that a German team had just taken advantage of the same period of fine weather to do the first winter ascent of the Eigerwand. Later I was to have the opportunity of meeting them all and expressing my admiration. Their names were Hiebeler, Mannhardt, Amberger and Toni Kinshoffer, who after the death of Kohlman was to become my best friend until he in his turn found eternal rest among the mountains.

We drove gaily back to Paris, singing for two nights and a day without leaving off.

This was a good period in my life, divided between a profound interest in my work, which restored my confidence, and weekends on rock or snow. Hoping to see something of that training ground of great climbers, we took a quick trip to Munich, but were foiled by the weather. It was a time when I shed all my tension, but also of preparation for the coming season. Incessantly, often solo, Pierre and I climbed up and down practically all the routes at Saussois and in the Ardennes. I remember a deliriously happy day at l'Ange, with Dany tied on between us, when in defiance of all the rules the three of us belayed to a single peg. But above all, Pierre and I thought about the central Pillar of Fresnay.

This was also the time of Pierre's first attempts to ski, apart from the descent from the Cengalo. The first day, coming down the red piste at Les Houches, the muscular monster schussed the Mur des Epines. On his first and last descent of the Vallée Blanche, I can still see him almost sobbing with the pain, asking me why on earth I had brought him there before he even knew how to turn. We were constantly together in the warmth of friendship. I had a terrible time getting him to take out a life insurance policy. Then there were our fantastic departures on Friday evenings; our simple childish joys; and as a kind of climax of happiness before it faded for eternity there were days of fulfilment in the Gorges of the Jonte and Tarn.

On two occasions, Pierre Kohlman had doubled for Jean Marais in climbing scenes, and the latter now asked him to find half-a-dozen friends to take part in a cloak-and-dagger movie. Naturally he thought of us, and so it was that Dany, Pipo, La Fouine, Habib, Vieille and I foregathered in the rue de la Victoire to receive the orders of Kohlman, our leader. We were already intrigued by this new kind of adventure. Our job was to do terrifying abseils over the high limestone crags of the Jonte Gorge, and also to teach the real actors to climb. This was how we came to meet Jean Marais.

Before going down to Meyrneis we took him to the Saussois where, thanks to his good nature, we soon had him climbing. He turned out to be exceptionally gifted. For several weekends running we crossed France in a 2 CV Citroen to set up the abseils. I remember one weekend in particular when, setting off from the rue de la Victoire on Saturday evening, we drove all through the night to arrive next morning in the bleak, splendid scenery of the Méjean moors, where we spent four hours pegging and preparing the scenario for the film before heading straight back to Paris so as to be in our offices by 8 a.m. next day. Thus we spent the ridiculous time of thirty hours driving for the sake of four hours' work.

Presently it was time to join the rest of the troop, so we hired cars and descended on Meyrneis. The hotel was friendly and the filming team truly remarkable. I well remember the horrifying 120 metre abseils among the overhangs, so different from anything in our ordinary climbing experience. There was one strand of rope and no top-rope, and in general it was the height of folly. Luckily everything worked out for the best, and "le Miracle des Loups" was a success. Due credit was given to Pierre Kohlman's team of climbers.

I will refrain from describing the delirious evenings at Meyrneis in company with Marais and his friends, but they were the foundation of a genuine friendship, and the famous actor was deeply affected when Pierre and Antoine met their deaths a few months later, an occasion on which he wrote me the most touching letter I have ever received. When not filming, we explored the countryside, one of the most austerely beautiful areas in France, hitherto unknown to us. Habib and I tried fishing for trout, but without success. As the only woman, Dany too had the time of her life, surrounding us all with kindness. Marais would talk of himself and Cocteau, while I talked mountaineering. When Pierre and I were together, however, our only subject of conversation was the central pillar of Fresnay. It must have been our destiny.

After ten days or so the filming was over, and we returned to Paris. As we drove back in our hired cars, we had the feeling of having lived through an adventure which could never be repeated.

CHAPTER XI

The Central Pillar of Fresnay

PERHAPS IT MAY seem inopportune to bring up the subject
of the central pillar of Fresnay once again. Nevertheless a
certain scruple of objectivity impels me to return towards an
event which was a school of life for those of us who survived;
and above all a sense of obligation towards our friends, great-
hearted mountaineers all.

The central pillar of Fresnay somehow represents an era in
the history of mountaineering, and for this reason it will be
well to place it in its proper geographical and historical setting.

There is no doubt that climbers see few sights so fine as the
colossal southern face of Mont Blanc viewed from Courmayeur.
Some of the sharpest struggles and some of the finest first
ascents in the annals of climbing have taken place on its icy
flanks. At the time of which I write this mountain stronghold
still harboured one of the last great problems of the Alps: the
central pillar.

The pillars of Fresnay are situated between the Innominata
and Peuterey ridges, which also have their place in mountaineering history. The left-hand pillar is really a direct continuation of the Innominata. That on the right, first climbed
during the Second World War by Giusto Gervasutti, most
human of mountaineers, is bounded by a great gully of ice
ascended by Walter Bonatti in 1961. At the time of which I
write, the grandiose central pillar remained virgin. From its
base in the upper Fresnay glacier it soars some 700 metres to
just below the crest of the Brouillard ridge where the latter
merges into the summital dome of Mont Blanc. From a
climber's point of view it divides into three parts. The first,
which is not vertical, gives mixed rock and ice work; the
second, which is almost vertical, gives mainly rock-climbing;
and the third, which overhangs in many places, can only be
climbed by artificial means.

By virtue of its scale and exceptional situation, it was
inevitable that the central pillar should attract the attention

The Fresnay face of Mont Blanc

of mountaineers, and it is easy to imagine Gervasutti glancing to his left when climbing the right-hand pillar. Similarly, climbers on the Innominata ridge must often have noticed it on their right. To the best of my knowledge, however, the first to think about it seriously were Bastien and Coutin when they made the second ascent of Gervasutti's route in 1952.* They took several photographs, but must have considered the problem insoluble as they did nothing about it.

The first serious attempt was made by Bonatti, Oggioni and Gallieni in August 1959. They carried equipment up to the Col de Peuterey via the Fresnay glacier and the Rochers Grüber. From the col they climbed to the top of the first step, but realizing the need for more equipment they then turned back.

In June the following year the French climbers Desmaison, Payot, Audibert, Lagesse, Laffont and Mazeaud made an attempt, but were overtaken by bad weather on the Rochers Grüber and had to retreat after two bivouacs without having reached the foot of the pillar.

As we drove down from Paris in June 1961 the continual rain did nothing to encourage our optimism, and when we reached Chamonix our fears were realized: the summits were covered in new snow, while in the valley it was still raining. Bored with having nothing to do, Kohlman and I walked up through the rain to the bivouac under the Dru, hoping to try the Bonatti pillar. Dany Badier kept us company as far as the foot of the couloir then returned alone, as we impatiently decided to attack at once. The bad weather delayed us a good deal, especially the storms, thus giving us a particularly good opportunity to appreciate the extraordinary qualities of Walter Bonatti, who had made the first ascent alone. We reached the quartz ledge at the top of the climb after two bivouacs; it was here that we had bivouacked after climbing the west face. The

* Translator's note: It may be relevant to add that when L. Terray, G. H. Francis and the translator made the third ascent of the right-hand pillar a few days after Bastien, they also noted the possibility. The latter spoke of it afterwards to Brown and Whillans, who were immediately interested. Thus Whillan's motivation in fact antedated that of the author, and was not aroused by the tragedy as suggested in the final chapter. The challenge was sufficiently obvious, and other attempts had in fact been planned and made.

weather was now splendid. It was time to hurry over to the Pillar of Fresnay.

So it was that a party of four set out on the first cable-car to the Aiguille du Midi on Saturday 8th July. There was Pierre Kohlman my best friend, with whom I had done all my best climbs. His strength made him a better free climber than I, but it was above all his intellectual and moral qualities that won my esteem and affection. He loved the mountains because there he could be alone, far from the madding crowd and close to God, whom he was destined to meet so soon. There was Robert Guillaume, an exceptional mountaineer who had given up everything to live at Chamonix in the shadow of the granite needles on which he had done practically all the climbs, often alone. The youngest of us was Antoine Vieille, the great hope of French mountaineering. A man of elemental energy and physically the most powerful of us, by some paradox he was to be the first to die. Though he had only been mountaineering for two years his list of achievements was already impressive, and he dreamed of the Dolomites which he was never to see. Finally there was myself, by far the oldest. Because of this, and because I had already made an attempt on the pillar, I assumed a certain responsibility.

We were full of confidence and joy, which overflowed into shouting and song as we crossed the Bedière in hot sunlight towards the Fourche hut where our kit was already stacked waiting for us. The last steep slope led us to the view of our kingdom, Brenva, Peuterey, and there beyond, in the distance, the pillar.

The day was spent in final preparations. As usual before a major undertaking, it was difficult to sleep. Tactical preparations or preparation of dreams . . . Pierre chatted away, happy like the rest of us, as can be seen from the photos we took at the door of the hut against the magnificent backdrop of the lower bay of the Brenva.

At midnight, heavily loaded, we abseiled from the hut down to the glacier. The weather was oppressive. It had not frozen, and we struggled along breaking through into the snow. Even the Col Moore presented difficulties, and the traverse under the dangerous overhanging séracs on either side of the Route Major and the Pear Buttress was made in fear and total darkness.

The snow was wet and heavy at daybreak as we began the climb up to the Col de Peuterey. Menacing clouds gathered over Italy so that we could no longer see down the Val d'Aosta, and when we were about half way to the col we decided to turn back to the hut. It was laborious kicking our way back up to the Col Moore. These were the first disappointments and lassitudes. Alas, they were to go unrewarded. By the time we reached the Col de la Fourche, Pierre and I were seriously worried about our friends, who had not yet appeared over the Col Moore, so we went back to help them. The rest of the day was spent lying in our bunks at the hut while it snowed outside. At about 8 p.m. it suddenly grew cold and the clouds vanished, renewing our hopes. Anxiously, unable to sleep, we waited for midnight, chatting of this and that, trying not to think of the pillar although we could think of nothing else.

The alarm went off at midnight. Another day: Monday 10th July 1961. Lazily we stretched, lit the primus and waited for our tea. There was a sound of voices outside to which we listened tensely. Metallic noises, ice-axes, crampons. The door opened and three men came in. It did not take long to understand what it was all about. In the semi-darkness we recognized Walter Bonatti, who could only be heading for the pillar. And we had thought he was in Peru! There were mutual introductions: he was with Andrea Oggioni, a name which spoke for itself, and Roberto Gallieni.

We came to the point without delay. The famous Bonatti charmed us from the outset and recognized our priority. He had come straight up from Courmayeur, not knowing we were ahead of him; now he offered to go somewhere else and repeat the climb after us. Antoine Vieille suggested that we join forces, and without any hesitation there was a general round of embraces. A Franco-Italian party to climb one of the last great problems on the grandiose southern face of this great mountain which belonged to their two countries: what a wonderful idea. The impulse of our hearts was the same, we shared one wild, profound joy. Henceforth friendship would be our only guide. It was to remain written on the faces of our four friends forever.

Immediately we worked out a plan of campaign. Walter had already cached all the necessary equipment on the Col de Peuterey, so we could climb up there with light sacks, thus gaining time. The Italians were to go ahead up to the col, then descend for their equipment to the top of the Rochers Grüber while we led the first step of the pillar. Next day they would lead the second step, and on the third day the two French parties would lead on to the top, equipping the last step. This plan was followed to the letter in an atmosphere of perfect mutual understanding right up to the beginning of the drama.

Bonatti then made a short entry in the hut book to indicate where we were going. This message was to be found by Gigi Panei, and enabled us to be located. We packed up the equipment we were leaving behind—100 pitons, 50 karabiners and 30 wooden wedges—and wrote our names on it. Nevertheless, some unscrupulous person made off with it, and when some of our friends went up to recover it towards the end of July, it was no longer there. It was now 1 o'clock, and Bonatti and his companions set off. We watched their head-torches going down the abseil rope we had left, then progressing rapidly towards the Col Moore. For us, there was something unforgettable about the moment. A friendship had been sealed; the great game was about to begin.

As I slowly closed the door of the refuge, I thought of the adventure ahead, full of enthusiasm at the idea of leading my friends towards this great first ascent. It was as though a film were running through my head, a flow of thoughts, a creative rapture of the imagination, mixed with apprehension and questioning. How would it all go? Mountaineers are familiar with this state of mind before a climb. Afterwards, in the heat of action, there is no more time for imagining except during bivouacs.

Being the oldest, I had a feeling of responsibility which indeed still troubles me. I was happy to be able to share it with Walter Bonatti, and somehow it has caused me to feel more strongly about Mont Blanc than about any other mountain, in spite of the tragedy.

Kohlman and I brought up the rear. The torches of the Italians disappeared over the Col Moore; our tracks from the previous day enabled them to make good time. Vieille and Guillaume being also well ahead, the cold, starlit silence became oppressive as we made that unforgettable crossing of the upper Brenva glacier to the foot of the Col de Peuterey.

Here we caught up with the Italians as Bonatti, with masterly technique, cut steps all the way up the couloir. The slope was sometimes very steep, but urged onward by our own desire and the enthusiasm of the Italians we moved ahead together, rarely stopping to belay. Dawn found us still committed to the slope, framed on the left by the beautiful north face of the Aiguille Blanche de Peuterey and on the right by the impressive Eckpfeiler buttress, another Bonatti route. Presently we came to the rocky barrier below the col. The loose rock provided a serious obstacle, and it proved impossible to protect ourselves, as the schist split whenever we tried to drive in a piton.

By 6 a.m. we were all on the Col de Peuterey, the pillar towering above us like a colossal arrow pointing to the summit of Mont Blanc de Courmayeur, a dream-world. Along the crest of the Peuterey Ridge were tracks left by the French guide Pierre Julien, who later was to break the traditions of mountaineering,* ignoring the example given after the death of Meier on the north face of the Grandes Jorasses, when other climbers left the face alone so that Peters might have the joy of returning to commemorate his friend. An omen. . . .

We spent some time on the col going over our plan of attack. Above us the ruddy granite was bright in the sunlight, and surely in the whole world there can be nowhere more beautiful than this lonely spot. Then Bonatti and Oggioni went down to the Rochers Grüber while Gallieni, who had not slept for three nights, took the opportunity to doze off. The rest of us set off towards the base of the pillar, intending to reach the top of the first step before evening.

I began the traverse at about 8 o'clock, sinking into the snow which was already softening, but I was hurrying so much in order to avoid stonefall in the couloir between the pillars that there was no time to think of anything else. Pierrot belayed me, watching my movements. He knew what to do. I had so much confidence in him that I never needed to give directions. He loved the mountains in the same way as me;

* Translator's note: It is difficult to understand why Julien should be singled out for this treatment, since numerous others mentioned in this book also took part in subsequent attempts on the pillar. And it must in all candour be remarked that the history of mountaineering reveals no such tradition as is here evoked; rather the contrary.

I knew that at this moment he would be vibrant with happiness to the depths of his being. Once across the rimaye, I kicked up a steep little slope to the first outcrops of rock, hammering in a couple of pitons and leaving a fixed line so that the Italian party could join us more quickly. Towards 11 o'clock, after the first difficult pitches, the four of us stopped for a rest. Below us, Bonatti and Oggioni were struggling slowly back towards Gallieni, bowed under heavy sacks. Above us towered the bare granite. It was good to take off our sacks and eat while snapping a few photos.

I was feeling on great form, and while Pierre belayed me I attacked a magnificent 40 metre slab, one of the finest pitches on the pillar and entirely free except for one wooden wedge. I felt free and happy. Pierre came up rapidly in his turn, an exceptional climber. He would have liked to be leading, but as he was the best of us I wanted him to save himself for the assault on the final step. Behind us, Antoine and Robert were fixing ropes and pitons for the benefit of the Italians, who were feeling somewhat tired, and whose strength should also be saved for the final push. It all seems so vivid as I write.

It was mixed ground and took time. Under the rather anxious gaze of my companions I had to fight my way up an icy chimney. Finally, at getting on for 4 o'clock, I reached the last pitch, an imposing overhang well plastered with ice. It took me two hours and a number of pitons, but at last I was able to pull over on to the top of the first step tired but happy. I remember calling down to Antoine "Le Mazeaud n'est pas fini!"*

By this time the Italians had caught up with my friends, and I could read the fatigue of the day in their faces. The first ones up to me prepared the bivouac while I safeguarded the others, and by 7 o'clock our cookers were humming. There was a lot of chatter and exchanges of songs from the Val d'Aosta and Montmartre. The weather was cold and splendidly clear.

From our perch we looked out over the Fresnay Glacier and the famous Aiguille Noire. Just beside us was the Innominata Ridge, and away in the distance the Gran Paradiso. There was a light, fine-weather haze, and I had a short discussion

* Translator's note: a pun. In French, "mazout" = fuel oil.

with Walter. Everything had gone well, and in two days' time we should be over the summit and on our way down to Chamonix. Antoine and I smoked a few Celtiques. We had never experienced such a perfect bivouac. Calmly and happily we dozed off. Pierre silently said his prayers as usual—it was our thirtieth bivouac together—then woke me, just after I had succeeded in getting to sleep, in order to wish me goodnight with a beaming smile.

At 3.30 a.m. on Tuesday 11th July, Walter and Andrea woke us up—as usual, no easy matter where Antoine was concerned. It was bitterly cold, so we waited for the sun to appear, which it did in great splendour half an hour later, recalling us to the struggle. Slowly and lazily we got ready, using the opportunity to take a few photos. Walter got perhaps the last picture of the four French climbers together. Then he was off; that day it was the job of the Italians to lead the second step. It was the kind of mixed climbing at which he excels. He placed very few pitons, but left behind ropes and étriers to help us. For my part, I brought up the rear with a heavy sackful of equipment, literally hoisted upwards by Kohlman, and I cannot claim to have got to grips with any difficult pitches. Far above me, I could hear Walter battling with icy runnels. When the artificial pitches began to appear, Antoine took his turn at the rear.

We got along quickly enough, with very few halts, and to be perfectly truthful we had little time to admire the scenery. I was bowed under the weight of the sack, and my friends helped me by hauling on a rope directly attached to it. Towards 2 o'clock, Bonatti called down that the final step was in sight. I stopped and looked up. It was a veritable apparition, overhanging and gradiose. We were all spellbound. Already it seemed clear that the route would go up the great crack in the right-hand face and that by the following evening we should be on the summit. Nothing was going to turn us back at this stage.

A difficult rock pitch and a very narrow ridge of ice brought us to the foot of these last difficulties. I took out the photographs, comparing them with the reality. We obviously had some artificial climbing in store for us, but for the time being we were together again, tired but happy at being face to face with the crux. After a few words it was decided that Pierre and I would prepare the first few pitches while the others got everything ready for the bivouac. I even had the secret idea of bivouacking in étriers half-way up the step in order to save time—it reminded me of the Cima Ovest.

Pierre set off in the lead. The first pitch proved to be artificial and led to the summit of a pillar we called "the candle". There we found such a comfortable ledge that we called down to our friends to quit their bulldozing operations and come up to join us. When we were all together again, it was my turn to lead. The rock was as trusty as a friend; I felt confident and safe. We were now at 4600 metres. It was another magnificent artificial pitch, and the pegs sang as they went in. I shouted my joy to the heavens, while Walter smiled up at me and admired my speed. Those moments of mastery and plenitude were the finest of my life.

Emerging from a line of crack, I made a delicate rightwards traverse, then, by a long exposed step, reached another crack which I started to peg. It was at this moment that the bell sounded for one of the greatest dramas in the history of mountain climbing.

The weather was splendid, the sky of an untroubled blue.

Seated in my étriers, I was hammering away when I heard a sound rather like the ringing of a telephone. Forty metres below me, my companions pricked up their ears. Suddenly there were pains in my hands and sparks began to flow out of the hammer, while the karabiners slung over my shoulder stuck to my fingers. Bonatti shouted up that an electric storm was about to strike. This rather astonished me, as the air was perfectly clear and there was not a breath of wind. Nevertheless, I attached all the equipment at the highest point reached and fixed the rope for an abseil. Before I had reached the bottom of this short descent, the space of a few seconds, I was caught in a violent squall, surrounded by swirling cloud and lashed by hail. Just as I swung across to join Pierre on the ledge, a flash of astonishing intensity struck him right on the ear. His hearing aid turned black and he fell haggard and inanimate into my arms.

Now the drama began in all its horror. We were trapped on the Candle, which was to be our torture chamber. Flash followed flash. At first there was thunder, then silence, but in an atmosphere dazzling with ozone. It was 5 o'clock. We did not move or prepare the bivouac, but just stood there leaning against the rock, Pierre and I together, the others below, transfixed with fear.

Fear remained with us all that interminable evening and yet more interminable night. Measuring our movements, we put the ironmongery as far away from us as possible and tried to sit down, but the strokes redoubled in frequency, making us jerk and jump helplessly, horribly. Only the ropes by which we were anchored prevented us from being catapulted over the 600 metre drop below. Pierrot was visibly the worst affected, so I gave him an injection of Coramine.

The Italians installed themselves as best they could in their bivouac tent, while we sat down under our plastic sheets. Each stroke of lightning stiffened us against the conducting rock and would have been fatal if we had not been completely soaked. The highest pillar on Mont Blanc was acting as our lightning conductor.

The fear of death possessed us. There was nothing to say or do but sit and wait for death to come. We all took Coramine to stimulate our resistance to our all-pervading weakness and nausea. When midnight came it was light as in a blast furnace. Every so often we were simultaneously convulsed, and one particularly violent shock banged our faces roughly against the rock and made the Italians leap. Sparks issued from our hands and feet, and later I was to find that I bore the marks on my ankles in the form of little black stars. Antoine did his best to reassure me, though in reality he was as scared as I was, while Robert looked after us all.

We wept not so much from weakness as from discouragement. It was inhuman. Pierre was struck again and slumped over my knees, sliding down the rock, and I grabbed the rope to hold him back. I spoke to him, but he did not reply; he was practically never to reply again. Now that his hearing aid was burnt out he was completely deaf. I held him in my arms and he looked at me with tears slowly running down his face. I had never loved him so much. What is so strong as friendship?

What did we think of? Each of us kept his inner thoughts to himself, but we all prayed, the Italians in their beautiful singing language, we in our rougher one. And we all thought of death, which was there before us. The continuous terror was burdensome, pressing, dismaying, as the storm persisted through the small hours of Wednesday, 12th July.

At 7 a.m. the electrical storm stopped, and it began to snow heavily. The calm seemed marvellous; soaked and exhausted as we were, we fell asleep in unbelievable attitudes, disturbed by nightmares. At 10 o'clock, a clearing enabled us to see Mont Fréty, white with snow. The wind had got round into the north, and we shouted our joy. The couloirs around the pillar were rumbling with incessant avalanches, but heavy clouds were still torn by the gusts from the summit of Mont Blanc and borne away over Italy at vertiginous speed.

We sorted things out, cleared the snow, moved the kit farther away, and had a hot meal. We were unanimous that there was no need to retreat. Our equipment was in perfect order, and we were so near the goal: 80 metres at most, and I should be at the top of the pillar. In July, bad weather never lasts more than 24 hours . . . what we did not know was that the storm was sweeping across France from the Channel to the Alps, and that many sailors, our comrades in peril, would never return to port.

So, though it had begun to snow again, we regained confidence. The day went by. We talked mountaineering, telling each other about our various climbs. Bonatti and his friends impressed us by their calmness, and I think that they were impressed by our resilience. I remember a lengthy discussion with him about "his" pillar, which Kohlman and I had done a few days before. Antoine was hungry and kept on cooking meals for us all. Still it went on snowing, but we waited, convinced that the nocturnal cold would improve the weather. Now and again I would look up at the wall that I had begun to peg, now covered in ice. The ropes were rigid, the étriers swung sadly in the wind. Forty metres above hung my hammer, marking the highest point attained. My karabiners clicked against their pitons. It was a sad enough picture: beaten climbers waiting for the end.

How could those who later stole our victory have failed to see all this equipment?

As evening fell hopes faded. Each of us withdrew into his own thoughts, hardly speaking any more, the Italians below us in their tent, we under our plastic sheet, backs to the rock, feet hanging in space.

That second evening was even more dramatic than the first. Towards 6 o'clock the sound of thunder was heard again.

We were literally transfixed with terror and lay there waiting for the worst, while Pierrot, who could hear nothing, slept peacefully on my shoulder. The white luminous atmosphere which is the precursor of lightning was not long in arriving. Soon came the first shocks, bringing with them the familiar sensation of feebleness. We lay passively, in an agony of fear, lost in that brightly lit inferno. Towards midnight it faded, only to give way to heavy snowfall, soon followed by a violent wind, a wind which made us believe that the longed-for miracle was about to happen. And alas, a miracle did happen.

Thursday 13th July began with bitter cold and a clear sky. Our clothes were rigid with the frost. As we sat there shivering the stars twinkled above us, the lights of Courmayeur far in the gulf below. All of us were now awake, filled with renewed hope. Tomorrow would be a day compounded of sunlight, victory, joy and the end of suffering. The day after would be a day of calm . . . shouting and singing with exultation, we lit our primuses for a brew, sending signals of encouragement towards Courmayeur with our head-torches. Yet, though Bianca Bonatti and Giovanna Gallieni were looking up at the pillar at that time, they saw nothing. We chatted about everything, made bets about the outcome of the Tour de France and jokes about the lightning. I got my equipment ready so that I could start with the first rays of the sun. Racked with cramps, Pierrot got up and stretched. He felt so happy that he suggested carrying on right away; after all, we had climbed together in the dark before, and had he not achieved the exceptional feat of climbing the final roof-overhang of the Cima Ovest at 1 o'clock in the morning?

Never had hope been so great. It was good to think that our friends would be reassured and would not need to organize any kind of rescue party. Presently, however, sloth overcame our frozen bodies, and we slept.

The awakening was perhaps the bitterest of my life. The next act of the drama had begun, crueller and more immediate than ever. At 10 o'clock we were woken by thunder. The snow was driven down the wind with such force that our plastic sheet was torn. Yet there was no wavering; we were all resolved to remain there, frozen to our "chandelle" which Andrea with his Milanese accent continued to call the "candella".

On the Col de Peuterey

Vieille on the central
pillar of Fresnay

Bonatti at the beginning of
the central pillar of Fresnay

I clambered down to Bonatti's tent for a chat. With four
of us lumped together in incredible positions on a ledge two
metres long we were so short of air that we had to tear the
fabric in order to breathe. I could not see outside, but hunched
up with Roberto Gallieni's arm over my shoulder I listened
while he calmed me by speaking of his children and mine, two
little girls who did not like to think that their daddy was up
in the mountains. Oggioni spoke of the sea and sunlight at
Portofino, sometimes praying or singing in his soft voice.
Walter sat impassively, as befitted a great man. During this
time my three friends, with whom I had made this pact for
what should have been a victory, seemed to grow drowsy,
using up their final reserves. When I climbed back up to them
that evening, however, they still wanted to hang on until the
following morning before coming to a decision. I then scrambled back down to Walter and we sat there talking while the
others slept.

It was then that we took the decision for everybody. If it
were fine in the morning we would go on, if not we would go
down. Already we knew what an ordeal the descent would be.
At last, despite the cold, the wind, the snow which fell upon
us like a shroud, we dozed off. In the absence of lightning we
almost felt well despite our growing exhaustion, and contorted
as we were we had a few hours of peace to sleep, to think of
ourselves, and above all of our impending fate. The hours
dragged by like years; our sagging eyelids did not quite close.

Why did we wait so long? Because we so much desired the
unattainable goal. Was it from pride? No, it was love of the
mountains which surely could not make us suffer any longer.
But it was also judgement. We had all read the tragic stories of
retreat, especially on the Eiger. It seemed most improbable
that the bad weather could persist indefinitely at this time
of the year. And above all, we shared a blind faith in Walter
Bonatti's ability to find the way up the ridge to the summit
and down to the Vallot hut. It was the unspoken desire of our
hearts to stand on the summit after the indescribable storm
which had held us prisoner.

And so another midnight came and went. It was Friday
14th July. The night stole on as we sat in a shallow cold bath,
our clothes clinging to our skin. At 4 o'clock Walter and I held
a council of war. I would force the pitches above, whatever the

E

weather; he, as the local expert, would then lead us over the summit and down. He knew the way better than anyone.

I got ready without delay. Outside, it was snowing. Everything was frozen hard. I seemed to have no strength left, and our few remaining karabiners stuck to my skin. Even the ropes froze on to it. Pierrot and the others regained a little warmth by sorting out the ropes. Knowing inwardly that it was impossible, everyone was secretly hoping for my success. But it was no good. Walter understood.

So that was it. We should just have to leave all non-essential equipment with our pains and memories there on the candle. Now drama was to give place to ordeal. Looking up at the pillar for the last time, or at least as much of it as remained visible through the snow, I think we all understood that. There was, after all, a certain nobility in renouncing our victory without having been beaten by the difficulties. Looking back, I can see the faces of the dead, Pierrot, Antoine, Robert, Andrea, and of the living, Roberto and Walter. All were fine with the fineness of men beaten neither by hopelessness nor despair, but who were simply victims of circumstance. There was a kind of victory in our retreat.

Walter led off, while I belayed him. The rappels were fully 80 metres long. Quickly the rhythm established itself: I followed second, and the others came after me silently, for throughout this infernal descent nobody spoke. The storm continued; visibility was under a metre. Andrea brought up the rear, always with a smile, as we lost height rappel by rappel. Before long we all lost control of our movements and had to belay each other. This meant that our progress was slower, but Walter insisted on calm. After one of the abseils, an 80 metre rope got stuck and would not yield even to our combined weight. Nobody spoke much. From time to time we would notice one of the pitches we had climbed.

There was one place where I remained motionless for two hours, my feet buried deep in the snow, belaying the others. When my turn came to abseil, I inadvertently struck my right foot against the rock. The pain was unbearable. A few moments later I struck the left and felt nothing. It was frozen. Well, we had worse things to worry about; but I noticed that Pierrot's hands were also literally blue.

So the day went by, and at last we reached the bottom of

the pillar. Walter belayed me across the rimaye, but buried in the snow up to the waist I did not even know when I had passed it. By the time the others reached me, we were all staggering like drunk men. It took me several hours to reach the Col de Peuterey, though I worked away like a robot, leaving a long trench behind as record of our suffering. Our movements had become mechanical. We were seven human animals struggling for life.

Darkness was falling as we reached the col, and we decided to bivouac in a crevasse which would at least shelter us from the worst of the storm. While Bonatti cooked our last remaining food, the others worked at clearing out a habitable site from this cruel environment. I gave several of them injections of Coramine and we gulped down our last remaining medicines, thinking of the rescue party that must be on its way and of our Italian, French, Swiss and other friends who must be worried about us. But in fact we had no conception of the general hopelessness that prevailed at Chamonix and in the Val d'Aosta.

I remember noticing the first signs. His hands black with frostbite, Pierrot sat immobile in the snow from utter fatigue. For four days he had been unable to hear anything. As the worst affected of us all, he spent the night in the tent with the Italians after having asked me for another injection, sleeping on Walter's knee. Most unusually for him, Robert too sat motionless in the crevasse. I offered him an ice-axe, but he refused it, and it was easy to understand. Only Antoine generated a little heat by hacking away at the ice to clear a site. Visibly exhausted, Andrea, who had brought up the rear all day, set about boiling water.

We did not bother to take off our crampons as we settled into our down-filled clothing to pass a night seated in icy water. There was no more singing. Robert slept, while Antoine and I chatted. Though the night was frightful it has a certain beauty in retrospect, since I made a friend. We talked of ourselves, of our friends and relations—he adored his brothers and sisters—and even of God. There was a last packet of cigarettes in my sack which we smoked right through, brewing tea until there was no more fuel left in the cooker. We were even able to joke about this and that, and to discuss women; there were some we had both known intimately. Bonatti called over that Pierrot had dropped off quietly to sleep, and that Andrea and Roberto were also resting, but Antoine and I gossiped on through the night.

At 3 a.m. on Saturday 15th July, I got up. Outside in the storm I somehow understood for the first time the drama which was about to play itself out, and felt mad with fear for us all. There was no time to waste. As I woke the others, I saw the same reaction written on their faces. Whether their feelings were conscious or not was of no importance now; what mattered was to get out. We tied on together, united for better or worse, seven men going to their fate, a symbol of friendship, our stations of the cross.

Walter set off in the lead, digging a veritable trench across the steep, snow-laden slopes to the Rochers Grüber, while we followed silently, conscious of the gravity of the situation. Each movement, even each word, counted. We tried not to think too much of our forced retreat. As rearguard came Andrea, followed by Roberto, and finally Antoine.

It was important to take care; on a slope as steep as this, the least slip would have been fatal. Having finally reached the top of the rocks after a delicate traverse, Walter at last stopped for a moment to safeguard the first few to follow. Then he threw down the ropes for an abseil and started down. Having seen all the others across the traverse, I got Robert to bring me across in my turn. Last of all came Antoine, unconcernedly keeping me informed about his progress along the deep trench. Suddenly he seemed to stagger, then sat down in the snow. Watching from below and fearing lest an avalanche should sweep us all away, Walter called out to me to be careful. I asked Antoine to get up and finish the traverse but received no reply beyond a few spasmodic movements. Without wasting any more time, Robert and I pulled him along the floor of the trench with the rope. He was dead.

Antoine Vieille, the youngest of us. He had died a man's death, master of himself, his gaze fixed on the deep well of love. Now he was to remain for a long time in this place where he had died. I thought how I had guided his first steps in the mountains, how I had introduced him to this world of splendour. Now he was struck down in his three-and-twentieth year, a young hero, but more, a man. His climbing partner Robert was standing beside me, crying. I asked him to begin his abseil, and was left alone with the mortal remains of this handsome prodigy. Walter understood and climbed back up to me. A piece of tent served as a shroud, a piton to anchor him there with the great pillar as his gravestone. As in some ancient ritual, we left his sack at his side. Our faces were wet with tears. The last, fatal scene had begun.

Now we must fight to limit the disaster, summoning our last resources to save our friends and ourselves. In our madness, we assumed responsibility for the survivors. When we reached them Robert was pale, but Roberto tried to comfort me. Pierrot asked me what had happened. When he understood, he too wept and prayed, wailing aloud and wishing to remain by the body of Antoine, but I forced him to go on. Comprehending my inner drama and the drama in which we were all placed, Andrea put an arm around my shoulders. Then the infernal descent continued.

Rappel after rappel, unthinkingly, we followed Walter like his shadow, knowing that our salvation lay in him. Without the reassurance of his presence we should all have died on the Fresnay glacier. We were now so weak that we begged him to let us abandon all the equipment. Joyously, crazily, I hurled my sack into the depths. All we kept was a few pegs and mousquetons to enable us to climb back over the Col de l'Innominata. Lighter now, we continued the descent. I began to waver, and but for Roberto's encouragement would gladly have sat down and died in my turn. Pierrot arranged the rope for me to abseil; he was willing me to survive.

Towards 4 p.m. we heard voices on the Innominata and called back, but the storm swept away our cries and the rescue party heard nothing. Why did it have to happen like that? We kept on hoping to meet them, but they never came.

With the last abseil came a glimmer of hope. Knowing the place, I thought we should reach the foot of the Col de l'Innominata in a few minutes. As I touched down on the glacier, belayed by Walter, my disappointment was bitter to find the snow shoulder deep. Together again on relatively flat ground, we wept for the knowledge that we would never reach our goal.

Walter now asked me to lead the party, which had grown apathetic. If I could manage the first half of the glacier, he would do the rest. So I began to labour like a navvy to clear a way forward through the snow, while Pierrot supported himself on my shoulders. So disorganized were we that we even neglected the rope, the symbol of human brotherhood. Little by little, we were heading towards death. The glacier seemed to have no ending as I laboured forward, up to my shoulders in snow, taking five minutes to consolidate each step, trampling the snow slowly and mechanically, while Pierre followed close behind.

I had stopped thinking. By now, all of us had stopped thinking. We were just six walking dead. From time to time one of us would glimpse the col. I concentrated on trying to find a way through successive mazes of crevasses. I knew nothing, I saw nothing, I just kept going. When Pierrot spoke to me, I did not reply. Since he could not hear anyway, what did it matter? Yet I felt more love for him than for anything in the world. Just now, on the descent of the Rochers Grüber, he had saved my life by not letting me stop. Now it was my turn to stop him sitting down to die. The snow was whirled along on the bitterly cold wind.

Thoughts of friends came confusedly into my head—at least, it seemed as though I could remember some—and of my father—at least, I supposed he was—this man who had taught me to love the mountains as I followed him from peak to peak in the ranges around Grenoble.

Then I fell, disappearing horribly and completely under the snow. Without a friend to help I could never have got out. That friend was Pierre. Then he too fell, and it was my turn to help him up. The suffering was unbearable, and yet somehow I kept on.

When we were halfway down the glacier, Walter took over the trail-breaking, with Roberto behind him. As he passed me I confessed my feeling of guilt at having left Antoine behind. His answer was to put an arm around me. Twelve years older than I, Roberto was like a big brother. Next came Pierrot, saying nothing, then Andrea, whom I held up by the shoulders, with Robert leaning on me from behind, a line of dying men.

One after another, we all fell. Each time was more exhausting than the last, and the hours went by full of suffering as we descended the second half of the glacier metre by metre, the blizzard veiling everything from our eyes, though I knew the Noire and the Gugliermina towered above us on our left and, far behind now, the pillar. Our fellow-climbers from

Paris, from all over the world, must be out anxiously looking for us.

Like an unchained elemental force, Walter ploughed on faster than ever, intent on saving us. Roberto and Pierrot followed, while the rest of us staggered half-demented in his wake. Presently Walter called me forward to help him fix ropes up to the Col de l'Innominata, on the other side of which, as all of us knew, lay safety—just 100 metres away. I left my two friends seated in the snow, happy in the knowledge that we had won the race against time.

But it was not to be. Silently and gravely, Walter climbed through the storm to the top of the col, pegging occasionally. Now I had to go back for my friends, a new ordeal. Then I slipped and fell a few metres. I wanted nothing so much as to remain where I was, and as my mind was a total blank I do not know where the force came from that enabled me to continue. Suddenly Andrea Oggioni was in front of me, crying and shouting "Robert! Robert!" at the top of his voice. I hurried forward, but where I had left them there was now no one. On all fours I scrabbled around in the snow. Robert was gone. Blinded by the tempest, I called and called, but no reply came. Just when I had believed him saved, he had fallen into a crevasse and now lay dead a few metres from my side.

Immediately after his partner, Robert had given his last energies to save us. All his friends used to call him "le Pâtissier". He had sacrificed everything to his love of the mountains, and now he had returned to them ennobled. They found him frozen in the snow, an expression of joy rather than pain on his face, the kind of joy that Beethoven translated into music. He had fulfilled himself, and now it was all over. May those who pass the spot where he died say a prayer for him. Those who pass his grave in the little cemetery at Chamonix should know that here was a man who lived out the life that he had chosen.

Crazed and shaken, I lurched back towards Pierrot, Roberto and Andrea. Now there were only five of us left. Walter had reached the col; I called up to him, and he shouted back that it could only be a couple of hours before a rescue party returned to look for Robert. Roberto did his best to console me. It was as though he knew something that I was unable to understand.

It was high time for us to cross the col and descend towards Gamba and safety. Walter threw down a rope to Roberto, who disappeared up into the murk. Pierrot looked at me, his eyes full of love; his face remains graven forever in my memory, the most beloved of all my friends. Then suddenly he seized the rope and climbed it hand over hand without a word, without any protection, an exceptional feat. At the time I felt nothing. It never occurred to me that I would not see him again. If only he could have known how much he meant to me. No words can express my loss and my pain.

So he went to his God, man, hero, saint. How many climbs, joys and sufferings we shared, as well as the everyday life of the city where we lived together as brothers. Perhaps I have never loved anyone else as truly. And there were so many things for which I would ask his pardon. On the Dru, the Badile, the Pouce, the Peigne, he was the strongest and best of us, his stature exceeded only by his generosity. When I learnt of his death, I seemed to die too. A few paces short of the hut he sank down on the snow, praying for death. When help reached him, anxious at not seeing me at his side, where I belonged, he found the strength to ask where I was, then died before the reply could come.

At his funeral at Ivry they played the Requiem of Mozart, whose music he loved, who also died young. Perhaps I shall not have the privilege to die as Pierre did, ennobled by suffering, but we were born the same day and somewhere we shall find each other again. My greatest pain is waiting for that day. He was my guide, he remains so forever.

So Andrea and I were left on the glacier. I tried to climb, safeguarding and hauling him. Above, on the col, Bonatti felt his strength beginning to ebb, and shouted down that we should have to wait while he took the others down to the hut and summoned help. It was now midnight. The storm had redoubled in strength, more dreadful than anything except death, which was all around us.

The hour turned, and it was Sunday 16th July. Unable to see anything, I took over an hour to climb a few metres. When I reached a piton I was too feeble to open the karabiner. I called down to Andrea to climb and pulled him towards me. He came obedient as a child, laying his head on my arm which was clamped to the ropes as they streamed out on the gale.

Mazeaud leading on the second day on the central pillar

The retreat from the pillar

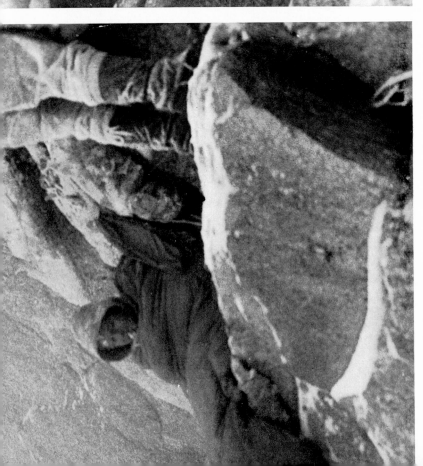

Bivouac in the storm

We were two walking dead in a Brueghelesque world. In-
ebriated, semiconscious, drained of all strength, we stood and
waited. Time must have gone by, but by now we were outside
time, the world, the storm, everything.

At 2 o'clock Andrea stirred, pulled my arm, and began to
mumble. I do not speak Italian, but semiconscious as I was,
I understood that he was telling me about his people in Monza,
a surburb of Milan to which I was later to make a pilgrimage.
He looked into my eyes questioningly and I took him into my
arms, speaking to him in a language which he did not know.
Two men, unable to hear or comprehend each other's words,
could yet understand one another. A quarter of an hour later
he died in my arms.

Andrea's name remains for me a kind of symbol, attached
to his great climb on the Brenta and to the southern flanks
of Mont Blanc, linked also with the name of Bonatti. If he died,
it was because he brought up the rear, safeguarding us so that
we should live. He was a small man with features which were
somehow extraordinarily tough and tender at the same time.
As I saw him die, he taught me that death is not something to
be feared. A few memories, a few prayers, and a light goes out.
Lying there dead on the mountainside, his face was the same
as the sculpted face which now watches over his grave—
profoundly human.

Now I was utterly alone.

Of the others, three were already dead, the fourth was
enduring his last moments. Only two . . . but I did not know
that, I was no longer able to know anything at all, even if I
had wanted to. I was horribly afraid of the silence, the heavy,
whirling snow, of death which stood beside me, overcoming
me little by little. Somehow my body suffered without feeling
anything. What was happening inside me? It was a time of
total blankness, with moments of lucidity. Each time I came
to, I saw before me a black, cold wall, sheathed in ice. I waited
without waiting.

Sometimes a crowd of thoughts would come into my head,
but mainly I wished dully that it would all end. Once, impelled by goodness knows what reflex, thinking of how Pierrot
had clambered up the rope, I tried to do the same. After a
metre or so I fell back, tearing out the piton to which Andrea
and I, the dead man and the living, were tied. We went flying

down the slopes of the col, till with a sudden jerk I fetched up short. Later I was to learn that a knot in the rope had saved me. The stiffened corpse of Andrea bounced on down to the glacier below. At the same time the sack which Walter had tried to lower slid down the rope to me, and this gave me something to occupy my mind and body. Bit by bit I pulled out the contents, looking at them, turning them over and dropping them into the storm. I was so thirsty that I sucked the fluid that oozed from my frost-bitten, swollen fingers.

Perhaps I dozed off. I remember yelling, calling for help while I swung there, the very rope that seemed to be choking me at the same time recalling me to life by the pain it caused. Perhaps Walter had not reached the hut, and I too would die where I hung. And while I waited the night paled into a livid dawn.

Today I realize that it was a privilege to endure those moments alone, face to face with death, to have prayed.

Thirty metres above me on the Col de l'Innominata I saw human forms and shouted to them to hurry. Soon they were beside me, and one of them, Ulysse Bruno, put his arm around me. At that I fainted. When they had hoisted me to the col, an injection brought me around and I was given hot drinks. All around me were friends, Courmayeur guides, and not a single person from Chamonix. My eyes dimmed. The hope and the effort back there on the Rochers Grüber: had it been worth it?

We started down. I tried to walk, but only succeeded in staggering. Later there would be photos showing me unconscious in their arms. It seemed never-ending. As we finally drew near to the Gamba hut there seemed to be crowds of people. I was thirsty; somebody gave me a drink. My fingers were swollen, numb, blue. My entire body was in pain, but that was as nothing to my state of mind.

As I entered the Gamba Hut there was Walter, without whom none of us would have survived, and Roberto at his side. I asked for Pierrot; there was no reply. Walter held me tightly in his arms. Looking into my eyes, he saw that Andrea also was dead. In that moment, the dead who had died to save us forged an unbreakable bond between us. Then somebody tore us apart.

Sunday 16th July. It was all over.

Potelle took me in his helicopter together with the body of

Oggioni. For several hours I went into a coma, with half-lucid intervals during which I seemed to see the faces of friends. I was in the hospital at Courmayeur, surrounded by whiteness. There were injections. From the softness of dreams I emerged into reality.

First came my father, squeezing me in his arms, holding back his tears. Gérard Géry could not restrain his. And there was Dany, looking so serious, and doctors Bassi and Crozoli. In the end it was Rébuffat who told me that Pierrot was dead. With all my strength I wished then to join him.

At this moment of drama, of life and death, one of the most trying in my entire life, my father's kindly gaze gave me the courage to go on living. My beloved Courmayeur seemed to be full of friends. As they took me off again to the helicopter-port, there was René Desmaison, who had chosen Pierrot and I to accompany him in his great adventure on the Cima Ovest. Then Potelle helped me again into the helicopter, considerate as ever, and I relapsed into coma, awakening in the Hôpital St Luc in Lyon, where I was placed under the care of Dr Colson.

My feet had turned black and begun to hurt, so I was constantly injected with Novocaine or Peridil. Everyone was very kind. Slowly I returned to life, though continuing to feel close to the dead. My father was at my side. The first letter from Walter arrived. Lionel came over from Grenoble, followed by Vaucher, Paragot, Berardini and many others whose smiles meant much to me.

They brought me the newspapers to read, an ordeal: our pictures, notably that taken before the door of the Fourche hut. Somebody pinned it to the wall of my room. Later, Jacques Sangnier was to return it to the hut, surrounded with flowers. There were pictures, too, of the dead being brought down, of the recovery of Antoine's body, of red roses in the snow at 4000 metres.

Another day of great pain was when my father brought me a copy of *L'homme foudroyé* by Blaise Cendrars. It was dedicated to his son, killed while flying in Morocco, and once again brought home what a privilege it is to die young amid beloved places, like my friends at the foot of the pillar. Had it been me, I would have found peace for the first time.

Piussi came to visit me, then Pierre Julien. When they let me out, I visited Walter in Courmayeur. Later there was to

be Trento, where I was constantly in the company of mountaineers who understood. Later again came my return to the
mountains, with an attempt on the north face of the Matterhorn in winter. There was also a slow, religious pilgrimage
with Walter and Roberto, going over the ground to recapture
memories. And there were and will be other fights.

But also, far away in Greenland, there are mountains
which now bear the name of our four Belgian friends who died
the same day, after having conquered eight of the highest
summits in the region. Eight names, Belgian, French, Italian
. . . but the nationalities do not matter; they are first and
foremost the names of men.

CHAPTER XII

Return to Life

In October 1961 I travelled to Trento. I am not sure if the festival there can ever really deserve the name, since so many mountaineers disappear from the ranks each year, but at any rate on this occasion it was just a meeting dedicated to our friends lost on the Pillar of Fresnay. It was still difficult for me to walk, and I had to be helped by Dany. The bandages on my feet needed changing every day.

For me the meeting proved a revelation, and I have not missed one since. The encounter with climbers from other countries brought great consolation. I struck up warm friendships with journalists like Tonella, Bernardi and in particular Roly Marchi, and with climbers from Trento, Lecco, Milan, Munich, Salzburg, Innsbruck and Vienna. These meetings had a profound effect on my philosophy of mountaineering. Among the foreign climbers I found nothing but understanding. Their enthusiasm enabled them to see the promise which the tragedy on the Pillar of Fresnay held for the future of mountaineering, and unlike some of my compatriots they did not seek to blame, or look for pretexts such as weakness or lack of preparation in order to justify their negative attitudes. Faith shone in the eyes of these youngsters from all over the world, united in their passion for mountaineering. Walter, Roberto and I were in some sense the tragic heroes of the scene, but everybody respected our feelings.

Roly Marchi's friendship played a special role. He spoke to me as man to man. In his company I met Cassin, Mauri, Piazza, Michielli, Aste, Zeni, Franceschini, Maestri, Stenico, Panei and Bassi, all of whom became my friends. I also met those who had first climbed the north face of the Eiger in winter. One evening, while I was dining with Walter Bonatti, John Harlin and others, Toni Hiebeler came over to introduce me to those who had been with him on the climb. My eyes encountered those of Toni Kinshofer, and a great friendship was born. That evening at Carlos' restaurant we all drank a great deal, and I forgot my troubles. Walter smiled at me across the room. We were both returning to life.

After talking for a while to Kinshofer, Hiebeler made me a proposal in which I could hardly believe, because my feet were still causing me horrible suffering. After swearing me to secrecy, they invited me to join them in January in an attempt on the north face of the Matterhorn, which had not yet been climbed in winter. Joy and hope came flooding back.

When later in the week I was presented with medals for my comrades who had died on the pillar, I wept. Henceforward, however, I had the conviction that their deaths had not been merely pointless, and that I had a message from them to transmit to the mountaineering world, which shared my emotion as their names were read out. Walter, standing at my side, had exactly the same feelings. How many of those I met that week have now vanished in their turn, leaving the same message and example.

Throughout the autumn, Toni Hiebeler and the others wrote to me regularly. As there was likely to be competition, I was to hold myself in readiness from 21st December on, this being the date on which the purists consider that winter climbing begins. I was presented with provisions and equipment lists of extreme precision. Clearly, Toni left nothing to chance. I trained with enthusiasm and slept soundly, an unusual thing for me, devoting particular care to my feet, on which I used the magic medicaments Duradilan and Peridil prescribed by Dr Colson. Walking was part of the programme.

My friends were astonished by my calmness. It is true that without Pierre the rue de la Victoire did not seem the same, and that I insisted on silence. My mind, my body, my whole being were concentrated on the Matterhorn. I read everything that had been written on it and traced the outline of the various routes on photographs. I was determined to succeed, not to avenge my friends, but to sort out the relationship between myself and the mountains.

During the evening of 19th December I received a telephone call from Toni. "Come quickly," he said. "An urgent situation has arisen. Hilti von Allmen and Paul Etter are already up at the Hörnli hut." An hour later I was on my way. My departure was effected with the same discretion which I had shown in my preparations. Only Dany knew where I had gone.

Once on the road I could give way to my excitement, and the kilometres flew by. Presently I turned off my usual route to Chamonix, turning left towards Dijon, over the Jura, through Lausanne, and on into the Valais. At St Niklaus I jumped on to the train heading up to Zermatt. At last I could relax. I felt happy. Now that the long car-drive was over, I could think calmly, mulling over the idea of success. My energy and will to conquer had returned, and, by the same token, my peace of mind.

By nature I am intuitive but also easily worried. Often I dream, imagine, glimpse, foresee, and presently I find that I have achieved. At certain depressed periods of my life it has often been an ordeal thus to have to create, to call upon the powers of the imagination.

At Zermatt station the snow was falling in huge, heavy flakes. Toni and I fell into each others' arms, dancing with exuberance. The others were already there. We strolled round to the Hotel Bahnhof, where I was congratulated by Biner himself. What had I done to deserve such kindness? He spoke to me about Lachenal, also about the pillar. His face, chiselled by the years, was magnificent. Once again I felt the freedom of communication between mountaineers, a prelude to friendship.

That evening we dined with our Austrian friend Krempke, who was to be the fourth member of the party. He was an architect whose passion for mountaineering had led him to quit Vienna for Zermatt. Toni Kinshofer, who had led the climbing on the first winter ascent of the Eigerwand, was a carpenter. He worked day and night to be able to escape into the mountains. Hiebeler, the planner and driving force of our team, was a journalist. Everything in his life was organized with an eye to climbing. Each of them had an impressive string of achievements to his name. It was a privilege to have been invited to join them.

For the next few days we had to settle for skiing as the weather got worse and worse. Sometimes, through a gap in the clouds, we would see the north face. As a change from interminable French and German lessons, and in order to break the monotony, Hiebeler and I decided to carry some equipment up to the hut. Von Allmen and Etter had already come down. Astonished as I was by Hiebeler's methodical preparation—he is truly a great expedition leader—I was still more so by his physical power. Labouring painfully through the snow, occasionally exchanging a few words in bad French or German, we reached the hut after dark, then spent a marvellous evening. More and more, I thought how there were no frontiers between mountaineers, and told Toni how our pan-European party fitted my conception of climbing. Our first ascent would be a European one. I thought of the photo of the Matterhorn that I had stuck up above my bed, pencilling in imaginary bivouac spots. Outside, it was still snowing.

For some reason I dreamt a lot that night. It was all quite incoherent, but expressed my joy at being back in the mountains, serene and eager to take my revenge, not on the mountains but on myself, for the sake of my friends whose memory was as vivid as ever.

The weather got worse, and so did the boredom. There were long conversations with Biner in his family hotel. He spoke to me about young Dieter Marchardt who climbed the north face of the Matterhorn solo, then got killed on the Eiger. In order to break the monotony, Toni Hiebeler showed his film on the Eiger in winter. It was enough to send shivers down my back, a beautiful, powerful but profoundly human document. Watching it, I realized what a feat the ascent had been. Kinshofer in action was a marvellous machine, and to be in his company was a great joy. His sensitivity was such that it was difficult to situate him. And yet is that not the essence of the mountaineer, the powerfully sculpted body containing the sensitive, passionate mind?

To give ourselves a break, Kinshofer and I decided to spend 48 hours at Chamonix carrying kit up to the foot of the Walker spur on the north face of the Grandes Jorasses. We set off in a snowstorm, and at Bonneville I had to buy chains for the car, which, however, neither Toni nor I knew how to put on. Finally we reached Chamonix and "le Bivouac". Toni's personality made itself felt at once, and many compared him with Pierre Kohlman. It is true that there was a resemblance.

Next morning we took the first cable-car up to the Aiguille du Midi, digging a tunnel out on to the ridge with the help of the workmen. We were so loaded that Trasimeni kindly took our sacks down to the point where one could put on skis. The snowstorm was still raging, and visibility was nil. Groping our way down the Vallée Blanche took us more than eight hours.

Eventually we left our sacks under a boulder, where I was to find them two years later, and climbed up to Montenvers. The ordeal was such that I wondered if I was going to die, but Toni helped me and presently my strength returned. Night fell, a night so black that as we descended the railway track we did not even notice as we walked into a tunnel. The other end of the tunnel was blocked with an enormous wooden barrier. It did not hold up Toni for long. Woodwork was after all his job, he said, as with his steely arms he tore away a couple of planks so that we could continue. We reached Chamonix exhausted after fifteen hours of effort, and slept deeply. I dreamt of the Matterhorn.

After this interlude we returned to Zermatt, but it was still snowing as hard as ever. Morale sank, I made a quick trip to Paris and back to reassure my father, who was worried about my being on the Matterhorn. Naturally the news had leaked out to the press, and he was afraid for my feet. Driving back for all I was worth, a few kilometres before the journey's end I saw a car skid wildly and bounce several times end over end. I stopped, got out, and promptly fell down—the road was covered in black ice, and I had not even noticed. The other car was lying crushed a few metres away. I pulled out two dying men, and some Swiss who had also seen the accident rushed them off to the nearest hospital. After that I drove on slowly.

Back at Zermatt the weather began to appear more hopeful, and we made plans to go up to the Hörnli hut. Next morning we set off on the cable-car to Schwarzsee. The weather was magnificent, and so was the snow-covered north face, where it was fascinating to pick out the route. Then we slowly made our zigzag way across under the east face, reaching the hut late in the afternoon. That evening I became acquainted with the diet of German climbers, notably Sanddorn, a kind of rose-hip pulp which is the basic food of German Himalayan expeditions. Everyone looked happy, and it was enough to see the confident faces of Eric and the two Tonis to be sure that the climb was as good as in the bag.

We attacked early. Getting over the first bergschrund gave me a good deal of trouble in snow so deep that at times only my head emerged. At the second, we formed up in battle order: Kinshofer first, then Hiebeler, then Krempke, with myself bringing up the rear. The ice-slope with which the climb begins is long and exceptionally steep, so that progress seemed slow, but I was full of good hope at being on the mountain with such men and the hours did not drag. Everything went smoothly. At certain stances I had to wait a long time in the cold, but my feet gave me no trouble. Our boots, specially designed by Hiebeler, proved miraculous.

When night came, it was intensely cold and constellated with stars. We made a platform in the snow, drank the eternal Sanddorn, and pulled on our sleeping bags. Below our feet shone the lights of Zermatt.

With the first light of dawn we were away again. The mountain scenery around us was magnificent, by contrast with the face itself, which was hideous, consisting of black crumbling rocks dusted with snow. In fact, the Matterhorn is only beautiful in the distance.

Kinshofer advanced quickly and safely, from time to time placing an ice-piton to safeguard his progress, but cutting no steps. He had an astonishing mastery of crampon technique, stepping up on the two front points only, and I forced myself to imitate him. As snow gave way to ice we slowed up. We were now reaching the difficult and dangerous section. To our left, the Hörnli ridge was bathed in sunlight, but on the face the cold was bitter. Thanks to the inadequacy of my German I learnt to hold my tongue and think for hours at a time. Almost the only words I spoke were to ask Erik for a tight rope occasionally.

Via a delicate traverse, where I seemed to be walking on glass and felt strangely drawn towards the gulf below, we reached the foot of the big open corner which is a feature of the central part of the face. The two Bavarians were already clearing the bivouac site. We fired a green flare to show that all was well, and below in the valley Eric's wife replied. The message had been taken. We drank our Sanddorn and slept.

But while we slept, the weather was changing, and before very long we awoke to wind, snow, and cold which penetrated to the marrow of our bones. Kinshofer and I shifted carefully from foot to foot to avoid cramp, sometimes talking, while snores emanating from a couple of metres lower down showed that Krempke and Hiebeler were serenely sleeping through the storm. What characters! All that night and the next day we waited for the weather to change, and then all the next night,

36 hours in all. Our will to win was in no way weakened. We heard our friend Dittert speaking about us on the Radio Suisse Romande; it seemed that the further weather outlook was bad, and down there they were worrying about us. A depression was drifting over from the Channel. The French radio criticized me, saying that my bad feet would slow down the party, thus causing additional risk. When I translated this to my friends they grinned, and as I knew that I was fully recovered, I could afford to do the same.

The following morning the storm was still at its height, so we decided to retreat. Tying all the ropes together, we rappelled 100 metres to another ledge. Unfortunately, despite our united efforts, the rope would not pull down. An hour later we had still had no success, and we looked at one another in apprehension. It was decided to climb down unroped. I knew that the end must soon come, and my face must have betrayed my fear. On this wall of ice, without belays, only a miracle could save us. Hiebeler started off; suddenly his foot skidded, and he saved himself *in extremis*. Kinshofer realized that the danger was too great. Knowing that my feet hindered my cramponning, he looked at me kindly and said: "Pierre, we're not going to let you get killed. I'll climb back up and free the rope." I shall never forget the expression on his face at that moment. He not only saved my life, he saved us all.

Two years later Toni Kinshofer was to be killed in the mountains, but not before he had written one of the finest pages in the history of mountaineering, carrying his friend Löwe near the summit of Nanga Parbat on his herculean shoulders despite frostbitten hands and feet. His death was personally felt by climbers everywhere. In Paris I wept silently, thinking of how he resembled Pierre Kohlman, and wired to his close friend Mannhardt to lay some flowers for me on his grave. His photo has pride of place in the too-well filled album of lost friends, and when I look at it, in waiting for the time when I can see him for eternity, his face, so noble in its greatness and goodness, bears the same smile it bore that day on the Matterhorn north face.

Fearing the worst at any moment, we watched him climb back up the rope with the help of a Prusik knot. After the strain we had put on it, would the peg hold? The storm was such that we could hardly make ourselves understood. It was three hours before Toni returned and the abseils began again. This time we had no further problems right down to the rimaye. By evening we were back in the Hörnli. I was completely exhausted, but the three preceding days had been such an intense experience that I was happy. The storm raged around the hut making the timbers crack like those of a haunted house, but we slept.

As we skied down next day, we were surprised to see two figures coming to meet us. Our friends had been worrying, and now Michel Vaucher and Guido Tonella were coming to see if they could help, bringing with them a heavy load of equipment for the north face. There had been just one little oversight in their preparations: Guido had forgotten to pack the food!

I skied down to them. Guido spoke to me in German: "Toni, wie geht es dir (how are you)?" Out of habit, I replied in German: "Aber, ich bin Pierre", and there was laughter all round. Wrapped up like space-men, we had not recognized each other. Soon we were back in Zermatt, feeling happy despite our lack of success. As though to salute the mountain's resistance, the sun burst out.

As we left Zermatt we were naturally disappointed, but there was consolation in the comradeship and in the thought of further projects to re-unite our international party. Personally, I was happy to have known such men and to find that love of the mountains is the same everywhere. I had admired their tactics and teamwork, and had begun to feel that I belonged. In fact, I had got beyond a certain sectarianism. We held each other in confidence; in reality, this failure was a major success.

When in Paris soon afterwards I learnt of the victory of the Swiss Hilti von Allmen and Paul Etter, the Austrians Schlömer and Krempke, and the Germans Siegert and Kauschke, I was glad, not because our attempt had paved the way for them, but because it had fallen to men of different nationalities.

Faithful to his promise, Toni Kinshofer came to stay with me in Paris for three weeks, tirelessly sightseeing. In order to keep fit for the coming expedition to Nanga Parbat, he sometimes walked over 40 kilometres per day in Paris. It was a real pleasure to help him broaden his knowledge.

In June I heard that Bonatti and Zapelli had made the first ascent of the north face of the Pilier d'Angle, perhaps the last great problem on Mont Blanc. Thinking of Walter and of days we had passed together, I felt a great desire to see him again. I had no idea that I was thinking so effectively, for the next thing I knew a telegram arrived from him, saying: "Pierre, come quickly. The east face of the Petites Jorasses is waiting for us. Affectionate greetings." That was exactly Walter's style. It was 7 p.m. I got straight into my car, and reached Chamonix in time to catch the first cable-car over to Entrèves in company with my brother. Walter was waiting for me. We embraced, aware that another great adventure was beginning.

Knowing that I must be tired, Walter left me to sleep while he got the equipment ready, then Bianca drove us up the Val Ferret in the little Topolino. My brother François found it difficult to understand how I could set off on such a climb in such a state of fatigue. He did not realize that with Walter I would have gone to the end of the world, even half dead.

The plod up to the Gervasutti hut was long and trying. Both of us suffered from fatigue, the heat, and above all the weight of the sacks. Nevertheless, we felt optimistic. It was late in the evening before we arrived at the brand-new hut, which had been placed fully assembled on its site by helicopter only a short time before. All that had been required was a small team of experts to anchor it to the rock. We spent a pleasant evening recalling memories and eating enough for ten, so as to be lighter next day. As we dozed off to sleep I felt happy to be here with one of my dearest friends and to affirm our friendship on the anniversary of last year's tragedy on the flanks of Mont Blanc, now pale under the light of the moon, while above us bulked the wild east face of the Grandes Jorasses.

We slept so well that the alarm clock did not even ruffle our slumbers, so that the Glacier de Fréboudze was already bathed in sunlight as we reached the east face of the Petites Jorasses. The only signs of passage were those of my attempt two years earlier with Alzetta, so tragically killed with his three companions in Greenland.

Quickly we clambered up the familiar pitches. At one stance, calmly and tactfully as always, Walter told me off for belaying to only one piton. The rope ran out steadily, the pegs sang as they went in, and the mousquetons gave reassuring clicks. I felt fine; we were both on form. Few words were exchanged beyond "tira" and "molla". The sunlight was warm, and everything went with the regularity of a metronome. Walter took some photos. As we climbed the artificial pitches there was time to joke. Far below in the valley we noticed the tiny white spot of Bianca's car. However, today we needed no reassurance. Everything was perfect, success was certain, and we were simply happy to be together again on a first ascent. The only problem was thirst. Our throats were already dry, our tongues stuck to the roofs of our mouths and our bodies began to feel dehydrated.

At the highest point reached two years before, I came to the final peg. It bore the name of Lionel Terray, and Walter removed it as a souvenir. From there on the climbing became more complicated. Above us was an impressive series of roof overhangs which had to be surmounted. It was difficult to get sound pegs, and I began to go slower on account of fatigue and the increasing difficulty, but I had perfect confidence in Walter and advanced nevertheless. The ropes glided across the rock, and the tinkling of the étriers lent a gay note to the otherwise severe struggle. The climbing was serious, the overhangs on a scale that reminded us of limestone. When we had to haul up the sacks they jammed maddeningly, and the crags re-echoed with the same oaths in French and Italian. The rock itself was magnificent, but so compact that it was difficult to find anywhere to place pitons, which often only went in a few inches.

Day was declining as I emerged from the zone of overhangs, only to find myself below a belt of boilerplate slabs which appeared to be of extreme difficulty. Were we going to be forced to use expansion bolts? Walter climbed up to me. I considered that we could bivouac where we were, but he knew that beyond the slabs there was a much better site. He had reconnoitred the face through field glasses on several occasions, and his mountain instinct was such that he could not be mistaken. I was afraid that we should find ourselves caught out by darkness on the slabs, but he would have none of it and said he would climb them quickly. This decisiveness is his exceptional quality on the mountain.

Dumping the kit, he took just a hammer and a few pegs. Then he was away, a horrifying series of moves of VI superior, without any doubt the hardest pitch I know of on granite. Sure of himself, he climbed up widely spaced holds, traversed on his hands for several metres, his feet in friction against the rock, and reached a crack. Quickly he placed one piton, then he was off again, climbing free. The whole pitch took him just ten minutes. I could hear him panting on the ledge above. It had been an astonishing demonstration of his qualities of calm, serenity, self-confidence, class and morale. It seems as though nothing can stop him. He sums up the chances, then just goes, playing with the difficulties. I had already had occasion to admire his exceptional gifts on mixed ground, but the last ten minutes had revealed his astonishing virtuosity as a rock climber. Anyone would be proud of his friendship.

After the sacks had been hauled up it was my turn. As I was climbing it grew dark. Suddenly I felt myself plucked upwards, with barely time to place my hands and feet on the holds as they went by, wondering by what prodigy Walter had managed to climb them unaided. Then I found myself on an ample ledge in the middle of the wall, the very one that he had picked out with the field glasses.

This is another point to emphasize. Walter's mountaineering instinct is such that he will always win against the mountain by divining its least obvious weaknesses. I might find some pitch impossible-looking and try to left or right, but he somehow knows that this is the place to attack, and up he goes. Witness to this are his beautiful and exceptional routes on the Capucin, the Dru and the southern flanks of Mont Blanc, with which his name will forever be associated, as it will with the Grandes Jorasses and with K2, Gasherbrum IV, Rondoy and, as a final return to the source, the Matterhorn.

There was nothing left to drink, and our throats were burning. As we settled into our little bivouac tent a storm of exceptional violence broke over our heads. The blackness had been total, but before long there was so much lightning that it was as though we were sitting in the middle of a fire. Our fear grew, and it seemed as though the mountains were seeking their revenge for our escape from the Pillar of Fresnay. The noise and confusion were like something from the Apocalypse. We trembled at the thought of the pitons and ice-axes at our sides, separated from us by no more than a fine cloth. Each time the lightning discharged through them it made us jump, and gradually nausea and weakness overcame us. In a moment of deadly intuition we seemed to see the faces of our friends. It was all so familiar, as one drama resembles another.

But miracles sometimes happen, and presently Walter

realized that the sound coming from the equipment was no longer that of electricity discharging but of water flowing down the face. It sounded practically the same. Hastily we clambered out and buried our heads in a miraculous runnel. And the miracle did not stop there. The storm rolled away; the stars emerged, and with them our smiles, our pleasure and our confidence. Walter spoke of Paris, I of coming to live in the Val Ferret, each of us taking pleasure in making himself better known to the other.

Next morning it became obvious that it had snowed a lot, just the sort of conditions in which Walter excels. The climbing remained mostly free, though there were a few artificial moves. We slanted across the face from right to left, following the line of a sort of depression. This led to an icy gully four pitches high, where Walter had to pull out all the stops. It was fascinating to see him at work, almost like a mathematician at grips with an equation, each gesture calculated, each piton a marvel of ingenuity. His movements radiated the same authority as those of a champion cyclist or sprinter, yet when he was spoken to his voice in reply was that of the most human and sensitive of men.

The gully ended in a black, disagreeable pitch of grade V and VI, from which Walter pulled out on to the summit. We were full of joy, and, as usual on these occasions, embraced. However, we were not to be left to enjoy our summit rest in peace. The mountain seemed to react immediately to our victory. Decidedly, Walter and I seem to have a faculty for attracting storms. Lightning began to strike from all sides, till the very mountain appeared to be flinching under the repeated shocks. All hell seemed to have broken loose. Walter's calm remained unshakeable as we hastened down, but his face wore its special expression of concern. When we reached the snow-slopes of the ordinary route I dashed off down them and he followed, though not without paying particular attention to security, for the strokes of lightning had become more frequent than ever. At the bottom of the slope, the bergschrund proved to be almost 15 metres wide. There could be no question of crossing it, and we paused in indecision. Finally we traversed along it for over a kilometre before finding a way over. At last we could turn and look back up at the face we had climbed, smiling and happy. The weather too had cleared. The tension

On the Walker spur

Recovery: Bonatti gives Mazeaud a ride on his back

The Matterhorn in winter: the ordinary route runs up the
ridge facing the camera, the north face is in shade on the right

was over. It was late. Far below, in the valley, Bianca's small white car set off back towards Courmayeur.

Once again we spent a night in the Gervasutti hut, this time without anxious thoughts. The fight was over, the desire achieved: those who had escaped with their lives from the Pillar were back in the battle, and winning. I looked across at Walter's sleeping form, then sank into sleep myself.

The sunlight was warm as we walked down next morning, taking pictures. One of my photographs of my companion was to become famous in the advertisement: "Wear a Millet rucksack like Walter Bonatti". The forest below was full of pleasant odours and the sound of the torrent. We played like children, hiding from each other, laughing and singing. Then there were men in front of us, a team from Italian television, and our faces hurriedly lost their joyous childish expression to adopt that of adults exhausted by their efforts. How often and rightly I had heard Walter say: "Pierre, one is only truly happy up in the mountains."

We dined at the Restaurant de la Brenva, kept by our friend Leo, entering our new climb on the page of his visitor's book following that which recorded last year's tragedy. Next day I crossed to Chamonix, picked up my car at the foot of the cable-car, and travelled the 600 kilometres back to Paris on the wings of joy. It was the end of my best, maddest and happiest adventure.

Once again I was full of hope, and it was Walter who had restored it to me. Later he was to tell me that I had performed the same service for him. Clearly, the climb had been a necessity to both of us. We named it the Voie de l'amitié, the Route of Friendship. There could be no finer name. It was dedicated to our friends who had died the year before, who had sometimes seemed to be climbing at our sides.

On 13th July I received a telephone call from Roberto Gallieni and set off immediately for Courmayeur. The parents of our friends were already there, and there was an anniversary mass. The gospel was that of peace on earth to men of good will. Next day we three survivors walked silently up to the Gamba hut, where, with great emotion, they showed me the spot where Pierre had fallen. Then we went on to the Col de l'Innominata, where the ordeal of Andrea returned vividly to my mind. Only bad weather prevented us from going on to the top of the

Rochers Grüber. With sad faces we shook each others' hands, sunk in memories and emotion.

Through a gap in the clouds we noticed the last Pillar of Brouillard, and a project was born. It became and remains a constant desire, but I know that it is only a matter of time before one or other of us does it.

Our friends in Courmayeur, Cazari, Panei, Bassi, Andrea's great friend Aiazzi, and many others, understood our distress. When the pilgrimage was over, Walter and Roberto escorted me back to the cable-car. Each year we would have the same sombre memories, but the mountains would be there to restore our confidence. Alone in the cable-car I could let my tears flow. During the crossing of the Vallée Blanche, the pillar showed for a moment through the cloud. Homage to the fallen. I prayed.

Exhausted from a series of sleepless nights, I stopped for a few hours in Geneva. The weather was bad, and up on the Walker spur of the Grandes Jorasses Cauderlier and Batkin were fighting for their lives. Nevertheless I wanted to return to Paris via Besançon, where there was an exhibition of paintings. Crossing the Jura I fell asleep at the wheel and collided head-on with a ten-ton truck. The car spun, bounced and somersaulted, throwing me out. I was woken up by the noise. There were seventeen fractures in my left foot, which later turned as black as it had done the previous year from frostbite, but I felt no pain at the time. I still have no idea how I escaped death, but I suppose my solid constitution must have had something to do with it.

Before long I was visiting Fontainebleau with my father to train on the rocks, and a month later, my leg still in a walking plaster, I was able to do some of the classic routes at Saussois. It had been a warning. In fact, I had deserved to die. There is a limit to how much one can demand of the human machine, which may revolt if overtaxed. I had got tired and fallen asleep, as I ought to have expected.

In October I returned to Trento to meet my old friends and make new ones. Toni Kinshofer, just back from Nanga Parbat and the hero of the occasion, was limping painfully. Already he was becoming a legend. Somehow I felt adopted by Trento, and talking with all these friends was thoroughly rejuvenating. It was interesting, too, to meet Herman Buhl's climbing companion Kurt Diemberger, and many others.

CHAPTER XIII

And not to cease from Loving

AT THE END of June 1963, I received a telephone call from Roberto Gallieni. If I could spare the time, he said, Walter and he and I could take a trip to the Dolomites.

We met at Milan airport. Between us, we are probably the three biggest ice-cream eaters in the world, and there was just time for a quick one before setting off for Cortina. We spent the evening at Trento, and next day Walter and I climbed on the Cinque Torri while Roberto shopped for our stay in a chalet belonging to my friend Giovanni Mariotti. The three of us then set out to climb the Tissi route on the Tofana under an unrelenting sun, but got diverted by the water falling from the summital overhangs. I remember a number of exposed pitches and one extremely difficult wall which was not on the route. But at heart we did not care whether we followed the route or not: all that mattered was to be back in the mountains and to be climbing.

From Cortina we went on to Alleghe in the Civetta range, the main wall of which is calculated to induce a shiver of apprehension in any climber, both by its size and by its history. It is, indeed, on a scale commensurate with the highest walls of the range of Mont Blanc. Though it was raining, we walked up to the Vazzoler hut singing happily. Suddenly encountering a young woman at a turning in the path, Walter stopped. As I caught up, they were speaking of Trieste. He introduced me to Bianca di Beaco. I was deeply impressed by her beauty, her friendliness, and above all by her smile which seemed to express her freshness and vitality. We were often to meet again, and her friendship was to become dear to me. As we went on towards the hut below the breath-taking walls of the Torre Trieste, up which Cassin and Carlesso had both forced routes, Walter told me that she was the best woman climber in Italy. Immediately I longed to climb with her, somewhere, somehow, and I felt a kind of certitude that this happiness would be given to me.

When we reached the hut there was another memorable

meeting, this time with Da Roit the warden, a man hewn from the rock, but with a kindly twinkle in his eye. Vazzoler must be one of the most beautiful places in the world, combining peace, softness and grandeur. The hut itself is a small cottage tucked in among pine trees, ringed round with imposing mountains.

Next day we did the magnificent Tissi route on the Torre Venezia in the pleasant company of Robert Wohlschlag and Erica Stagni from Geneva. The famous traverse really calls for concentration, and I recall annoying Walter, who at this point was closing the march, by taking in the rope too energetically. Owing to my clumsiness, he had to put in an extra piton.

Then our too-short stay was over, and we tramped triumphantly back down to Alleghe, howling songs in every language under the sun until we lost our voices. Back at Milan airport we did not—and never will—say goodbye, but just "au revoir" as though we should see each other next day. The Alitalia Caravelle had the Italian bicycle-racing team on board and flew up past Lecco to the Piz Badile, then along the whole chain of the Alps to the Meije. It was a fantastic vision of known and loved places from a new angle. The plane was just half an hour late at Paris!

That summer of 1963 began with bad weather and snow all over the Alps, and I decided in consequence to take no more than two weeks' holiday. I had a lot of work to do, and in the middle of August I was due in Reunion Island. When I went to Chamonix in mid-July it was no longer to the Hotel de Paris, which had changed since the death of Antoine, who had been responsible for all its atmosphere. This time I had a tiny, beautiful chalet of my own. Marysette Agnel and her husband had had it built just a few days before their death on the old Brenva, and their young son Oliver had inherited it. Marysette's mother, who had lost all three of her children in climbing accidents, kindly leased it to me.

From then on it became the scene of international meetings between climbers, for whom there was open house when they visited Chamonix. One year there were seventeen of us, French, English, American, Italian, Austrian, German, and also a Czech, my friend Kratochvil, whom I had discovered in Paris wandering from hotel to hotel before I invited him back to the rue de la Victoire, where he remained for over a year. One day

Mme. Agnel wrote to me: "It was very strange, but having taken a stroll round by the chalet to see if you needed anything, I found a great crowd of young men, none of whom spoke any French. I had the feeling that I was a foreigner!"

Looking back, I remember how, a few days before his death on the Eiger, John Harlin went to the chalet to look for some equipment. The exceptional weight of snow on the roof made him fear for the rafters, and he took the trouble to clear it all off. Later, Gary Hemming added a fine photo of John to the long gallery of lost friends on the wall of the chalet—Gary who was so tragically to disappear in his turn.

Together with Robert Wohlschlag (usually known as "Pellebrosse") of Geneva, and Antoine Tsinant, I made an attempt on the Pointe de Saussure. We were foiled by bad weather, but I shall always remember our two bivouacs. Pellebrosse looked like a twin brother of Harpo Marx endowed with herculean strength. He was one of the finest climbers of his generation, and no difficulty ever stopped him. Intending to return, we left a lot of kit at the foot of the climb, where, so far as I know, it still lies.

Between two storms I made a quick ascent of the Kohlman route on the Aiguille du Midi, imagining Pierre in action on the first ascent. The line is a great open corner, barred at one point by a roof overhang formed by a smooth block wedged there by some curious trick of nature. Kohlman had taken just two hours. I thought of his exceptional gifts.

Another time I went up to the Cosmic Research Laboratory hut with Tsinant. At this time he was passionately addicted to mountaineering and seemed from his exceptional gifts to be on the threshold of a remarkable career; then one day, no one knew why, he just gave it all up. That year the "Cosmiques" was a second home to me, and we spent happy evenings with Jacquot the warden. The hut has one of the finest settings in the whole range, looking out past Mont Blanc de Tacul and the Capucin towards the north face of the Grandes Jorasses. Our objective was to climb the Pointe Durier by its west face, a project that had been fascinating me ever since my attempt on the Aiguille de Saussure. Its two parallel faces are respectively turned towards the Mont Blanc de Tacul and the Mont Maudit.

Aerial photographs had shown that the bulk of the climbing

would probably be artificial, and as we prepared our heavy sacks that evening we had an agreeable feeling of excitement. That done, we settled down to read; in the Cosmiques you can find everything from comic strips to Balzac, a complete set of Tintin, and a voluminous collection of whodunnits. Among the latter, *Murder on the Summit,* by our friend Giovanni, took pride of place, though to tell the truth it is more devoted to the fauna of the Hotel de Paris than to crime.

It did not take us long to get to the top of Mont Blanc de Tacul. We were fit by now, and it was the fourth time that season that we had been up or down this particular slope. From there we walked across to Mont Maudit, where things became more serious. In order to reach the foot of the west face, a sort of mountaineering ultima thule, it is necessary to descend a series of steep ice gulleys in the direction of the Grands Mulets. Abseil followed abseil, all highly impressive, linked by pendulums and daring, risky traverses, and it was not until late in the afternoon that we reached the base of the Pointe Durier, which soared into the sky like an arrow. In those savage surroundings we felt like first-comers. Yet it was anything but calm; the séracs on Mont Blanc toppled and rumbled unceasingly. Sometimes we had to shout to make ourselves understood.

The pedestal forming the base of the aiguille was not easy. The cracks were white seams of ice and snow. The cold bit deeper as the sun sank, and the Vallot hut blazed as though on fire. An icy corner led to some choked-up chimneys, all strenuous and violent climbing, after which the sacks had to be hauled. As darkness fell we set up our bivouac on the end of a narrow blade of snow that would lead us from the pedestal to the foot of the face proper, a 300 metre curving line of great purity. At this altitude the granite is bright red. I could already see that the upper part of the face was so smooth and compact that we should be unable to climb it direct without using an immoderate number of expansion bolts, and would therefore be forced on to the north-west ridge. But what did it matter? The important thing was to be there.

It was a cold bivouac. Over on the Grand Plateau we could see lights, no doubt from the head-torches of climbers delayed by heavy snow on one of the routes on the Italian side of Mont Blanc. We could even hear them talking, and made signals with our torches. Presently they saw us, and seemed to wonder

if we were a couple of idiots who had lost their way on Mont
Maudit. We reassured them, and they went on their way down
to the Grands Mulets, where the lights of the hut shone like a
beacon.

After a substantial meal of steak we felt drowsy, and it was
comforting to slide into our warm sleeping bags in the middle
of that icy, lunar landscape.

The cold was bitter next morning as I brewed the tea and
Antoine got the equipment ready. Then I started up the crest
of snow that led to the rocks above. It was astonishingly fine,
a real knife-blade. The face began with a system of two parallel
cracks. The pegs sang as they penetrated the granite, and an
impressive weight of equipment swung at my waist. Presently
the rock became rotten, no doubt owing to the effect of cold
at this great altitude. Neither wooden wedges nor coupled
pitons seemed to solve the problem, and with every movement I
risked falling, in which case the pitons below would have come
out like a zip-fastener. Tsinant belayed me carefully, following
my gestures with concentration.

After two pitches of artificial climbing rendered trying by the
quality of the rock I came out on to the ridge. On my left was
the gully we had descended the previous day. I stood bathed in
the soft, warming rays of the morning sun, while the gully
remained locked in frost and shadow, another world, like
certain mountain faces which never receive any sunlight. Then
it was time to haul the sacks and bring up Antoine. He did not
seem altogether at ease as he removed the pitons, no doubt on
account of the bad rock. There followed several pitches of free
climbing up the ridge while I looked in vain for a way back on
to the face, which consisted of one enormous vertical boilerplate. After a while I was even forced on to the dark, hostile
north face, from which we were unable to escape until we
reached the col ten metres below the summit. The holds were
coated in ice, and only the red colour of the rope lent a human
touch to this morbid, alien world.

Night overtook us, and it became necessary to look for another
bivouac site. There seemed to be no alternative to some ledges
in the gully, and after an excessively delicate traverse I reached
one which was fairly comfortable. Again the night was cold,
and again we saw the lights at Grands Mulets, les Houches and
Les Bossons. Later I was to meet climbers who had been

descending Mont Blanc that night and had heard the sound of our hammering, then located us on the arête. My repose was troubled by the thought that our climb was at best only a very winding line, and that I should have to return and straighten it. In the event, I was to leave this for the delectation of the expansion-bolt experts.

In the morning we climbed up the remainder of the north face to the col, not bothering with the summit, which consists of a pile of easy blocks some ten metres high. As we returned to the Cosmiques and then Chamonix we were happy but not entirely satisfied.

However, it was not long before I succeeded in overcoming this feeling. A meeting with André Contamine led to a project to put up a new route on the north-west face of Mont Blanc de Tacul. It seems to have been written in the stars that in 1963 my destiny should be linked with that mountain. Once again, therefore, I found myself in the cable-car heading for les Cosmiques. Our projected route, a 500 metre triangle of snow and ice, with here and there a few outcrops of rock, blazed in the light of the setting sun. I was delighted to be climbing with André. I had repeated a number of his routes in the Mont Blanc range and had found them all of high quality. He is still one of the best ice-climbers in France, but he remains unconceited and friendly. We had long been hoping to do a climb together, and now at last the opportunity was given to us.

It was very early in the morning we said goodbye to Jacquot, who, as usual, had got up to make us a substantial breakfast. Our crampons squeaked on the ice of the glacier, and barely half an hour later we were climbing up the steepening slopes towards the bergschrund, which it fell to me to cross. Thereafter, we led through with clockwork regularity all the way to the summit. Right away, a gully between two lines of rocks called for a major effort on André's part. Several ice-pitons were needed, and even a few nicks with the axe to give the feet some illusion of support. Getting the pitons out again was surprisingly difficult. As the sun rose we saw that we had already climbed about half the route, but nevertheless went on without stopping. A two-pitch traverse through soft snow lying on ice then brought us on to a kind of false ridge up the middle of the face. It was my turn to lead, and as, unlike my companion, I am in no way an ace ice-climber, I zigzagged

The second day on the north face of the Matterhorn

The west face of the Dru

The north face of the Grands Charmoz at Chamonix

from outcrop to outcrop, desperately looking for somewhere
to plant a rock piton. My tracks looked as though I had been
sleepwalking.

On the summit we unroped, and after taking a few quick
photos dashed off down. To our own surprise, we reached the
hut exactly four hours after leaving it. On the occasion of the
second ascent, a Belgian party took eleven hours for the face
alone.

By 10 a.m. we were back in Chamonix, where I succeeded
in persuading Dany and a few others to go up to the Cosmiques
the same evening. During the course of my numerous descents
of the Mont Blanc de Tacul that summer I had noticed a
possible line up the south pillar of the Aiguille du Midi, and I
wanted to knock it off before returning to Paris. I had exactly
three days left.

The whole south face of the mountain is a magnificent
climbing ground, but several fruitless attempts on the pillar
had shown it to be undeniably the hardest problem there.
There were already four other routes, and as I was the only
person to have climbed them all, I felt I owed it to myself to
have a try at the outstanding problem. Looking up at the
pillar as we passed below it on our way to the hut, I could see
that so much artificial climbing would be called for that with
five of us in the party we were bound to bivouac at least twice.
We dumped the kit at the bottom of the climb and went on.

That night we sat up late playing cards with Jacquot, who
was unbeatable. Shortly after 2 a.m. we were up again. Dany
was enchanted to be taking part at last in an Alpine first ascent,
and on a face she already knew well and liked. Outside it was
bitingly cold. This sensation was not to last for long, however,
for as I started up the first pitch the pillar was bathed in the
morning sun.

The difficulties were not long in appearing. A sloping slab
led to a series of vertical blades which I climbed with the help
of étriers. Next came a narrow chimney, with a strenuous
mantelshelf on to a ledge at the top. This was the first stance,
and I brought up Dany and Pipo. The other two were to look
after the de-pegging and pass up the equipment as required.

Above rose a magnificent corner between two enormous,
smooth, utterly unbroken walls. Right in the back was a thin
crack which I was able to climb with knife-blade pitons. I

F

left the étriers on the pegs in order to make life easier for the second man. The top overhung, and although some rotten rock made the spot somewhat disagreeable, lack of rope forced me to take a stance in slings. The sun blazed down. Below me— I overhung them—my companions had stripped to the waist and were sun-bathing. Changing the order of the rope, I asked Pipo to come up first, while Dany sat on the ledge below and watched.

Pipo was obviously expecting a long wait, for when he arrived he produced a swing seat. He always thinks of everything. Now I had to make a leftward traverse along two thin parallel cracks, both of which were blind in places and called for both maximum concentration and effort. The pegs would only go in a few centimetres and then had to be bent over so as to reduce the leverage. Gradually I got farther and farther away from Pipo, who was watching me like a hawk. After three hours of exposed, nerve-racking effort I found myself under a sharply overhanging prow of rock. Below, on the ledge, the others were still stretched in the sun. With a great deal of difficulty I got round the corner and climbed the roof. The crack was icy, and the wooden wedges could get no secure grip. Two of them were plucked out when I asked Pipo to give me tension. I was now in a critical and acrobatic position, starting from which I had to make a free mantleshelf. The toes of my boots scraped down the holdless rock, seeking friction. My strength was draining away. A few moments more and I should be off. Desperately I launched myself upwards, swung up my body, and at last found a hold. The rope cut into me cruelly; it was clipped into too many karabiners and would not run free. I worked my way up a chimney, and at last, jammed in between two vertical flakes, found something which could be described as a stance. Above me, two parallel cracks led upwards for 30 metres, after which it looked as though a few pitches of free climbing would lead to the top of the Rébuffat route.

I could no longer see my companions, but I knew that they were getting ready. Pipo brought up Dany; I could hear her exclamations of delight. The second rope also began to climb the corner. Pipo passed Dany through on the middle of the rope so that she could be better protected. In spite of her lightness she pulled out two of the pegs on the traverse, causing Pipo to shout a warning. It was astonishing how agile and supple she was as she scrambled up to join me. I gave Pipo a tight rope, but he nevertheless came off on the overhang, so that his 75 kilos suddenly came on to my shoulders.

The light was failing, and as the weather was also threatening I decided to abseil off. Pipo started off down and immediately organised the second abseil, followed by Dany. By this time the second party had reached me, so they went down in their turn. Altogether there were three abseils of 40 metres each, and presently they were reunited on the glacier. It was now pitch dark, and I had to take infinite precautions as I descended, as I had no torch on me and had to grope around for the next rope each time I had pulled down the preceding one. By the time I reached them it was snowing, and we hurried back to the hut. Jacquot had followed our progress, and like a true friend had cooked us a monstrous supper.

It snowed all night, so in the morning we descended forlornly to Chamonix and spent the day listening to the rain. Dany made lunch for fifteen, as only she can. In the evening the weather brightened up, and I decided to set off again on the first cable-car in the morning. Only Pipo and Antoine elected to come with me. The others were still too tired, but I could not wait any longer, as I had to be back in Paris for the following day.

As we were all in the same chalet, there was no problem about the rendezvous. From the top of the Aiguille du Midi we descended in four rappels to the highest point reached two days before. Without any delay we climbed the parallel cracks. They required an impressive number of wedges, but went quite quickly. The rock was sound, and several fine pitches of free climbing brought us to the summit towards 3 p.m.

That evening in Chamonix we celebrated our success in company with those who had been with us on the first and most difficult part of the climb. After we had downed a few bottles at le Bivouac I climbed into the car and set off back to Paris. The holidays were over, yet I was happy. They had been short and the weather unfavourable, but I felt that I had fulfilled my contract with the mountain.

CHAPTER XIV

Marine Interlude

ONE DAY EARLY in December 1963, while I was working in my office in the Ministry, I received a phone call from the photographer Gérard Géry saying that he wanted to see me urgently. I told him to come around, and he wasted no time in getting to the point.

"Pierre," he said, "a new volcanic island has just broken the surface in the sea to the north of Iceland. It is in continual eruption. I think we should go and land on it."

I was slightly taken aback, but agreed at once. We should need a party of three, and Pipo was the very man to make up the number. None of us knew anything about the dangers of the sea. Climbers we might be, but not sailors. Gérard and Pipo were to set off in advance with the equipment, and I was to catch them up in Iceland: the former assured me that I would not need to be away more than ten days. Three days later they had everything packed up and were off.

From Orly I flew via London to Keflavik, arriving towards evening after a journey alone in an enormous Boeing. A 50 kilometre taxi ride took me to Reykjavik, where I found instructions waiting for me from Gérard. Although they had had difficulty getting the inflatable boat and outboard motor through the customs, everything had gone well and was now ready.

At dawn next morning, which at this time of the year in these latitudes is at about 10 o'clock, I flew in a light aircraft to join them at the airstrip at Vestmannaeyjar. On the way, the pilot kindly flew me around the volcanic island, a speck lost in the middle of the ocean. It was frightening to see how it continually fumed and spat, but I forgot my fear in the pleasure of meeting the others.

We spent the day sleeping, organizing the equipment, calculating our chances, and concealing our intentions as best we could from the local sailors, who seemed to guess what we were up to and probably wanted to forestall us. Was there going to be an international competition to be first on the island? Pipo went through the movements of starting the motor again and again. The homework did not seem to have been perfectly memorized, and from time to time he would dive back into the instructions.

We were too nervous to sleep much that night. Pipo and I chatted about first ascents, notably the south pillar of the Aiguille du Midi, and agreed that we would feel a lot safer if something like that were on the books for next day rather than an encounter with the sea.

Friday morning before dawn, three men half dazed with fear carried their boat down to a beach well away from the port so as not to appear too ridiculous in the eyes of the locals. We pumped up the boat, attached the motor, checked the petrol and the photographic gear. We had dressed in our climbing clothes, including crash-helmets and even ropes so that we could belay to the boat—after all, you never know, if it got rough. . . . Over the top of everything we wore real oilskins worthy of old salts, and, as crowning glory, sou'westers which would inflate automatically if we fell in the water. We had too much confidence in the manufacturers to want to try them out.

At first light, under the horrified gaze of some small children, we pushed the big air-bed into the water, telling each other that we were just going to take a quick spin round for test purposes. The motor fired at once, and as everything seemed to be all right we decided unanimously to continue. We felt somewhat stupefied by our own decision. There in the bottom of the boat lay the flags of France and of *Paris-Match*. Eighteen kilometres ahead lay the volcano, smoking.

Pipo was at the helm, Gérard and I sat clutching the edge of the boat with the energy of despair. Fortunately the sea was calm and everything seemed to be all right. Along the coast rose the craters of volcanoes which had been extinct for thousands of years, a moon-like landscape. Our little craft bobbed gaily past great cliffs where the gulls looked like innumerable splashes of white. The water was cold, the wind positively glacial. After all it was December, and in this arctic volcanic region winter reigns most of the time.

Before long there were no more rocks and extinct volcanoes around us, just water, the illimitable expanses of the ocean. We felt apprehensive, and sang to keep our minds off the unfamiliarity of it all to us, more accustomed to snow, ice and granite.

So far behind us that we hardly dared to turn and look at it, Westmann Island was sinking below the horizon. Ahead, the volcano appeared to have calmed itself in welcome. A long way off to starboard, a trawler seemed to be heading towards us. Probably the crew were inquisitive and wanted to watch our landing, and maybe to help us if necessary.

We were oppressed by our own silence. Gérard tried cracking jokes. I was busy asking myself what on earth I was doing in this predicament, while Pipo had retreated into a watchful taciturnity befitting to a captain responsible for his ship and the safety of his crew.

Now we were only a few hundred metres away. The trip had taken two hours. The surprising thing was the calm. It seemed almost ominous. Pipo steered us in close, and we leapt ashore like commandos. The ground was shifting underfoot. In our delirium we yelled and howled with such joy that we forgot to hold on to the boat, and Pipo had to plunge in up to the waist to save it.

We were in ecstasy to be standing on untrodden ground. There is not so much of it left in the 20th century, and even less which is destined to disappear so soon under the waves as this. Out came the cameras. I waved the French flag, Gérard that of *Paris-Match*. The silence weighed heavily on our nerves, a kind of unease. Wanting to see the crater, we set off to run up the few hundred metres to the summit. The lava underfoot was soft and inconstant. I forgot my fear entirely, swinging to the other extreme and losing all sense of danger. Supposing we were to spend the night on the island? And supposing . . . but my inner monologue was suddenly broken off as Gérard saw a puff of smoke and shouted to me to come back. In panic I sprinted back to the boat. Pipo and Gérard were already pushing off, and I had no desire to be left on the island alone.

It was like the end of the world. The earth shook, the noise was deafening, showers of ash shot into the air, lightning flashed and struck; it was as though all the elements at once were pouring out of the bowels of the earth. The volcano was erupting again, and death seemed certain. Both land and sea appeared ready to engulf us, and as I leapt frenziedly aboard they did indeed succeed in swallowing up my Leica.

Reunited in our frail rubber craft, we tried desperately but in vain to get farther away from the shore. Everything was enveloped in ash, and we looked more like miners than mariners or mountaineers. While I attempted clumsily to row and Gérard bailed, Pipo tried in vain to start the motor, each of us cursing the other two ineffectually, since nothing could be heard above the monstrous roaring of the volcano. Ash rained thickly around us, including more solid chunks, a few of which I stowed away in my pockets to give to friends in the apparently unlikely event of surviving. Still the motor refused to start. Our faces were pale, and we began to tremble and sweat with fear.

The waves quickly grew to terrifying proportions, tossing us around like a nutshell. From trough to crest they were some four to five metres high, and we swooped from the heavy, ash-laden crest to the coal-black trough in a matter of seconds. The sky above grew blacker and blacker, while lightning slashed across it as though from an incandescent retort. This time we were for it, without any doubt. The sea moved with the energy of an unchained wild beast, the waves building up to a height of six or seven metres. And if the sea did not swallow us up, surely we must be suffocated or borne down by the weight of ash. And Gérard could sit there taking photos!

I lost an oar and nearly tipped out of the boat, grabbed something and hung on grimly. A pair of ruffians like that were capable of anything. Supposing they cut the safety line? "Two out of three return . . ." Think of the publicity! No, no, I was booked for the round trip. Later we were to learn that the trawler which had been observing us had reported our death to Reykjavik, and it was announced on the news that evening.

Slightly more cheerful noises emanated from Pipo. The motor had fired for a moment. We swung wildly from trough to crest, from crest to trough. It was enough to make anyone seasick and give them a fear of heights at the same time. Seen from the top of each wave the drop into the oncoming hollow was highly impressive, while when the hollow was reached the view of the next roller was appalling. What would happen if one of them broke over us?

Pipo had forgotten the starter. We implored him not to jerk the cord with such violence. If that broke it would be goodbye friends, and only the winds and waves would decide whether we fetched up in South America or at the North Pole. The petrol did not seem to be coming through; Pipo got out the book of instructions. Everything was coated in slag, but we seemed to be getting out of the worst of it. Luckily, the horsehoe-shaped crater was half submerged, so that the lava emerged as a fine spray containing a few solid lumps. If the crater closed up all this matter would be spewed out solid, and that would be the end of our little trip. It was true, of course, that we were wearing our inflatables, and then there was the climbing rope . . . I had a vision of three little black forms bobbing around in the sea.

Suddenly the motor roared into life: Pipo had remembered the trick. Now it purred away smoothly whenever the propeller happened to be in the water, which was not all that often. As long as it went well Pipo spoke to it politely, begging it to be kind and see us through. If it faltered for a second his manner became truculent: "You stupid bugger, you keep on working or else . . ." And it kept on working, taking us out to sea away from the inferno of the island. The size of the waves became less alarming, the rigid lines on our faces eased, our bodies no longer trembled. The din faded to a distant rumble. And we suddenly burst out laughing, knowing that we were safe and sound.

Vestmannaeyjar lay 18 kilometres ahead. Once again the crossing took two hours, and at 4 o'clock, just as darkness was falling, we landed. Now we were hero-worshipped by the children, congratulated by the fisherman, and stared at by all. If they had guessed that it was the first time any of us had put to sea, they would probably have regarded us as a bunch of idiots—and rightly.

The light plane took us back to Reykjavik, where we received a delirious welcome. Our escapade became a national event. That evening we were admired by pretty girls and treated to innumerable rounds of drinks and the stories of seafarers—real ones—for the Icelanders are men of iron, but also of great sensitivity. On the French news we heard that there was talk of an international dispute. The island was French!

Next day I returned to Paris by air.

Precisely one year later, from the other side of the world, I sent Gérard and Philippe a telegram saying: "When are we going to look for another Ile des Français?" And the following day, 6th December, a second volcano arose from the Icelandic seas!

CHAPTER XV

The Unending Continued

FOR CHRISTMAS I went to Chamonix, where I ran into Desmaison in the street. The weather was set fair, there was relatively little snow, and altogether there seemed to be no reason for not doing a climb. The only training I had had was a single day's skiing at Lognan, but who cared? In company with José Giovanni, the author of *Trou* and of the script of the film, Jacques Becker's astonishing last work, we decided to make the first complete ascent of the north spur of the central summit of the Aiguille du Midi on Christmas Day. This route had not been climbed even in summer.

At that time of the year the first cable-car does not reach the Aiguille du Midi until 8 a.m. Quickly we turned the Arête des Cosmiques and descended the couloir which runs straight down from the north between the two summits. Two hours later we were at the start of our climb. It began with a magnificent, slightly overhanging corner which called for artificial means and had to be climbed in its entirety. René climbed with his usual mastery. As for José, it was his first big climb, and he hauled himself upwards as best he could in a tangle of ropes, étriers and jumars.* It was my job to take out the pitons. Under the horrified gaze of the tourists who could see us from the terrace of the aiguille we made our way up the corner, which looks as though it were hewn out of the spur, reaching the top as darkness fell. The cable-car was waiting for us. It was just a short climb, but it was good to be back in contact with solid rock after the Icelandic episode.

Back in Paris I could not stop thinking about the first winter ascent of the Walker. There was going to be competition. On one side were Walter Bonatti and Cosimo Zapelli, on the other Michael Darbellay, Michel Vaucher and I. Naturally, the

* Translator's note: a device for climbing ropes with a minimum of effort. Foot-loops are attached to a pistol-grip which can be moved up the rope when the trigger is pulled, but grips when it is released.

competition was of the friendliest kind. Walter had known that
I had work to do, and had not realized that I could get away
so easily. Moreover, the two Michels and I had long had a
project to attempt the climb together.

At the beginning of January, the three of us were bivouacking
in the tunnels on top of the Aiguille du Midi, sharing the lives
of the workmen. We were surrounded with mounds of equipment which I had brought with me from Paris, by train for
once. The only person who knew of our project was Guido
Tonella, who had discreetly driven us from Geneva to Chamonix,
where we had taken the téléphérique without stopping in the
town. There was only one thing wrong, and that was the
weather. It would not stop snowing.

In this way we spent four days. I taught my Swiss friends to
play belotte, and we calculated our chances on the basis of how
the games worked out. On the fifth day the weather showed
signs of improving. We shouldered our sacks and set out to ski
down the Vallée Blanche with the object of reaching the
Leschaux hut, or what was left of it. The snow was heavy.
Vaucher and I fell an uncountable number of times, while
Darbellay skied behind and helped us up.

Opposite in the Combe de la Vierge there were no tracks to
be seen, which seemed to indicate that Walter had not come
over from Courmayeur. Our hopes rose accordingly. But when
we reached the ice-fall, there were two beautiful tracks. It
could only be Walter and Cosimo, who were thus ahead of us
in the silent competition and had marked up some valuable
points. As darkness fell we lost the tracks in the ice-fall, which
for us was hardly surprising. Again, it was one up to Walter.
We decided to spend the night at the Requin hut, arriving
worn out. It was snowing again, and despite a mountain of
blankets we were stiff with the cold.

Next morning the bad weather set in again, so we left our
kit at the hut and skied on down. At the point where the
glaciers join we found tracks descending from Leschaux,
showing that Walter was several moves ahead. We followed his
trail right down to Chamonix, where I learnt that he had not
made himself known, but had taken a taxi up to the tunnel and
then continued on foot to keep in training. He never missed an
opportunity to train.

Back in Paris I followed the weather reports, which announced non-stop snow all over the Alps. Then one evening I heard that the Italians had attacked anyway. Before long followed the news of their victory. I was delighted with it; without any doubt Walter was the best of us all, and it was right that he should win. It gave me particular pleasure when he sent me a greetings telegram from Courmayeur. Michel Vaucher went up to Requin to bring down the kit. We had failed through inadequate preparation and lack of time, but we were all glad that it was Walter and Cosimo who had succeeded.

There was a lot of work to do, and I could only get away from Paris for a few weekends. On one of these our friend Ziegler flew Dany, Claude Languepin and me up to the Col du Dôme from where we climbed Mont Blanc and skied down through perfect snow. Down at the Grands Mulets we rejoiced like excited children over this easy mode of mountaineering.

In June Walter came to Paris, and I had a fantastic week showing him around my favourite haunts. He was like a happy child, wanting to see and know everything, taking photographs of all he saw. These were his first footsteps as a reporter. As his journeys in Africa and Alaska have since shown, he was to become one of the best in the world. It was a great joy to introduce him to my father. The two men had a lot in common, including faith in life, the will to succeed, and a reluctance to grow old, which I share.

Whatever my success in mountaineering, I could at least reasonably claim to be interested in my fellow men. I had climbed a lot with mountaineers from the various Alpine countries and was keen to make friends with and learn from the Americans who had put up some great routes in Yosemite and more recently also in the Alps. Just lately they had made the first ascent of the south face of the Fou, an exceptional achievement.

I had met John Harlin at the Trento mountain-film festivals, and we had often talked of doing a climb together. When I got back from my trip to the Indian Ocean, we decided to put these plans into practice. I knew John's doctrine, which was to climb faces by the most direct routes, as it were following a plumb-line from the summit. Knowing that mountain-climbing had passed into a new era, I shared his views.

We arranged by telephone to meet at my chalet, and the ten

days we spent there laid the basis of a solid friendship. We had various projects in mind, but the prevailing conditions ruled out climbs at very high altitude. Finally it was the idea of doing a direct route on the west face of the Blaitière which dragged us away from our delightful idleness among the flowery meadows that surrounded the little chalet Gigi Panei had nicknamed Concord, with its growing reputation as an international port of call.

Once again it was the téléphérique. Getting off at Plan de l'Aiguille, we took the path towards Montenvers, then struck off to the right. Apart from the pleasure of being in the mountains, there is nothing very pleasant about grinding up moraines and glaciers unless that is the aim in itself, and this occasion proved no exception. Presently we stood at our chosen starting point directly below the summit, to the left of the celebrated "fissure Brown". The first few pitches were easy, and we climbed together without belaying, moving fast. Presently the going got tougher, and the sack-haulage began. Open walls and cracks succeeded each other; the route remained rigorously in the plumb-line from the summit. By 11 a.m. we were about half way, and it seemed reasonable to take an hour's rest. The view over the Peigne and the north face of the Aiguille du Plan was fantastic.

From here on, the character of the climbing changed, becoming entirely artificial and very technical. I now saw the American method in action. A single rope was used for climbing, while another strand remained free of the karabiners so that the second could jumar up. There were also pitons of high-grade undeformable steel. The face was impressively vertical. We were climbing on the scar left when part of the mountain had fallen away, so that the rock was light grey. Here and there were large blocks, delicately poised on small bases or none-too-securely wedged in cracks, which it was essential to avoid touching. Water oozed from a line of ascending cracks which we followed through the final overhang. It was this which had caused the landslide, and one could not help wondering if it might not happen again, a really horrible feeling. Each time the hammer touched the rock the whole structure sounded hollow, and the last major difficulty of this magnificent climb thus left a sinister impression.

We bivouacked at nightfall above that final overhang, chatting about our projects and formulating new ones. John told me about El Capitan and the Aiguille du Fou, confessing that for the next two or three years he only wanted to make first ascents, and revealing his plans for the Dru and the Eiger. Next morning we traversed the Vires Fontaine and descended to Chamonix via the Nantillons Glacier, happy at having been able to do this first ascent in ideal conditions. We had got along together perfectly, and the difficulties of the climb had seemed to flow away beneath us. Neither of us could think of many climbs that had gone so smoothly and pleasantly, and I felt that I had gained another friend.

After a day off, as conditions at high altitude seemed no better than before, we decided to try for another first ascent in the Aiguilles. Seen from the Blaitière, the Chamonix face of the Fou had looked impressive. Again we went up to Plan de l'Aiguille and trudged up under the west face of the Blaitière, stopping for a moment to look up at the place where, four days earlier, we had started our climb.

At the very top of the glacier stands a monstrous wall of ice dividing the west face of the Blaitière from the first bulwarks of the north face of the Aiguille du Plan. My idea was to turn the ice on the left, but, purist as ever, John insisted that I attack it direct. It took the whole morning to climb that 150 metres, using a lot of ice-pitons and sometimes étriers. Sometimes I even had to hammer the ice-axe into the slope as a further aid. At times it seemed as though the whole shaky construction of colossal blocks tremored and tottered. After five excessively trying pitches I finally pulled over on to the top, which consisted of a broad terrace of soggy snow on which the sunlight beat down. Above us the north face of the Fou stabbed upwards like a spear out of a wilderness of ice.

Suddenly there was a deep roar which rapidly became ear-splitting. Imagining a gigantic rockfall we stood transfixed. Then we saw the helicopter, piloted by François Charlet. He hovered within 10 or 20 metres of our terrace, waving and taking pictures, while the draught blew streamers of snow up into the sunlight. It was really beautiful. Then suddenly he dived down along the ice-wall we had just climbed, leaving us in silence for a moment, before soaring again up across the west face of the Blaitière as if to inspect our route, and finally disappearing.

We set off again up a series of steep snow bands which led us to the Vires Reynier, a line of ledges which runs right across the face, where we set up a kind of comfortable base camp. The summits around us were still resplendent with spring snow, and the north faces of the Peigne and Pélérins looked like an ice-rink tipped on its side. We had a snack; this time the provisions were American. Then we sorted out the equipment. That afternoon we would climb as far as we could, fixing ropes and returning to the ledge for our bivouac, so we could leave the bulk of the gear behind for the moment. Next day we would regain the highest point so far attained by jumaring back up the ropes.

The rock was compact, but nevertheless revealed some lines of weakness. A row of disconnected cracks led directly up under the summit, and the big problem would be getting from one to another. It did not look as though there were many overhangs, but there was no doubt that the face was rigorously and continuously vertical. It looked as though the major difficulties would be concentrated in the last few pitches, where the rock was monolithic. Well, there would be time to worry about that when we got there. John led off up the wall.

It proved to be strenuous artificial climbing, calling for a lot of thick wedges. Much of the time we used American wedges made of metal. John clipped only one rope through the pegs for security, the other hanging free from the belay. When my turn came to follow, he gave me tension on the free rope while I jumared up the other from peg to peg, taking them out as I advanced. I seemed less good at this than I had on the Blaitière, maybe because the rock was steeper.

We led through, and I must admit that on the pitches which it was my turn to lead I found that a single rope for security did not seem much. I therefore used a couple of slings to give myself tension on the pegs. Standing in American tape étriers, I thought wistfully of the rigid metal rungs to which I was accustomed. For his part, John considered that no other equipment was up to the job, and even went so far as to throw away an Allain karabiner just because the gate was stiff. I could find no excuse for this gesture but fatigue, for by this time we had indeed been struggling for hours to climb a few short pitches. As we went, we fixed hemp cord on which to slide back to the Vires Reynier, where our light-blue sleeping bags began to look more and more inviting.

Some of the traverses from one system of cracks to another proved ticklish, and we were forced to resort to pendulum rappels. After another couple of pitches we reached the base of the final tower, some 200 metres high. The more we looked at it, the more monolithic it appeared, and it seemed that next day we should require a considerable number of expansion bolts unless we took a more roundabout line to the right, which in John's eyes would have been cheating. There was only one way to climb the face: direct!

It was about 7 p.m. as we sat in our étriers picking out the line for next day and preparing to descend by means of a few abseils and the fixed line, when in a matter of moments a violent wind began to blow. It was rapidly followed by the rumbling of thunder, which in this horseshoe of mountains between the Blaitière and the Peigne reverberates worse than anywhere else. Swiftly a curtain of hail swept over us. Without any further delay I grabbed the rope and started down the first abseil, hindered by the hailstones pouring heavily down the rock and the wind which kept on trying to spin me. John shouted at me, using a vocabulary I had never heard before. I gave him equal change, and when he started down I redoubled my efforts so as to let him know that I in my turn had no objection to his moving faster. As I sat in the étriers pulling down the rope a great mass of hailstones began to build up on my knees and shoulders. In a matter of seconds it piled up to a height of one or two metres and I had to push off from the face with my feet to let it slide away. It was impossible to see anything at all, even the equipment. All our attention was centred on getting the rope down, which was the only thing that mattered.

Conditions were even worse by the time we were ready to start the second abseil. The wind had grown so strong that the ropes streamed out horizontally, and to stop the two strands twisting I attached karabiners and pitons and anything else I could find to their ends. When we reached the bottom of this abseil it was pitch dark, and we were still far from the bivouac ledge. It was impossible to get any farther; we were stuck in painfully uncomfortable positions in a streaming crack, soaked and chilled to the bone. Our clothes were literally frozen stiff, yet we felt as though we were in an icy-cold bath. The wind, hail and snow continued all through the night, and it seemed as though time had come to a stop. Only the lightning seemed to have passed over. As the hours dragged on, hope of finishing the climb gradually ebbed away. Our fine first ascent was doomed to become a mere attempt, as too often happens. We should just have to come back.

The storm was still raging at dawn as we abseiled on down to the snow-covered Vires Reynier. Our sleeping bags and equipment were buried. Exhausted by our punishing bivouac, we crammed everything into the sacks. We were in a hurry to get it over with. Harassed by the elements we traversed and descended to the Vires Fontaine which finally led us to the north-west ridge of the Blaitière. From there we gained the Nantillons Glacier and descended to Chamonix and the chalet. We had not eaten for twenty-four hours, and now we slept for eighteen.

As though to make a game of us, when we awoke the sun was shining on the Chamonix face of the Fou. However, so much snow had fallen that we decided to cut short our vacation. John returned to Leysin, where he was on the point of setting up an international climbing school. I went back to Paris. We agreed to meet again when conditions were more favourable.

I had often explained to my friend Tonella, who is a veritable mountain historian, my theory that, in order to get to know each other better, climbers should climb with people from other countries. I tried to put the theory into practice, and it was a private ambition of mine to form European and even international teams. This dream was about to be realized.

At the beginning of July I received a letter from Tonella. It seemed that Lothar Brandler, whom I knew well, wanted to make a film featuring just such a European team. The idea was to record an ascent of his own route on the Cima Grande. Shooting would begin on 14th July and would last two weeks. There would be three actors, Roberto Sorgato from Italy, Wino Ender from Germany, and myself. To help him with the filming, Brandler had three of the best climbers of the day, Bittner, Uhner and Scheffler. Tonella knew in advance that I would agree, and I wasted no time in wiring: "See you Locatelli 14 July."

In my Triumph I sped over the Arlberg, through the Tyrol, and over the Brenner to Cortina, where I stopped for the first time in 1200 kilometres to eat ice-cream on a terrace. Suddenly it occurred to me that I could hardly keep my eyes open, which after all was natural enough. Before long the car was climbing the white hairpins of the road to Misurina. At Auronzo I went up to say hello to the Mazzoranas, stopped again for a few minutes at the Tre Cime hut, and at last reached the col with its fantastic vision of the north faces.

Loaded like a donkey, I walked down to Locatelli, where Rieder welcomed me in the midst of a monster sing-song. An impressive number of beer bottles were in evidence, ready to play their part in helping me to sleep. I heard my name being whispered all around the room and shook innumerable hands without always being sure if I could put names to the faces. The atmosphere was the same as ever, cosmopolitan and international. The only element missing, as so often in the Dolomites, was French. Well, I should just have to make up for that myself.

Over in the far corner of the room, an athletically built man caught my eye. I knew at once that it was Roberto Sorgato, the devourer of the Dolomites. As he made his way towards me I was staggered by his physique, and indeed I was soon to learn that his strength was only equalled by his kindness. He spoke French with the gravelly accent of Belluno, which took me aback. Sometimes I feel a kind of reserve when I meet people, and it was so now: so many first ascents, such strength, such radiance of character. His hand crushed mine as they met; when he smiled, his features seemed to have been carved out with an axe. All I could find to say was: "Bon jour, Roberto."

"Bonjour, Pierre," he replied. "Pleased to meet Mazeaud at last." My reserve evaporated. We grinned at each other and drank a lot of grappa. Before long we were firm friends.

As evening came on, Lothar and the team returned from a technical reconnaissance of the face, where they had been investigating camera angles. General delirium broke loose, and Roberto and I joined in the Bavarian songs with a will. Sensing that a historic chapter in mountain film-making was being written under his roof, Rieder sat up late with us, paying more attention to our intoxication than to the repose of his other guests. As filming was to start next morning we staggered to our room towards 2 a.m. There was not a minute to waste if we were to get everything done in the time available, and we had to allow for weather.

Roberto and I shared a room and went on chatting in the darkness. I was deeply impressed by his simplicity and total confidence, and felt that I had made a real discovery in getting to know him. He confessed that he had been wanting to meet me; I did not dare to admit how eager I had been. We spoke of the Cima Ovest, where he had made the first winter ascent of our route, a dreadful adventure in the course of which he had hung for more than ten hours under the overhangs on a single rope with only one piton. And indeed I knew that his courage and strength were legendary.

Lothar woke us early next morning. Filming was about to begin. The two weeks were to go by in an atmosphere of confidence, friendship, fun and continual banter. For the first week we shot sequences of the lower pitches and a number of minor scenes, returning each evening to the hut for the eternal "Bouillon mit Ei" and goulash. During the day the three actors obediently followed the draconian orders of the director and producer, who was emerging as not only a great climber but also a great man of the cinema. During the prize-giving at the Trento Mountain-Film Festival, at which Lothar's film received first prize, my friend Luc Moullet, editor of the well-known *Cahiers du Cinéma*, was to say: "Orson Welles might well be jealous of him. Pans like this have never been filmed before." It was no accident. As Lothar filmed us he was suspended beneath the overhangs, so that he had the climbers, the face and the screes hundreds of metres below all in the lens at the same time. The result on film was an amazing sense of space and exposure, so that the climbers almost seemed to be flying.

Each evening we descended a couple of hundred metres in a series of impressive rappels. I began to have doubts whether such a film could be a success. The idea of doing the whole route in these circumstances seemed far-fetched. But I underrated the determination of Lothar and his team, Bittner who was shortly to be Daisy Voog's climbing partner when she made the first feminine ascent of the Eiger, Uhner who put up the fantastic Saxon route on the Cima Grande just a few metres to the right of where we were now climbing, and Scheffler who had led his sixty-year-old father up the north face of the Cima Ovest. As we reached the screes at nightfall another Lothar would be there before us—Lothar Kosmerhel, who was filming the whole performance for television from the Comici route. Then we would all trot happily back to the hut together.

The prestigious Tre Cime di Laveredo will always have a special place in my heart. There I have passed not only this exciting interlude but some of the most wonderful moments of my mountaineering life. It was on the Cima Ovest that, thanks to René, I first discovered my possibilities.

When a rest day came along, Roberto and I went down to Cortina to gobble ices and other delicacies and to visit friends. Above all we wanted a change of scene. At Misurina I left my car in the garage of Valerio Quinz, an old friend of Cima Ovest days, and that evening we went back up in Roberto's famous Topolino, now venerable in old age, which had to be pushed when the going got steep.

Came the big day. Very early in the morning we set out with the object of filming the ascent of the big overhangs. Six of us were to climb, Scheffler and Lothar Kosmerhel remaining below to send up vital supplies of food and film. The climbers we met along the familiar track could not conceal their curiosity. Each of us made an effort to speak the languages of the others, and we had evolved a kind of international jargon. Altogether we had nearly 600 kilos of equipment as we reached the foot of the climb, 33 mm camera, reels, batteries, food and drink, mountaineering kit including a lot of expansion bolts, and goodness knows what else. Above all we had the famous "Kassete" of which we were to hear so much in the course of the climb as one Lothar yelled to the other. "Bitte Kassete, schnell, es ist sehr *important.*"

German, Italian and French, Wino, Roberto and I were to take turns at leading that day under the eye of the camera. Sometimes Lothar, like a maestro, would make us repeat a series of moves five or six times. He was cursed for his pains, but good-humouredly. The line to the support team on the ground was in constant employment, and Lothar filmed away in unbelievably acrobatic positions. Meanwhile the others combined climber's with camera crew's work, improving Lothar's belay with expansion bolts, preparing the next pitch, hauling and lowering reels, or reloading. The teamwork was at once merry and efficient. When dialogue was being recorded all had to remain silent save those actually engaged in expressing their suffering or rejoicing in the beauty of the climb, but the rest of the time the air was filled with happy shouts. Parties on the Comici route were hailed with ribald gaiety, especially that led by our friend Carlesso, who only seems to get younger as he grows older.

By this time we knew the first few pitches so well that they had become a game. It was true that acting as though we found it difficult called for no special effort. The climbing is of a high standard and will always call for skill however often it is repeated. But we now knew the moves and could afford the luxury of cracking jokes, in the course of which the languages of Schiller, Dante and Diderot were murdered with equal cheerfulness. Lothar and his team were pleased with these first shots of the climb done as a whole. Gert Bittner is a natural joker and Mac Uhner hardly less so. Thus there were smiles all round.

The darkness caught us a pitch below the famous traverse, and we bivouacked there. Gert and Mac were above, Lothar and I squashed together on the same étriers in the middle, and Roberto and Wino below. An impressive quantity of equipment hung all around, swinging on ropes. Two hundred metres lower, the other Lothar and Wolf Scheffler loaded food and drink on to the supply line. Farther off, over at the Locatelli, Rieder was making light signals to us. We replied with our head-torches.

Next morning, for purposes of the film, I had several times to repeat the traverse where I had so much difficulty a few years before. It was interesting enough in the right direction, but still more so in reverse! We ended the day all together on the big ledges at the foot of the artificial pitches, hauling up kit, learning our lines for next day, or teaching each other bits of slang in our respective languages. Everything was fine and morale could not have been higher. The friendship between us grew warmer all the time, and everyone made an effort to get to know all the others.

Filming next day among the overhangs was impressive in the extreme, and the scenes shot that day were to prove the most sensational of the lot. The cameraman made us repeat sections ten times over, which in such positions is not always a matter of pure pleasure. First the light would be bad, then he would run out of film, then the actor did not look natural, then the composition was wrong. . . . "Noch einmal," he kept repeating. We gained sympathy for the sufferings of the Chaplins and

Bogarts of this world, and from there it was an easy step to thinking about the fabulous bodies of actresses like Brigitte Bardot, the finest French export of them all. Roberto was insistent that I should procure him an introduction, whereas I felt that nothing could be pleasanter than a confidential discussion with Sophia Loren or Monica Viti.

After a tiring day (we had spent almost six hours on one stance alone) we bivouacked again on the ledges. Once more we hauled up the gear and discussed everything under the sun before falling into a heavy sleep. The moonlight glittered on the small lake below the Cima Ovest.

Grand exodus on the fourth morning. We left our comfortable ledges and climbed back into the overhangs, where we were treated to a display of Lothar's astonishing mastery as he had himself lowered over the overhangs, hanging clear several metres behind us as he filmed. The skill of Gert and Mac was equally amazing, enabling the boss to carry out incredible manoeuvres. The result was some gripping sequences of Roberto climbing on his étriers, where one hardly feels sure if he is actually hanging in space or swimming. The camera really gives the sense of something phenomenal, and this is at the heart of Brandler's extraordinary achievement.

Presently the camera team ran out of film and vanished upwards; later we heard them below on the track back to the hut. As for the European rope, it had to bivouac again, and this time in shirtsleeves, as the heavy kit had all been lowered off earlier. The cold was glacial. On the fifth day we quickly reached the summit, but had to return a day later to shoot the final scene under the summit cross, which dominates the range.

While this was going on, Harlin had started another competition over on the Cima Ovest. He was attempting the overhangs direct, while the French pair Berardini and Paragot contented themselves with the Couzy route.

All good things come to an end, and at last it was time to leave. In the meantime Dany had arrived, and we all left in a general happy bedlam. The baggage mule had several hundred kilos to carry over to the Tre Cime hut. Everyone drank himself silly, and the one universal wish was to meet again, in the valley, in the city, anywhere, but most of all in the mountains.

Cordée européenne deserved its first prize at Trento. Its exceptional quality is due to the mastery of Lothar and his team of climber-technicians, and also to the atmosphere of fraternity that reigned throughout its making and which can be discerned on the screen, reflected on three faces.

I drove back to Chamonix via Courmayeur, where I dined with Gigi Panei and a number of friends. When I reached my chalet I found that John Harlin had got there before me, having travelled round via Grindelwald. Conditions were ideal for an attempt on the Eigerwand direct, and there was no time to be lost; the competition was hot. John and the other Americans had formed a team with Sorgato and Piussi from Italy. Against them were ranged Germans, Austrians, and the French climbers Desmaison and Bertrand. There were also said to be Poles, Japanese and a dozen or more Chinese milling around at Kleine Scheidegg.

In no more time than it took to get the equipment together we were off to Leysin, and that same evening we arrived at Kleine Scheidegg. There was the Eiger, with all its pageantry and symbolism. The thought of attempting a direct route up the north face was enough to fill anyone with feelings of apprehension. Desmaison had just given up, and as the weather was bad and the face full of waterfalls, we decided not to risk it. Twelve hours after our arrival we were on our way back to Leysin. I still wonder when I shall climb the face. I am too old for the direct now, but Heckmair's original route still calls.

Back at Chamonix we found Sorgato with Lito Tajda de Flores, an American whose name sounded Mexican although in fact his mother was Bolivian, comfortably installed in the chalet. They were being looked after by Dany, in return for which they had to play with Lucas, a poodle puppy who was to grow up all too soon.

John was still dreaming of direct routes, so the four of us went up to the foot of the west face of the Dru to have a look around. We climbed the couloir in the small hours of the morning in order to avoid stonefall and struck straight upwards from the ledges leading across to the original route. It took us a day to climb four pitches, though John showed great mastery in the lead. Roberto and I followed, slightly disconcerted by the techniques employed as Lito jumared up the fixed ropes left by the leader. Finally it was time to bivouac: at this rate we should have to bivouac at least ten times. Maybe we should just move up here for the winter.

That night the weather broke, in accordance with tradition. In the morning we had to abseil off. The stone-falls were unremitting, and it was a miracle that no one got hurt. All the ropes were cut through. The rain was dissolving the very cement of the mountain and it seemed as though the rocks were enjoying themselves hugely, surrounding us with an odour of exploded stone.

A number of people in Chamonix seemed inclined to smile at our setback. I did not care for their attitude, but after all what did it matter? For us, the main thing was to try. The direct route was in fact climbed a year later by Harlin and Robbins, and at the time was certainly the toughest route on granite in the Alps. The score was one up to the Americans, whose ability had been questioned by certain French climbers.

Back at the chalet an international gathering of climbers sat waiting for better weather. Krakotchvil turned up, and together with Petit Claude and François Hess spirited Dany away to the east face of the Grand Capucin. As for Roberto and I, we decided to have a shot at the Walker, which would be his first climb in the Mont Blanc range.

There seemed no point in hanging around. We crammed a rope, a few pegs and karabiners and a duvet jacket each into the sacks, and away we went. The sacks were light—too light: we had forgotten the food.

From Montenvers we wandered slowly up the glacier, giving ourselves plenty of time to scrutinize the Walker. Someone behind seemed to be trying to catch us up, so we stopped and waited. It was Michel Vaucher. He was on his way up to join Walter Bonatti in an attempt on the north face of the Pointe Whymper, which would be a new route up the north face of the Grandes Jorasses.

Up at the Leschaux hut there were a number of French climbers and also a cross-section of the international community: Walter and Michel, and also John Harlin and Clarke, who were heading for the Linceul. Walter and I chatted late into the night while Roberto and Michel slept deep. Walter said that he had wanted me to be with them, but had been unable to get hold of me as I was in the Dolomites. Before we dropped off to sleep he gave me food for the climb from his own badly needed supplies.

Walter and Michel left the hut at midnight, closely followed

by John and Clarke and the French party who were heading
for the Walker. Roberto and I were fond of our beauty sleep,
and waited till a more reasonable hour. When we finally set
off at 2 o'clock the points of light far ahead showed how much
time we had lost. We moved rapidly up the glacier and found
the French party asleep at the foot of the face. It was still dark
as we tiptoed past, and not until we were a couple of pitches up
the climb did we reveal our presence. They gave chase immediately, but we left them far behind and ultimately they had
to bivouac.

The first few pitches are not difficult, but already we could
feel that we were on great form. As we went by we duly glanced
at the Cassin crack, which is nowadays usually by-passed. At
the Allain crack we overtook a party of English climbers.
Already we could feel that the climb was going to live up to its
reputation, and that it was going to be a great day. Our morale
and our physical condition had never been so good. I led up
the corner above the crack, then Roberto led through, and so
it went on the whole day. It was all quite automatic: there was
no need to speak. At the ice-bands we overtook another
English rope—there seemed to be a crowd today on one of the
most prestigious routes in the Alps—and so came to the 70
metre corner. Below us the other parties were spread out like
little black dots. Over on the right we could see Walter and
Michel who were just at the point of transition from ice to rock.
I called across to them. They replied that everything was
going well for them, and I could say the same for us.

The corner gave magnificent climbing, but I hardly had
time to notice it. I had never felt so at home, and Roberto too
was smiling to himself. Presently we reached the pendulum,
which was followed by a rather unpleasant pitch where I had
to get a bit tough on account of the ice. At the Cassin bivouac
we took half an hour off to enjoy the nuts and chocolate
Walter had given us. Before starting off again we were able to
call across to the others for the last time. They were surprised
by how fast we had got on. Over where they were the rock was
loose and the way ahead looked difficult. Their rope had been
cut by stonefall, but all was well and they were going on. I felt
worried about them.

Roberto and I now had to tackle the black slabs, a famous
section of the climb much redoubted by climbers on account

of the epic struggles that have taken place there. Nevertheless we encountered no special difficulty. The rock was splendidly sound and we experienced no feeling of hostility. There were a few pitons, but even these seemed unnecessary. Metre followed metre, and half an hour after starting the slabs we stood at the top of them. Again we stopped for a few minutes to look up the route ahead and inspect the Rébuffat bivouac, where Terray and Lachenal lost their way. There were some bits of rope and an old sack. Others must have bivouacked there more recently.

A pitch which we found unexpectedly difficult next led back to the ridge, and there began a kind of royal progress. We literally ran up the easy pitches, often moving together. An exhausted-looking German party which had already bivouacked twice was speedily overhauled and left behind. Still we did not speak, except once when Roberto broke the silence to say what a great climb it was, and how glad he was that we could do it together.

As we reached the triangular snow-patch we began to feel the pace for the first time. The red chimneys above were covered in ice and, though only three pitches long, took us three hours to climb. The holds and pitons had to be cleared of ice with the hammer, and we regretted not having brought crampons. The final ridge leading to the summit seemed long owing to fatigue, and on this easy but highly treacherous and iced-up ground we took extra care. At last we broke through the cornice on to the summit and fell into each others' arms, radiantly happy. Roberto had stopped talking about the Dolomites for once, and now swore only by the Grandes Jorasses and by granite. And indeed, for a first climb on granite it was quite something.

It was 5 o'clock. We had taken just twelve hours. In view of the time wasted in the red chimneys we felt satisfied with our performance.

After a short rest to savour our victory, we followed the ridge to the Pointe Whymper, the appalling verticality of which we were able to appreciate through a gap in the cornice. We thought of Walter and Michel.

As we turned to the descent the weather suddenly changed. Cloud formed around us, and it began to snow. Despite the excellent plan which Cabri had drawn me in Chamonix I lost the way, and as we were wandering around in circles we decided to bivouac, cursing the weather for preventing us from reaching the hut or perhaps even Courmayeur the same evening. Well, after all, it was only one bivouac the more, and a lot better than some we had known. The difficulties were behind us, and it was all over bar the shouting. With nothing to eat or drink but snow there was small temptation to sleep, so we sat and talked.

We had climbed the Walker spur in a veritable state of grace. Neither Roberto nor I had ever felt such mastery, climbed so fast, or enjoyed a more perfect entente. We had hardly spoken at all during the climb; everything had come about automatically, and the pitches had succeeded each other with the rhythm of a metronome. I later remarked to Dany that at times I felt as though I were on my own, and when we met again at the Trento festival Roberto commented that he had only really noticed my presence when we reached the summit. This state of grace has been referred to by Gervasutti, by Lachenal, and also by Bonatti in his descriptions of K2, the Innominata and the Bonatti pillar on the Dru. Roberto and I experienced it together, and it has left an indelible impression.

In the morning the sky was black, but seemed disposed to accord us a short respite. Down at the hut we slaked our thirst with hot wine and added our names to the long list of those who had done the Walker. We smiled to see that the name immediately before ours was that of Wino Ender. The cunning old snake had said nothing of his projects while we were filming. So we descended to Entrèves and caught the téléphérique up to the Col du Géant. As we crossed the Vallée Blanche the weather grew worse. We thought of Dany and the others on the Capucin, hoping that they were already down. And so we reached Chamonix and the chalet.

In fact, the party on the Capucin had to descend through the storm, and only arrived next day. Roberto went back to Belluno. The weather had me seriously worried, and during a lull I took a helicopter to see how Walter and Michel were getting on. Trotskiar had added to my disquietude with the news that their ropes had been cut again by another rockfall. All morning we searched the north face of the Jorasses from end to end and from bottom to top, but without seeing anything except a couple of climbers at the summit of the Walker. We approached to within a couple of metres, but the wind made it impossible to land. One of the pair seemed to recognize me. Later I was to learn that it was my friend Scheffler.

I was seriously worried by this time, but that evening I heard that Walter and Michel had finished their climb in good order. I was therefore able to return to Paris, where I was due for an operation. Just before going in, I learnt that Dany and Lito were stuck in a violent storm on the west face of the Petites Jorasses. There was nothing I could do, but Gary Hemming and Yannick Seigneur were to find them safe and sound. It had been a bad moment, but the relief was correspondingly great.

In October I returned to Trento for the film festival. The first prize which Lothar received for *Cordée européenne* seemed no more than justice. The whole team was there, and a gayer time would be difficult to imagine.

I brought Claude Deck, one of the best of the younger French climbers, along with me in my car. He seemed quite overcome with my senile energy—I was thirty-four—and in view of our timetable took me for a veritable monster. In effect, we left Paris at 9 p.m. and reached Trento at lunchtime next day after a nonstop drive. There followed four days of living it up in Trento. We left on Sunday at midday, called at Chamonix on the way, and arrived at Paris in time for me to be at work by 8 a.m.

Once again the festival had left an enduring impression, and I had met all the climbers from Trieste.

Back in Paris, Robert Paragot told me that I had been selected to take part in an expedition to the Baltoro Glacier which was being organized by the Fédération Française de la montagne. Immediately I began to read all the literature about the famous region and its chain of 8000 metre giants, dreaming of adding my name to the prestigious list of those who had climbed them. Alas, the Indo-Pakistani conflict put an end to that particular dream.

CHAPTER XVI

The Civetta

FROM JANUARY 1965 on, Roberto and I kept up a long correspondence. The two of us and Ignazio Piussi held ourselves in a state of constant readiness to travel to Grindelwald the moment conditions for the Eiger seemed promising. Unfortunately they remained obstinately unfavourable, and as Piussi first fell ill and then got married, our plans came to nothing. In a way I found this quite useful, as my time was much taken up with work at the Ministry in Paris and with municipal elections in Limoges.

So spring followed winter, and we began to train for our various summer projects. On Thursday 22nd July I was jerked out of my preoccupations in the private council of the Ministry by a telephone call from Chamonix: it was Roberto. I was to come at once to join him at the centre of the known world (my chalet), from where we would go on to Belluno and the Civetta. Conditions in the western Alps were hopeless. It was better to head for the Dolomites. Next day, however, I was due in Limoges, so I did the return trip by car—two nights running in a TR4—dealt with my post early on the Saturday morning, and set off at once for Chamonix.

When I reached the chalet Roberto was waiting. All around stood the tents of Italians, Germans, Poles and Czechs. There too stood the remarkable figure of our American born in Bolivia, resident in France, whose dream it was to die in Florence, and who, on top of all this, bore the incredible name of Tajda Lito de Flores.

We decided to set off without delay, using both cars—Roberto's with Diana as passenger and mine with Dany and the poodle Lucas. Before long we were through the Mont Blanc tunnel and leaving the granite behind us as we headed away towards the limestone. While waiting for Piussi to appear we spent two days of calm amid the flowers at a beautiful country house outside Belluno.

I have to admit that I was in two minds about meeting

Piussi. On more than one occasion I had stated in public my opinion of the climbers who, starting only a few days after the tragedy, had sought to rob Bonatti and me of our victory. I can only explain this emotion as stemming from one of the most shattering experiences of my life. My climbing friends, especially the foreign ones, have been good enough to understand and forgive. Walter Bonatti had set me the proper example by congratulating René Desmaison on the second winter ascent of the Walker spur.

So we lay around sleeping, unwinding and generally doing nothing, all the pleasures which one never gets around to in Paris. On Tuesday 27th July we decided to go up to the Tissi hut. Ignazio could follow us up, and in the meantime it would be nice for Dany, who had developed into the best woman climber in France, to make the first feminine ascent of the Philipp-Flamm route. Once again the car was loaded up, including the ineffable Lucas, and before long we were at Alleghe. The sacks went up to the hut on the téléphérique, while we walked up via Coldai so that we could walk along under "the face of faces" which I had not yet seen from close up. My visit two years earlier with Bonatti and Gallieni had been cut short by bad weather, and we had got no further than the Vazzoler hut and the Torre Venezia. From that visit two main impressions remained, namely the beauty of the Tissi route and the gracefulness of Bianca de Beaco, whom I had then met for the first time. I did not then know that she was to become a great friend, and that one day I should drive all the way from Paris to Trieste to visit her in hospital.

From Coldai the sight of that seven kilometre-long wall is truly breath-taking. No photograph can suggest the grandeur of its successive buttresses, ranging from the Torre d'Alleghe to the Cima Su Alto. I thought of some of the epic battles that had taken place on it: that of Solleder and Lettenbauer in 1925, and more recently those of Carlesso on the Valgrande, Aste on the Punta Civetta and Livanos on the Su Alto. The path to the Tissi hut goes uphill away from the face, but one keeps on turning around to look at it. We took the walk slowly. Up at the hut we were captivated by the charm of the warden Livio and his wife, and also of a party of young English climbers who had bicycled all the way from Dunkerque. There too I had the great pleasure of running into my friend Anderl Mannhardt again. On the Eigerwand and on Nanga Parbat he had been the comrade of Toni Kinshofer, outstanding even among mountaineers for his human qualities, who had saved my life during our attempt on the north face of the Matterhorn in winter. Too often, for climbers, such memories bring sadness in their train.

As we lounged singing around the fire that evening, the expected telephone call from Piussi arrived. He was already at Alleghe and would be with us in two hours. It was a disappointment for Dany, who would now have to wait for the Philipp-Flamm, but for Roberto and me it was a moment of joy. In my case, however, the joy was mixed with a certain nagging doubt as to how the meeting would go off.

In the event it passed off easily: Ignazio just embraced me. We were friends straight away, and despite my unorthodox Italian and his equally peculiar French we had no trouble in understanding each other. I have rarely seen such a massively powerful man—it seemed as though he could brush any obstacle aside—yet his voice was soft, expressing a deeply sensitive nature which I was soon to learn to appreciate.

Next morning, as we waited for the landlord of the "Coldai Arms" to look out some equipment, we had a long conversation about the Pillar of Fresnay, Walter Bonatti and our dead friends. Ignazio knew all about Pierre Kohlman's exceptional ability as a climber and told me how much he would like to repeat some of his routes in the Mont Blanc range. Presently we began to study our projected route on the Civetta. It did not seem beyond the powers of the party, and I kept to myself my fears that, unfit as I was after an exhausting year, I might not be up to doing the climb. When the kit was all ready we packed our sacks, then spent the day enjoying the company of others, especially Diana and Dany.

The night was short but calm, without too much anxiety about the difficulties to come. There would be a couple of bivouacs, but the weather was fine, nothing could go wrong, and in three days we would be back again. With a couple of giants like Roberto and Ignazio I would go to the ends of the earth.

It was still dark when we left the hut on Thursday 29th July, heavily loaded. Two hours later we reached the foot of the rocks after ploughing up a snow-slope; there was a lot of snow that year. After the ritual pause to sort out the gear we roped up. Roberto was to lead the first day, I the second, and Ignazio the third. We would haul the sacks up the difficult pitches, which in practice turned out to mean practically the whole time, as grades V and VI were a lot more frequent than grade II.

Right from the outset we were confronted with difficulties of a somewhat unpleasant kind. The rock in the lower tiers was rotten, and we had to take care not to start stone-falls which might have caused injury or cut the rope. Only Piussi, who was climbing last, could afford to let himself go, and his size 47 boots—needed to support his 90 kg—sent everything he found suspect thundering down the face.

As we rose higher the rock improved and we began to get whole pitches of magnificent free climbing of every variety, cracks, corners and walls. It was exactly as we had planned it. Our line remained rigorously in the vertical from the summit known as the Punta Tissi or Quota* 2992. The lower section was of grey rock which should go free, the central zone was yellow and would probably require artificial means, while the last part consisted of chimneys from which water was streaming even at this hot time of the year.

The views from the stances were magnificent. Already we were high enough to see the Marmolada, the Sasso Lungo, the Tofana. Closer at hand to our left was the Andrich-Fae route, to the right the Philipp-Flamm hiding the original Solleder route, the final grey towers of which could, however, be seen 1000 metres above.

Sorgato climbed with his usual class and calm. Some pitches called for concentration, but with him somehow there is always time to laugh and joke, so that we seemed to find ourselves in the atmosphere of the Boyard or the Brasserie Nationale at each stance. He knew the Civetta by heart, having climbed practically all the routes, including the first winter ascents of the Solleder and the Su Alto. From behind me came Piussi's voice with the time-honoured instructions "tira" and "molla", which echoed across to Mannhardt and his companion on the Andrich-Fae route, while their "zug"

* Translator's note: equivalent here to "point", or in military terms "hill".

and "frei"* echoed back to us. The international atmosphere was full of charm, and a feeling of deep friendship reigned among us. I experienced an emotion of great joy, wishing that somehow the moment could be perpetuated and preserved in its freshness before fatigue intervened. The time had not yet come to long for a plunge in the beautiful little lake of Alleghe, where we could already see a few boats. Our thoughts strayed to pretty women bronzing themselves in the sun, to hours of idleness. At this stage it was still a laughing matter.

Towards 2 o'clock we stopped to eat some cold bacon and taste the cheese which Ignazio had brought with him from Friuli, a rite which was performed in an almost religious atmosphere. Above us rose a great pillar, at the base of which we seemed to discern a good bivouac site, so when lunch was over we climbed off in that direction, imagining wide terraces, perhaps even a bed! At the same time the difficulties were becoming more serious. The wall had been growing steadily steeper and was now vertical, while above us great yellow roof overhangs seemed to mock our temerity. Roberto surpassed himself, and we did our best to follow. Presently he called down that the ledges at the foot of the pillar were as wide as the Place Vendôme . . . no, as the Place de la Concorde. A more perfect bivouac site could not be found. It was already 6 o'clock, and Ignazio and I floated upwards as though on wings at the thought that this evening, at least, there would be no bivouac on étriers. In certain respects the Civetta seemed to compare more than favourably with the Cima Ovest.

Speaking as a connoisseur, Roberto decided that the site was less comfortable than he had originally thought. Piussi, however, toiled away until he had cleared three perfect places where we could all stretch out full length. The cooker hummed and we ate, finishing off the water in our flasks. Tomorrow we should find snow. To top it all off, we had Italian dolci. On the path 400 metres below we could see Diana and Dany trying to make out where we had got to, while that little black dot frisking around in front of them must be Lucas. We could hear him barking. So we chatted philosophically as the sun disappeared behind the Marmolada. Down in Alleghe, the first lights began to wink out.

* Translator's note: "tight" and "slack" in both languages.

The Aiguille du Midi, showing the Mazeaud route

The west face of the Aiguille Durier

On the west face of the Blaitière

I lay there staring at the roof overhangs which jutted above us. Tomorrow was to be my day. At 9 p.m. my alarm watch went off. It was time to exchange light signals with those down at the Tissi hut, a link with the everyday world. We felt comforted and less isolated, bound by the great chain of mountaineering friendship; the climbers at one end, those who cared for them on the other, and open-heartedness on both sides.

It is always difficult to get under way after a good bivouac. Roberto had not slept well, but Ignazio was on great form, laughing and joking from the moment we woke up. It was my turn to lead, and at first there was a series of pitches of free climbing. I used very few pitons and indeed rather astonished myself by the way in which I dealt with the cracks, chimneys and corners. Behind me the others coped with the sack-haulage. Their teamwork was so good that we forged ahead quickly. The difficulties increased as we got nearer the overhangs, and at one point Roberto was somewhat astonished to see me take off my shirt in order to get up a particularly tight chimney, blaming the hut-warden's excellent spaghetti for my troubles. I left a rope hanging down the pitch to make life easier for the others, especially Ignazio, so much more strongly built than myself.

The weather seemed set fair, and at the stances, where I hammered in several pitons each time, the view grew finer and finer the higher we rose. Alleghe was shrinking to a group of dots, while the Marmolada revealed ever more of its beauties. Already we could see the summit of the Torre di Valgrande, but the yellow walls of the Pan di Zucchero showed us that we still had a long way to go. We climbed pitch after pitch of magnificent grade V, with here and there a step of VI. On one of these I nearly peeled off on account of the rope-drag, Roberto being unable to help despite my anguished cries of "molla". I recommend this particular bit of wall to the reader: there are hardly any holds, and it is easy to imagine oneself redescending the pitch at terminal velocity, the last piton being 30 metres below.

At about 3 p.m. we crossed the Comici ledges, not without a certain longing for the relatively easy ways off which they offered. It was Ignazio who recalled us to a sense of duty, reminding us that we were there to do a first ascent, not to follow an escape route. Inwardly I was entirely of the same opinion, and thought respectfully of the great Comici and his companion Benedetti.

More pitches of grey, solid rock led me to a little gash, sharp-cut as though by a knife. Now we were right up against the overhangs. Solidly moored to our pitons, we held a short discussion while looking up at the next section. It was 5 o'clock. Piussi was feeling the most on form, so it was decided that he would prepare the first pitch. It was a treat to watch him. The rope hung out clear of the face as he made his way upwards, climbing with great care. Thanks to the strength behind his blows the pitons seemed very sound. Each of us looked after one of his ropes, and despite the treacherousness of such over-hanging pitches where the rock is loose we found time to take a few pictures, reminding him as we did so that after all a beautiful woman was the best thing in the world, and that he would look pretty silly if one should happen to pay Roberto and me a visit while he was on the pitch. For his part he regretted not having a Havana cigar on him instead of a tasteless Nazionale "Export".

A leftward traverse where the pitons seemed less solid led him to a small cave which he stated to be ideal for a bivouac. The Civetta was certainly full of surprises. Bivouacks without étriers in mid-overhang—it was enough to make you ask if you were really in the Dolomites. No doubt tomorrow would remind us that we were.

This difficult 40 metre pitch had taken time, and it was now late. Roberto set off, removing the pegs as he went; as for me, I should have to Jumar up the rope, an idea which never exactly fills me with pleasure, but in such circumstances one has to sacrifice any little prejudices. Having reached the grotto, Roberto announced that there was not enough room for three. Ignazio therefore climbed on again, and after 15 metres reached his quarters for the night: a narrow ledge with uninter-rupted view and running water. The latter even descended directly on to his head, so that in the morning he was completely soaked.

Meanwhile Roberto installed himself in the cave and threw me down the end of a fixed rope. Jumars are a wonderful invention when you think of them in the valley, but not so great when you have to use them. With a piercing cry of "tira" I launched myself into space and, as Roberto was not only

above me but away out to the left, described a horrifying
pendulum. First I seemed to be getting very close to the Pan
di Zucchero, then, as it receded again, I wondered if I was
going to fetch up on the Philipp-Flamm. To top it all off I
began to spin, so that views of the yellow rock-face alternated
with Alleghe and the Tissi hut. Finally I was able to start
climbing and reached the "ideal" bivouac. It turned out to be
a small, sloping hole, in which it was going to be no easy
matter to sleep. I arranged my hammock as best I could, while
Roberto fixed himself in a web of slings, his climbing boots
resting delicately on my head. Next we played téléphériques
with Ignazio so that he could sample the culinary delights of
his country. The mouth of the grotto became a window on a
marvellously starry sky, and at last we slept.

At dawn we were woken from our slumbers by the yells of
Ignazio. The snow-slope at the foot of the face seemed dis-
concertingly close, but it was an optical illusion caused by a
change in the wind, which had gone round to the south. In
fact we had climbed two-thirds of the face and hoped to finish
that day as planned.

There was just time for a cigarette as we got ready, and then
we were off. Roberto climbed quickly up to Ignazio, and managed to find arguments to convince him that he must be on
better form than us. I came up last, depegging and hauling the
sack. A pitch starting with a large overhang then led us into
what would have been a pleasant chimney but for the water
tumbling down it. Not only were the summital cornices melting
in the warm wind, but it had begun to rain. The view was
out, and for the first time we found ourselves surrounded by
cloud. It was Roberto's turn to lead, but in his view water was
only pleasant on the Riviera and he had no ambition to tackle
the remaining 300 metres in their present streaming condition.
Nevertheless, protected by a hat worthy of John Wayne, he set
off under the downpour. By taking a great care and using
plenty of pitons he was able to make progress, and the double
rope ran out through our hands.

While Roberto was busy with this exposed and disagreeable
pitch, which had turned into a veritable waterfall, Ignazio and
I were making plans for the future, still happily convinced that
we should be off the mountain by evening. Linked by a similar
sense of humour our party of three had proved a success, and

it seemed a pity to break it up. We also spoke about climbers, and I explained to him that I liked climbing with people from other countries because it made the competition seem more natural. I said that it was a pity that there could not be international expeditions, and regretted that small-minded mountaineering authorities seemed unable to see beyond the bounds of nationalism. It would be a fine thing if the best mountaineers would climb occasionally with somebody other than their usual companions from their local outcrops. Ignazio shared my opinion, and I must say that he, Roberto and I have put our theories into practice in our various undertakings. It is by climbing with Americans, Austrians, Germans, Italians and Swiss that we French can best enrich ourselves. Our own point of view is well known; now we should learn to understand that of others.

Roberto's voice arrived as though from another world. The rain was falling so thickly that it made communication difficult. Our voices were drowned out, so that manoeuvres with the ropes were slowed down. It was as though all the rain in the sky were pouring down the chimney as I began to climb. The higher I got, the more respect I felt for Sorgato's lead. It came to my mind that a few years earlier Paragot and Berardini had told me that they had turned back off the Solleder route on account of the water. I could well understand. The only salvation seemed to lie in faith.

Another difficult and exposed pitch brought Roberto to the foot of the final gully, where the major difficulties were supposed to be over. It was about 11 o'clock when we joined him, so taking advantage of a pause in the rain we finished off our provisions. There was no trouble about finding something to drink—we had only to set our lips to the thick film of water that streamed down between the rock and our frozen bodies. As sometimes happens in the euphoria of victory, the last 100 metres to the summital ledges looked comparatively easy, so that we were in no hurry to start again and hardly noticed the storm coming up. Our sacks and ropes lay around in a muddle, while we applied all our ingenuity to lighting our last dry cigarettes.

At midday Roberto started off again. We reckoned that if all went well we should be at the top in three hours. If all went well. . . .

Although a number of big climbs go by without any undue excitement, the Civetta had no intention of becoming one of them or of pardoning us for having violated one of the last weaknesses in its 1000 metre wall. The mountain's reaction was as violent as it had up to now been welcoming. As in certain ancient tragedies there was no warning of calamity. It just struck out of the blue, 100 metres from the end of the climb.

The gully was barred by three large overhangs. It seemed best to climb the left wall, returning to the gully after each overhang to make a stance. We would lead one pitch each. This, however, proved to be no easy matter. The rock was compact, and it was difficult to get pegs to go in. Roberto hoisted up some more kit on a length of line, then prepared to begin the traverse to the right which would take him back to the gully above the overhang, where he said he could see a stance sheltered from the rain. I was holding on to a karabiner.

Suddenly there was a flash and a shock that made me jump. Was I more sensitized than the others as a result of the Fresnay adventure? Immediately, with an appalling crash, the storm broke loose over our heads. Ignazio, who had not felt the shock, yelled desperately to watch out. There was a special note of impending disaster in his voice. Thinking Roberto struck by lightning, I seized the ropes, which, however, came as though there were nothing at the end of them. Then a heavy sound made me look up. A more terrible sight would be hard to imagine: frozen with horror, I saw an 80 metre pillar of rock above us sway outwards and plunge into space, crashing and exploding against the face of the mountain as it fell towards me at tremendous speed. The instinct of self-preservation made each of us forget everything but himself. There could be no escape this time. The tons of rock were funnelled into the gully at the bottom of which we stood waiting, the whirring and bursting drew closer. I felt not so much fear as an utter certainty of death. Then came the first blows.

Thousands of rocks exploded all around us. I was quickly hit and my crash-helmet shattered. With spinning head I cowered under Ignazio, who protected his head with his hands. Then I was hit again, and it was as though my skull exploded. The rock was red with our blood. The bombardment appeared to be going on forever. We held our breath. It seemed as though our hearts had stopped beating. My back and legs were one enormous pain. Ignazio's hand was laid open and bled abundantly, while a huge block had injured his shoulder. Completely dazed, I wavered, then buckled at the knees. I told Ignazio it was all up with me; I was on my way out. Through the haze I saw him smile at me and say: "Pierre, pull yourself together. Breathe deeply." I took his instructions and immediately fainted, crumpling on to one of the sacks. When I came to I was firmly jammed between his powerful legs and the face. I hardly breathed, thinking dimly that Roberto was dead, I dying, and Ignazio injured and alone.

My head whirled, and what were in fact moments seemed endlessly long. The cataclysm was over, leaving us stunned and astonished to be still there. We were shaken out of our daze by the sound of Roberto calling. He was alive too! I heard Ignazio shout to him: "Pierre's going to die", which, since there was still hope, I immediately contradicted. The human animal does not give up so easily. Ignazio was to tell me later that at that moment my face was the colour of wax, my lips violet, my eyes unfocused, and that he really did think I was dying. For my part I wonder if I might not indeed have given up without his words and his presence.

Gradually, as our wits came back to us, we took stock. It was anything but encouraging. Not only were we badly injured, but all three ropes were cut in many places. Roberto was isolated, suspended in his étriers from a single piton; his rope, to which we were still hanging on grimly, swung free. The sacks at our feet were ripped to shreds. Slowly we tied the bits of rope together, watching Roberto as he soloed across the traverse to find a bivouac site where we could attend to our wounds sheltered from further rockfalls.

The waterfall was foaming down the gully more heavily than ever, bringing with it the remaining loose stones. Roberto had made it across the terrace to a big ledge on the far side. There followed an interminable wait while he knotted together bits of rope to throw down to us. When this had been done we jumared up to him and it appeared as though the nightmare were over. The rain had stopped, and as we prepared the bivouac we looked forward to the next day with more confidence.

It had been a close escape from death. The last couple of pitches up to the summital ledges were slightly overhanging, but did not look too bad. We should have to go slowly on account of the ropes, but we would make it. The bivouac was as comfortable as we could hope for in the circumstances. We patched up our wounds and made a hot drink, stamping our feet. It was good to be alive, to smoke a cigarette. Slowly we dropped off to sleep. During the night another stone struck Roberto and I heard him groan with pain.

The morning of Sunday 1st August, held yet another sight in store for us. The Civetta was sparing no pains to remind us that it was the face of faces. There were ten centimetres of new snow and the waterfall had frozen. The frost bit through our damp clothing; we were to hear later that two climbers had died of the cold that night on the Campanile Basso.

Roberto being the least injured, it was up to him to lead us to the top. However, he considered it impossible in these conditions. He knew the face perfectly; in these circumstances it was more difficult and dangerous than in winter. We should have to wait a day, and if necessary two.

So perforce we rested our bodies, but not our minds. There were no cigarettes or food left, though we still had fuel to heat water. We felt a great lassitude, but made a shelter of our red bivouac sacks which our friends would see from below. After that there was nothing left but to talk. At such times men are most truly themselves, and their presence comforted me greatly. We discussed mountains and mountaineering, memories of first ascents, bivouacs, and living and dead friends. All three of us were determined that this would be our last climb. Yesterday's warning had been too clear to ignore. We swore that from now on we would be content to take our wives and children for nice walks and pick flowers by the sides of paths. Naturally we knew that we would break our oath, but we swore just the same. Gradually our jokes became more subdued and graver, reflecting our situation.

It continued snowing. The bitter cold froze us to the marrow, and for lack of proper treatment our wounds hurt horribly. We thought with apprehension of the energy we should need next day or the day after to escape from this trap. There could be no question of retreating down 800 metres with the ropes and ourselves in their present state.

So each of us retired into his own thoughts. At the age of thirty-six, surely it was absurd to keep up the competition; yet weighing on the opposite end of the scale were the joy and the exaltation, and the pride of belonging to the international brotherhood of mountaineering. To climb mountains is to love them, and it is human to be unable to renounce what we love. Finally, there was the image of those who had gone before us, faithful to their passion unto death.

As evening fell it stopped snowing, and despite the increasing cold our faces looked a little less drawn. There was a glimmer of hope.

As the sky grew paler in the east, Roberto began to get ready. He was calm, but we could feel the weight of his decision. Aware of the state we were in, he intended to reach the top that evening, and was giving himself as much time as possible. The remaining 90 metres were covered in ice, and the overhangs frowned down at us black and forbidding. Behind them one could sense the ledges that would be our salvation.

The plan was that I would climb second, and as the state of our ropes made it impossible to climb a normal rope's length each time we should have to keep the pitches short. Ignazio would try to jumar up with his one good hand while we hoisted. We quit our bivouac ledge with some difficulty, but without regret. Our clothes were frozen hard. Ignazio watched us disappear behind the overhangs; henceforward the only link would be audible.

Roberto's willpower was astonishing as he dealt with the iced-up pitches. Most of our stances were on étriers, sometimes in uncomfortable positions where we were soaked again. Some of the overhangs were decorated with icicles two metres long and it called for all his skill to surmount them. When my turn came the pitons slipped out too easily and the wooden wedges needed only one light tap with the hammer to dislodge them from the frost-glazed cracks. It took our leader twelve hours to surmount the 90 metres leading to the ledges, and when I rejoined him I was exhausted but happy. The last ten metres were of extreme difficulty, and before any pegs could be placed for security it was necessary to chip the ice off the rock.

The ledges were covered with a thick layer of snow, but over on the left we saw the smiles of Livio the hut warden and two of his friends who had come up to meet us. It was difficult to communicate with Ignazio, but eventually he started up, bruised and battered as he was. It was an hour before he rejoined

The north-east face of Mont Blanc de Tacul

The north face of the Grandes Jorasses. The Walker spur
descends towards the camera from the highest point

us, pale with pain, semi-conscious, unable to speak. He just sat and waited while we hoisted the sacks.

Then, slowly, things brightened up. The sun came out, so that the mountain lost its threatening aspect and the great yellow walls began to glow. We had made a new route, and we had come through. Already we began to feel the first stirrings of desire to break our oath, to return to the combat.

From the summit of the Civetta we went down the Ferrata,* helped by Livio and his friends. Now that we were relaxed, the details of the climb passed before our minds like a film. The long nightmare of the last two days already seemed less terrifying, and we began to forget the miraculous chain of luck.

Presently we reached the Coldai hut and the faces of our friends, including the slightly shaken ones of Diana and Dany. At last we could tell each other of our secret fears and bad dreams. Next day we walked down to Alleghe and then drove back to the peace and quiet of the house by the River Piave near Belluno.

* Translator's note: a way down equipped with cables, pegs, ladders, etc.

CHAPTER XVII

The Hoggar

ONE DAY AFTER my usual swim at the Racing Club I began to think of my father, and how grateful I was to him for having taught me to compete on the sports field, in the mountains and in life. He had stimulated in me a taste for competition, not for the sake of the exploit but for myself. I hope he will forgive me if I say that nowadays publicity is the price one has to pay for success.

There is indeed a certain personal satisfaction in being well known and receiving the deference which goes with it, but the real joy comes from knowing that every experience is, and should be, useful. It is not a question of pride, except in so far as it is a pleasure to be of interest to the public—why deny it?—and thus worthy of publicity. But there are things which one hoards jealously, the infinitely various sensations that none but ourselves can tell: a mountain flower, a grade VI pitch, a vertical wall of ice, a path winding among pines, a sky in which the sun blazes, light breaths of wind and all-powerful storms. What matters is to love, then to communicate.

Once again I was caught up in the whirl of Paris life, with all its threats and madness. Always the same memories, the same hopes for the future, the same loneliness, the same passions. In the end one acquires a sort of maturity which predominates, in which one believes, and which instils life with a new rhythm so that in some paradoxical way one can love both the serenity of the mountains and the fitful contrasts of Paris. I had a feeling of alienation from the march of time, of clinging desperately to certain outmoded values. It seemed that life should consist of simplicities, yet I found myself side-tracked by many problems. Though I loved life, there was no time left to enjoy it, to read, to listen to music, to learn to know new people and things; and all this waste of precious days for the poor benefit of joining in the general rout.

There are periods in life when time passes slowly, as at

school when we long for the holidays or for our schooling to draw to an end; as in our university days; in moments of joy as with Claude, Marie-Edith, and Danielle; in furtive contacts as with Hélène and Sylvie and a hundred others; but with the assumption of adulthood the monster time devours all our days.

On my return from the Civetta that month of August 1965 I found Paris deserted, silent and beautiful. There was leisure to mull things over and to divide my spare time between the swimming pool, the cinema and—at last—reading. For the time being I recaptured a certain inner serenity, though it was to be disturbed again during the course of the coming months. When September came I began political campaigning in Limoges, and by autumn was caught up again in the feverish whirl as in previous years.

In November I presented *Cordée européenne* at the Salle Pleyel. For a moment I seemed to sense a breath of pure air in the labyrinth of my life, and, more important, had the impression that Roberto's smile and Wino's gaiety had conveyed something of the real meaning and atmosphere of mountaineering to the public.

The four years that I had been in my office in the Place Vendôme seemed no more than a few days. The view from my window was one of the finest in Paris, a world of factories, cranes, giant machines painted by Léger and sung by Ferré, an image of modern life.

Darbellay came to stay for a few days, bringing with him another breath of fresh air, remaining as calm in the night-clubs of the left bank as on the north face of the Eiger. The plans we made have so far remained unrealized.

Around Christmas the political battle grew hotter. My name was bandied about—but what of it? After the presidential elections, in which the coalition of our opponents at Limoges was beaten, the important thing was not to lose faith. I knew that the fever would return.

There were personal problems too, as always: my family, Sophia, Dany, the sweet letters of Bianca, the others, a complexity of claims. If only I could get down to the chalet and sleep, there among the wintry mountains. At least there was the Hoggar to look forward to, where my nerves would get some respite from the ringing of the telephone.

Two years earlier, in the course of dinner at our friend

Poincenot's, Jacques Ertaud had brought up the idea of making a film of a first ascent in the Hoggar. Lucien Berardini and I were there; both of us thought the project reasonable, and that it would be fun to go together. However, no definite date was arranged, and as time went by we more or less forgot the whole thing. Then at the beginning of February 1966 Ertaud rang up to say that if we could get free, the whole outfit could be under way in two weeks.

The hunt was up. I tore around from ministry to ministry and from equipment supplier to supplier, and at the end of the month the team met for the first time on the Caravelle heading for Algiers. Paris and all its cares seemed far away; the change of scene could hardly be more complete. Already I had metamorphosed into the different being that I become each time I get away to the mountains. The other members of the team were our friend Vernadet, the cameraman Michel Parbot, and the sound-engineer Harald Maury, both experts in their field: six friends setting off on a great adventure.

It was painful to land in Algiers, a city so full of memories, now lifeless, soulless, desolate. I felt in a hurry to get away. The plane winged from oasis to oasis, and the Sahara opened up before us, the only landscape that could excite me as much as the mountains, that perhaps had something even more noble about it. The names of the oases sang: Ghardaïa, In Salah, El Golea. On and on we flew towards Tamanrasset. Sometimes, far below, we saw the tracks of vehicles. Was there nowhere left in the world where one could get away from human beings? Yes, where we were heading: Garet El Djenoun.

Our objective was Takouba, a sort of granite spire, the last unclimbed peak in the Hoggar and probably in all Africa. None of us knew it except from photographs. Several French and Italian expeditions had attempted it without success, but we hoped to have better luck. So far there was no feeling of apprehension, the goal being as yet a long way off. Night fell and we slept until awoken by the landing, which was rather violent owing, we were told, to the lack of humidity in this pitilessly hot climate. Apparently there were days when it was impossible to take off at all from Tamanrasset. We had a sudden vision of spending the rest of our lives among the Tuaregs.

An open truck was waiting for us, and the cold of the desert night lost no time in making itself felt. The amenities of this capital of the central Sahara were on a par with its poverty, and what passed for the hotel was scarcely deserving of the name. Nevertheless, in spite of all the events, the departures and regrets, people still seemed to think of the French as friends. Down here we were in the land of legionaries and camel troops, several thousand kilometres south of Algiers and its echoes of revolution.

We wandered around "Tam" under a sun and sky limpid as you see them nowhere else. Everything was baked dry, from the chiselled features of the Tuaregs to the mud huts, real dwellings of adversity. A visit to the local authorities was in order; also one to Boub-a-Kers, our guide to the Sahara; and finally to the bistrot, where Lucien and I wrote dozens of postcards, and then began to chat about Takouba, enjoying our idleness. What a difference between this and other parts of the African continent! The fiery sun burns down continually, but casts a kind of spell. All around stand the famous summits of the Hoggar, the Iharen, the Assekrem and many others, reminding me of Kohlman, who once succeeded in making 18 first ascents in 14 days in this region. In former times the Tuaregs would capture black slaves in the lands to the south, then drive them in long caravans across the Sahara to sell in Egypt. Here too lived Father de Foucault, martyred in front of his dwelling. Nowadays the flag of the Algerian Republic and the National Army of Liberation has replaced those of the Legion, on tales of which we were brought up.

As we prepared to start at 5 o'clock next morning the sun was already lifting over the horizon, immediately warming and then superheating the atmosphere in a matter of minutes. We made quite a caravan: two trucks and a Landrover. There were so many accidents and delays that it took us a full three days to cover 300 kilometres. Indeed, the threadbareness of the tyres was equalled only by that of the garments of our guides. The Tuaregs are splendid men who live like aristocrats, refusing to admit the poverty by which they are weighed down, concealing hardship behind noble features.

After a brief halt to buy a couple of sheep which would provide us with meat we set off on our long and difficult but beautiful safari across the sand and rock. A sun-tan is no problem here. Perched in commanding attitudes on our truck and framed against the unending wastes where only the tracks of tyres remain to record the passing of man, Lucien and I began our career as film stars. Our inexpertly wrapped turbans failed to protect us either from sand or sun.

During the afternoon, we passed by the French atomic-bomb testing base at In Ekker, a veritable town with a population of 4000.

Later we came upon groups of gazelle, which we drove after until they fell exhausted, a wild chase which served to stock up our larder. That evening we had our first bivouac in the Sahara. Our thirst was such that it seemed as though it would need thousands of litres to satisfy it. We cooked our kebabs over the fire and listened to the Tuareg songs, while the desert lay calm under the moonlight. The spell of the place was too strong for memories to prevail. Even at night all was luminous, and we heard the howling of jackals. It was difficult to sleep. Lucien and I talked in low voices, as though out of respect for the silence and emptiness of this immense desert, now abandoned in death with only a few thorn-bushes to recall that it was once fertile and alive.

It was a first bivouac in the proper sense of the term. No doubt it was in such surroundings that man experienced his first real feelings and the first stirrings of philosophy, the sole reflection of the scale of nature. How could these tribesmen be other than noble?

In the early morning we started again towards the horizon. The tracks left by our vehicles reflected the nature of the terrain, sometimes long and straight, sometimes sweeping in curves, although the flatness never varied. Only far away on our right a bump on the horizon varied the desperate monotony: it was the Garet El Djenoun, the mountain of spirits, the home of Sahara mythology, a world of poetry and the unreal. Lucien sat silent, communing with nature. It was his second visit to the area, so that he had no questions, but I still had everything to learn.

The landscape began to change, to acquire relief, seeming to became more harmonious to our eyes at the very moment that it was becoming more chaotic for our guides. As we drew closer to the great granite block of the Garet, Takouba began to loom in the distance. Far off as it was, it could already inspire fear.

At Base Camp we found traces of the previous year's Italian expedition. The sun seemed to be made of molten brass, but we immediately set about unloading the equipment, after which it all had to be packed into our rucksacks, together with jerricans of water, the liquid gold of the desert. That night we slept more fitfully, as before battle, troubled by that restlessness to which one becomes so strangely addicted.

Before dawn, Lucien and I shared out our kit by the light of our head-torches. We wondered about our chances; defeat would be unpardonable. Ertaud was also busy, while Harald's sallies made us all laugh. Parbot was bent over his camera adjusting things. Crouched by the fire the Tuaregs sang to themselves. Only Vernadet, the picture of the unruffled mountaineer, snored serenely on.

Loaded like mules we plodded up a wadi towards our mountain, leaving the Tuaregs behind us to cope with the camp and the trucks, which appeared to be dying of fatigue, hunger (for petrol) and thirst (for oil). As the sun grew hotter, seeming to devour our bodies with its flames, our pace grew even slower. The sheer weight of the sacks forced us to halt often. We were too exhausted to speak, yet the air was so dry that we did not sweat. One wondered how animals could survive at all. When rain does fall it is torrential and the wadis fill with swirling, roaring floods that sweep everything before them, then soak away into the sand, leaving a red mark on the rocks as a sign of their passing. It is a Dantean landscape, combining paradise, purgatory and inferno.

There was a single bush on the way up, and there we sat down for a drink of brackish, tepid water from the goat-skin. I fell asleep and began to dream. . . .

. . . what a contrast between the attitudes of certain mountaineers and the calm of Gary Hemming, who was a guest at the rue de la Victoire for two years. Down at a bistrot in the rue Descartes we used to talk about the past, about John Harlin, about plans for the future. It would be quiet there on the terrace of this café I had just rediscovered after 15 years. There was a view out over the rue Clovis, bathed in spring sunshine. Farther off was the Place du Panthéon, with the church and library of Sainte-Geneviève. What a beautiful city Paris is, and what fine walks I used to take from the Quartier de la Cité to Marais, where the dramas of life seemed far away. So much of

our life between these stones; for me the Place de la Contres-
carpe is almost synonymous with happiness.

My dream went on to Chamonix and skiing down the slopes
of Lognan with Sophia. Then the scene changed to Cervinia
and seeing the Matterhorn from the other side, whizzing down
from the Plateau Rosa, and stopping over that night in Courmayeur, naturally at Filippo's.

And another day I skied down Mont Blanc with Edmond
Denis and some friends. Up in the mountains one is far away
from care. When we reached Grands Mulets there was Fanton
to welcome us. Knowing that he had similar ideas, I revealed
some of my plans to him. From his kitchen window in the hut
he gazes all year round at the Aiguille de Saussure and can
even see the Durier. Then the sensations of the flight up and
the ski-run down faded, and I was back in Paris. . . .

At this point I woke up. Harald was still beside me but the
others had gone on, and we started after them, feeling lonely,
small and exhausted. Half-way up we found them collapsed
over their loads for utter weariness, so with one accord we
dumped the kit there and went back down. First round to
Takouba.

Next morning and for the following three days we trudged
up from Base Camp to the foot of the rocks, a seven or eight
hour effort spiced with fear of the horned viper, which
abounded. At last we had everything assembled at the base
of the climb, and for Lucien and me the ordeal was ready to
begin.

At this point Parbot discovered that he had forgotten to
bring up a lens hood, so everything had to be held up for a day.
Somebody had to go down to Base Camp and come up again
the same day. I took this on myself and, as everything in this
country is paradoxical, carried with me water against the heat
of the day and rum against the chill of night. It would after all
be a pity to catch cold in the Sahara. I also packed two phials
of serum which turned out to be not for viper but for cobra
bites. It took me ten hours to make the round trip, singing or
thinking as I went. In the end I felt happy and confided to
Lucien my conviction that we should succeed, making fun of
the earlier parties for lack of determination.

We sat up late around the fire, listening to Jackie as he
explained the plan of attack. Far away over the desert we could

see other fires lit by the nomads. We had four days left. In the moonlight Takouba looked more hostile than ever, but I felt quite calm as I went to sleep, dreaming neither more nor less than usual.

Perched on the flank of Takouba more than 1000 metres above the surrounding desert, our camp was dramatic in the extreme. We had a simultaneous impression of dominance and insignificance. The contrasts were striking. Each dawn and dusk there were the brusque changes of temperature. By night there was utter silence, by day the mountain rang with happy voices. The bright blue of our sleeping bags and down jackets stood out against the tawny rock, and around the tents were heaped jerricans of water, climbing gear and photographic equipment.

Next morning early, Lucien and I scrambled up with all the heavy equipment to what we called the Col de la Garet. The real attack was about to begin. The scene was striking in its desolation and grandeur. In front, the great granite pillar of Takouba loomed over us, its summit guarded by immense overhangs, frightening in the hot morning sunlight. All around, the yellows and greys of the Sahara stretched to the horizon. Behind stood the imposing bulk of the Garet El Djenoun, casting no shadow because the sun was vertically above.

Pabot and Vernadet were impatient to start filming. Lucien and I had agreed that he would lead the free climbing and I the artificial. We would fix ropes to enable the photographers to climb up and down as needed. I was thirsty, my throat was dry and I felt suffocated by the heat, but it was up to me to start. I found a few pitons left by our predecessors, and the difficulties were such that there was no need to act for the camera and sound recorder as I called instructions to Lucien, who was helping me with the ropes. Jackie wanted me to perform some spectacular acrobatics, but I refused, my mind being totally set on the main objective. Metre by metre I progressed up the impressive wall, encountering bands of loose rock between the sound, so that the ring of the hammer would change suddenly to a hollow note. The cracks were either blind or too wide. Ordinary pitons would not hold, and I was obliged either to couple my biggest wooden wedges or drill holes for expansion bolts. The rock was hostile and beautiful as our surroundings, but the heat made it exhausting to climb and I halted frequently to rest and drink. My whole body felt dry as an old boot and it was difficult to speak. On the ground they were filming busily, and Lucien gave a commentary explaining what I was doing.

At last I reached a stance and could bring up Lucien. Still one of the best mountaineers in France, he has the strongest personality of all the Parisian climbers and a completely unshakeable morale. Climbing is his one and only passion, although he is an industrial designer by profession. He and his friend Paragot were among the explorers of the Saussois and put up most of the major routes there, later going on to climb an impressive number of routes in the Alps, where his most notable feat was the first ascent of the west face of the Dru. After this he went to the Andes and climbed the south face of Aconcagua, no doubt one of the most difficult climbs ever done. Unfortunately he was frostbitten during the course of it and lost his toes and parts of his fingers as a result; nevertheless he continues to climb every weekend and to go on expeditions. He is a wonderful friend and companion, whose human qualities are well known. During the Fresnay disaster he was in Chamonix, impatiently trying to organize a rescue party.

As he came up the wall towards me, stepping up in the étriers and unclipping karabiners with his legendary calm, he was talking about Peru, where we were both due to go on an expedition three months later. I told him that I hoped we would be able to climb together on the same rope, not knowing then that politics at Limoges and my job would make it impossible for me to go.

When Lucien had joined me I set off again, loaded with ropes, karabiners, all shapes and sizes of pitons, expansion bolts, hammer, étriers, slings, in short the whole tool-kit of the artisan climber. Our conversation was unvarying: "Hold it: tension" or "Slack on blue, watch red, the peg's not very good". But with Lucien there is always good humour and time to joke. The sun blazed down hotter than ever. The gestures one makes in the course of climbing have a certain theatricality about them, but here progress was desperately slow as we had to reconcile safety with the needs of the cameramen and the director, who shouted up his instructions from below. There was a certain vulgarity in the tone and content of our replies.

At the second stance I brought up Vernadet, his film camera hanging on a sling over his shoulder, so that he could shoot

Lucien climbing the pitch. Taking scant notice of the normal rules of security, he leant far out over the drop with incredible casualness and began filming. I safeguarded him as best I could, but he pulled out so hard on the pitons that I wondered if they would resist the strain. His weight alone was enough to frighten anybody. Between my feet I could see Lucien grinning as he climbed, while Vernadet shot miles of film. My task was to manage the ropes and protect both of them. Then Lucien had to go down and start again. Such is the life of a movie star.

The sun was more implacable than ever as I began the third pitch, but we were too involved to pay it much attention. Vernadet rappelled back down, and I could see the camera team putting up awnings in an attempt to obtain some shade. I moved slowly from piton to piton, leaving behind the étriers for "Lulu" to recover. The rock was firm and the pegs sang honestly and agreeably as I drove them in. The angle was about vertical, interrupted with little overhangs, and the only thing that detracted from the magnificence of the climbing was the heat. Eventually I reached the highest point attained by our predecessors. Above me an enormous roof jutted out several metres; this must have been the obstacle that had defeated them. Between it and me was an almost holdless wall with a piton sticking out of it. From the piton hung a mousqueton marked with the letters "R.S.", the initials of Roger Salson, leader of the last French expedition. Here I installed a regular advance base with several pegs, slings and hammocks, hauling up water and the rest of the climbing gear. Soon after Lucien reached me the sun went down, and with no transition at all it was night. The temperature plummeted from 40°C to below zero in a few minutes, a contrast which was hard to bear. By the light of our head-torches we slid down the fixed ropes and joined our companions at the camp, a few hundred metres below the col.

In the faint starlight Lucien and I sat and discussed the remainder of the route while the others made a fire and got supper ready. From our ledge high above the desert we could see a Tuareg fire twinkling away in the distance like a symbol of the smallness and greatness of man. Our thoughts drifted away and returned to ourselves in face of this immensity. Then we slept.

. . . I dreamed of a recent long weekend when I had gone four days and three nights without sleep. I had suddenly felt suffocated with Paris and Limoges and needed to get away to the mountains at all costs. There was a magnificent day's skiing with Gigi Panei on the Plateau Rosa. Sophia was quite overcome by his charm and the kindliness that shone out of his eyes. Another day we were turned back by a gale on the ordinary route of Mont Blanc, a reminder of how the unchained elements can change the course of things—in life also. Back at the Grands Mulets hut, however, I had the consolation of at last meeting Anderl Heckmair, the conqueror of the Eigerwand. It seemed almost a solemn event, but after a few minutes we were chatting happily about climbs and climbers. His features were as though hewn out of the living rock, whether you thought of him as the thrusting pioneer of the 1930s or the calm inhabitant of Oberstdorf. For me it was one friendship the more, and as nothing matters to me so much as friendship I was happy.

If it matters to me so much, why do I not feel that way about everybody? No doubt on account of all the snide gossip and criticism of which I seem fated to be the object, perhaps out of jealousy. Petit Claude used to reassure me, saying that what mattered was to have a personality of one's own and to fight. I believe that the formula fits, as I love to compete.

Driving back to Paris, my third sleepless night, I grew drowsy and only just avoided an accident. Sophie slept peacefully through it all. I drew into the side of the road for a rest, thinking that I was growing old. A few years earlier I would have carried off such a weekend without effort. . . .

Lucien and I were up before daybreak, and as the sun rose we were already Jumaring back up the fixed ropes. For once it seemed fun to swing off into space, and as we passed by the places where we had struggled we could look them over without having to go through the experience again. It did not take long to reach the last stance of the previous day. This was where the real test would begin.

As we slung the kit around our waists and shoulders we could see our companions preparing for the day's filming. We reckoned that there must be five or six pitches to the summit, and we hoped to reach it that day.

It was Lucien's lead. The wall above, eight metres of smooth, vertical rock, was the obstacle that had stopped all previous attempts. Half-way up began a loose, awkward crack, the wrong width for jamming. It looked to me as though an expansion bolt would be needed, but Lucien preferred to try it free and climb fast. Nevertheless his progress was measured up to the foot of the crack. As he reached it he swung his body violently to one side and wedged a foot, the other remaining in friction on the wall, a prodigious feat of strength and balance. Metre by metre he fought his way up the rock, which looked impossible without rawlbolting. I was panting with tension as I watched his movements. Finally a mantelshelf over an overhang brought him to a ledge where he could rest. I shouted my congratulations, but for the time being he was too overcome to reply. Lucien had cracked the crux of the climb; now it was up to me to finish it off.

As soon as he had recovered I was literally hauled up the slab. Despite the fact that we were now under the huge roof there was not a speck of shade. Here we discussed where to go next, our dialogue being transmitted to the ground by the microphones about our necks. It was decided to traverse left in order to attack the roof at its weakest point, then climb an overhanging section which would lead to the final cracks. I took my time getting ready, then left Lucien practically expiring in the heat on the stance. To start with there was a short tension traverse in order to reach a crack where I could place a piton. From here on it was to be pegging practically all the way to the summit.

The piton did not exactly inspire blind confidence. It was hammered in upside-down, and the crack itself was in flakey, fissile rock. Gently I clipped in the rope and an étrier, then still more gently eased my weight on to it. Everything held, but the drop below was frightening. Quickly, another piton. As the number of pegs increases so does one's confidence; this is one of the facts of life. I was still quite close to Lucien, so we could commiserate mutually about the heat that seemed to be scorching each individual pore of the skin.

The pegs were all as bad as each other. Nevertheless I had to get on to the top rung of my étriers in order to grope around above the overhang for the continuation of the crack. As I could see nothing, it was a curious combination of methodical search and guessing game. Presently I found a place, although it felt more like sand than rock. Leaning back outwards as far as I could in tension from a series of pegs that asked nothing better than a chance to pop out, I chose my longest piton and held it in place with my left hand, hammering blindly with my right. The piton sounded hollow, so, still without seeing anything, I had to drive in another beside it. Placing the karabiner and étrier on the unseen pegs was another little work of art. The étrier hung down behind me, and with a sort of surging movement I transferred my weight to it, holding my breath in suspense. Would the piton hold? It did. Quickly I added another étrier and moved up them; now I was around the angle of the overhang, out of sight of Lucien. We could communicate only by shouting, and it proved easier to relay instructions by radio via the team on the ground. Anxiously they asked how it was going, the ritual phrase of worried onlookers. In the sort of circumstances in which I found myself there is always a temptation to let off steam by answering rudely. The French language is rich in the appropriate vocabulary and I did not spare them, bellowing that if they wanted to change places it was all right by me.

Teetering on the bad piton, picturing to myself what would happen if it came out, in which case it seemed likely that all the others would too, I searched desperately but in vain for a place to put a sound peg so that my nerves could relax. Everywhere the rock was not completely solid it was eroded by the blown sand. The walls of the crack were not parallel but opened outwards, and the interior was filled with fine sand like ball-bearings so that even wooden wedges would not grip in it. There was no alternative but to place an expansion bolt. Seated in my étriers I resigned myself to the hard labour of drilling a hole in the rock. It was nearly an hour before I could hammer in the bolt, after which I tested it with all my force. Satisfied at last, I could now concentrate on the climbing ahead. My shoulders were pushed up against the next overhang, and as I leant out backwards I was exerting dangerous traction on the bolt. Feverishly I searched for somewhere to place a wedge. Finally I got round the overhang on the left. I was climbing farther and farther away from my second, the rock still overhung, the positions were uniformly strenuous and I did not trust a single one of the pitons. The light was ebbing, and darkness would come rapidly. Suddenly I felt cold. I banged in a last wedge, then quickly climbed back down to Lucien, leaving my étriers swinging in the wind. Together we slid back down the fixed ropes to the col, where our friends were waiting. Takouba was putting up a good fight and had won another round.

Neither Lucien nor I slept much that night. Both of us knew that if we did not succeed in climbing the mountain next day it meant defeat, as the aeroplane would be leaving Tamanrasset in three days' time. I tried to imagine the final grooves . . . surely they must start to lean back from the vertical quite soon. So one starts by imagining, goes on to believing, and ends up convinced. Late in the night the moon rose, shining on Takouba. It was freezing hard and I curled up inside my sleeping bag as in the course of a bivouac in the Alps, padding my sides with rucksacks and clothing. A flannel liberty bodice would have been welcome. At last my thoughts wandered and I dozed uneasily.

It was still night when Lucien shook me awake. Hastily we swallowed something hot. Just as night fell like a shutter when the sun set, so now it was broad daylight within a few moments of dawn. From the col we Jumared back up the climb, both of us feeling an urgent need to have done with the mountain, and presently I was hanging again from my last wedge of the day before. Meanwhile the camera team had also regained their posts and from time to time asked questions which we were too keyed up to answer.

Confidently I trusted my whole weight to the étriers, hauling on the wedge as I moved up to place another peg above me to the left so that I could start the traverse which would lead to the way over the last overhang. The ropes were running badly, so I gave a series of sharp jerks. Without warning the wedge came out and I fell. Several pegs unzipped and I found myself hanging in space from the expansion bolt, the only point of attachment which had withstood the shock. Lucien was staring up at me wide-eyed. All he had had time to do was hold on to the rope and hope that I would stop.

Pulling myself together, I wondered what to do next. In point of fact there was only one course open to me: to get back up to the expansion bolt and start pegging all over again. With a lot of help from Lucien's rope-manoeuvres and many precautions I finally reached the angle of the roof overhang, but this time instead of risking another wedge I placed a second expansion bolt. The granite was so hard that the exercise took over an hour, but in the circumstances this was the only kind of attachment in which I had much confidence. Once the bolt was well and truly in I could lean back and reach for other cracks above the edge of the roof.

By the time I had surmounted the roof I was so exhausted that I was unable to answer Ertaud and Parbot, who were asking me to record my impressions. I just did not have the strength to speak. It seemed as though the mountain was incandescent; there was not a spot of shade to be found anywhere. I sagged from the last piton and laid my head against the rock. Respecting my feelings, Lucien said nothing. He knew the cost of such efforts and left me alone. In moments of silence like this men understand each other.

Presently I felt able to start moving again, still a matter of continuous pegging. After a while the crack widened out enough for me to take a stance which I sprinkled liberally with pitons in the hope of gaining a little security. In order to save time Berardini decided not to depeg, but as he climbed up to me a number of them just came out in his hands. The pitch which followed was still artificial, but easier. We also felt easier in our minds, and once again responded to the requests of the camera team. The next stance was clearly going to be the last. Calm as ever, Lucien watched, helped and encouraged as I went through the ritual motions with the double ropes. The angle seemed to be getting easier over on my right, and as soon as I could I left the system of vertical cracks and traversed in that direction. The last few pitons seemed to be really firm, so hauling in some slack I called down to Lucien to let the rope go free and started free climbing. The first few moves were hard, then suddenly it was as though the mountain had given up. Shouting with joy I ran forward to the summit, dragging the ropes after me. Right on the top there was an astonishing little bunch of flowers which I picked for a souvenir. Standing there, dominating the desert, I felt a true conqueror. It was a moment of supreme happiness, and I wanted to savour it alone for a few minutes.

This was my first virgin summit, and I felt moved to tears. I drove in a piton as a sign of victory. All this while the microphones were recording my monologue as I talked to myself.

Takouba

Above: The north-west face of the Civetta

Below: Mazeaud after the stonefall on the north-west face of the Punta Tissi

A hundred thoughts flashed through my mind, the joy of conquest, the beauty of my surroundings, the satisfaction of having accomplished the mission, myself, all my friends, life itself.

Then I took in the rope, literally towing Lucien up the final slopes. The impassive master-climber turned into a human being again as he came forward with tears in his eyes and flung his arms around me. In our earphones we could also hear Ertaud's voice thanking us. The film was made; our adventure was over.

Or almost. In effect, the abseils back down the mountain still held emotions in store. At one point, the rope would not pull down and we were overtaken by cold and darkness. Our friends below waited helplessly. It was as though Takouba wanted to keep us for itself. At last we felt the rope yield, and in total darkness we abseiled on down to the col. That night we slept deeply and dreamlessly for the first time.

Next morning, after a last salute to the mountain, we descended to Base Camp and prepared to leave this enchanted place which had suddenly become dear to us. As the trucks bumped and trundled back towards Tamanrasset we watched first Takouba and then Garet El Djenoun fade and disappear, each of us revolving his own memories and regrets. By evening we had reached In Ekker; next day found us at Tamanrasset under the same torrid skies; and then we were winging homeward from oasis to oasis, Algiers, and at last Paris.

It had been a fine adventure and a new aspect of the mountains. Do we need to account for our passions? For my part I have many, and they add up to the whole of life. But I love mountaineering above all because I have faith in it as a touchstone and a source, whence my fear of the time when I shall no longer be able to practise it. Yet even then I shall be able to walk among the mountains, too look at and love them. And I shall have my memories.

For the time being I have other projects, and I am not yet prepared to renounce the terrifying rhythm of the life I have chosen. I refuse to yield to its pressures. Absorbed in new problems, I look forward to next summer and the profound joy of teaming up again with Sorgato, Piussi and Bonatti. But in the background waits the more distant project that I once spoke of with Gigi Panei: an old house in the Val Ferret at the foot of the Jorasses, in the evening shadow of the south face of Mont Blanc. The idea of spending my old age in that place is a sort of leitmotiv which renders bearable the mad life I now lead. As in a trance I foresee the end of the sound and fury. There will be music, books and memories, and solitary walks from Entrèves to Planpincieux.

CHAPTER XVIII

Mountains and Motivations

AT TRENTO THAT year there was a novelty in the form of a round-table conference, chaired by Tonella, where I at last had a platform for explaining my philosophy of mountaineering. But first of all there was the pleasure of meeting Bianca, Baldessari, Maestri and all my other friends over a bottle of Ferrana at Spiro's.

I was anxious to express myself sincerely, and had therefore prepared a text while staying with Roberto Sorgato near Belluno. I wanted to make known the motives of my joy and my distress in climbing, my purpose in living. Lying in the field in front of the old farmhouse I found reasons to hope. Mountains, life: one could be carried away by them as by any conflict, for example between one's own problems and inner contradictions or between an old love and a new, in short any dialectic.

Why do we climb?

Before even trying to answer this incomplete question, I would like to point out that climbers ask themselves this after each narrow escape or each time they lose a friend. Why should a valuable life be sacrificed to this crazy obsession? The dead friend had often asked himself this question, and just as he went on nevertheless, we know that we shall go on. But the non-mountaineer asks the question not only after reading the sensationalized reports of tragedies in the newspapers, but also after major first ascents and other successes, of which he hears more and more often owing to the development of information media.

There are two types of answer. The first is the confession of personal motives, and is thus subjective. The second is the justification of the sport and those who practise it as a whole, and is thus ethical and objective. The public believes that we climb for one reason or another, often either glory or stupidity, and finds the whole performance perfectly pointless. But in fact do climbers in general climb for any particular reason? We find ourselves in the position of having to justify our enthusiasm in the eyes of others.

Both types of answer call for great frankness. It is high time that the popular image of the mountaineer as an exceptional being was done away with, although it would also be wrong to fall into the trap of thinking him an inferior one. Quite simply, climbers are men like any others. They have good qualities and faults, and if sometimes the dead can be thought of as heroes, a hero is not a superman.

To deal with the personal question first, then, why do I climb?

Let us think of the subjective and objective answers as the two panels of a diptych. I repeat that the first is a form of confession, and it follows that if I am not completely honest in my analysis I shall not succeed in answering the question.

In fact I have a number of motives, which I shall name without making any attempt to rank in order for the sufficient reason that I do not know if any one predominates. When I think about them they seem to combine, and I think that this is the case with any passion or feeling the unity of which defies dissection. Moreover it is a fact that for me, as for most climbers, climbing is a passion. To this extent, then, we have a common starting-point for our analysis.

Climbing is a sport. Certainly it is a complex one, bringing with it satisfactions unknown to others; but the converse also applies, and the 400 metre runner has satisfactions unknown to us in our solitude. I climb for the sport and all its satisfactions. One of these is to remain in good physical shape through the hard exercise involved, which also tests the human machine to the maximum.

There is also the legitimate drive to win. I am speaking now of competition, for I like the competitive struggle. My combat is with the mountain, but it has a triple victory in view: over the mountain, over myself and over others. This desire to surpass others gives rise to various forms of competition.

The first of these is the achievement itself, the performance, the search for new ground which in the Alps, at least, has perforce succeeded the search for unclimbed summits. Naturally one must preserve a sense of proportion, but essentially this is the equivalent of the spirit of the pioneers. For the sake of making a first ascent one puts up with anything, and nowadays that ineluctably entails publicity of various kinds. First of all your name becomes known, and you may become a member of the GHM.* Then your techniques may be copied, since the news spreads quickly. Finally you are known and judged by the public at large. For my part—I promised to be frank—I rather like this kind of prestige.

For me there is also an intellectual satisfaction in any first ascent, stemming from the creative imagination, the spirit of enterprise, the research, the uncertainty and the application. A certain philosophy is bound to be inherent in the concept; thus, for example, people speak of the Munich school of climbing, the dilettante attitude of the French, and so on. In the actual execution the desire to finish it off and get down safely manifests itself, and it is by no means unknown for the climber to speak uncharitably of the rock and vow to spend future holidays at the seaside. It is from first ascents that my spirit of competition gets the biggest satisfaction, as they seem to me the touchstone of mountaineering performance.

It is also interesting to repeat great climbs such as the north face of the Eiger, the Cassin routes, and the like, though they are often devalued by the different conditions obtaining and an excessive number of pitons. I am not criticizing the latter by saying this, and if one happens to be on particularly good form there is, after all, no need to use them. Nevertheless, unlike some other climbers, I do not feel much poetry in repeating routes. For me the poetry is in the walk up to the hut, the flowers by the path, or the return back down through the glades and pastures, not in the weather, lightning, or simply a difficult pitch.

First winter ascents are an extension of the above. There are not all that many first ascents left in the Alps, and the competitive instincts thus frustrated have found this new outlet. Naturally, therefore, I owe it to myself to take part.

Very much the same can be said concerning first solo ascents. But in this case I am inhibited by lack of confidence—call it fear if you like—and personal factors such as having two children.

It seems to me that first feminine ascents have similar justifications.

* Translator's note: the Groupe de Haute Montagne, an offshoot of the French Alpine Club reserved for outstanding climbers.

To round off this theme of competition and first ascents, I will add that the idea and the execution are in practice linked by a period of secrecy. There is a certain malicious intellectual pleasure in hiding your true intentions and even letting it be thought that you have something quite different in mind, while at the same time doing your best to find out what your rivals are up to.

Climbing is also a pleasure; there is a sense of well-being when one is up in the mountains. We find ourselves restored to the stone age, up against the facts of nature. The values of so-called civilized life are effaced, and we feel at home because we are back in an animal world. In this connexion I would note that there is a pleasure in hardship, even—may I be excused—a certain masochism. The mountains form an immense playground or stadium, with all the appropriate pains and joys. One could say that pleasure is found both in mastery, as when climbing an enjoyable stretch of rock, and in effort, as when finishing out a strenuous chimney. Finally there are the pleasures of the climb as a whole and those of reaching the summit, a compound of happiness at being alone in the beauty of the mountains.

The running of risks has a definite place in my mountaineering philosophy. In the same way I would enjoy motor racing, although the car itself would be an encumbrance coming between me and the achievement. It is true that I enjoy risking my neck, though I believe that I know how to calculate the danger and control my rashness when necessary.

This taste for danger entails a contact with death. Although I am afraid of dying, the idea of doing so in the mountains is somehow less alien, and that would indeed be my preferred end. I admit that, like Madier, I would like "a swift and dazzling death". Moreover, death is something we learn. Our dead friends are not only an example but a symbol, and—I think of the Fresnay disaster when I looked death in the face—our reactions in the dramatic moments when it seems that death may overwhelm us are the same as those of sailors. In those moments life seems less important than at other times, so that one is closer to the supreme being. There is no pretention in saying this, because this is what I mean by having faith in the mountains, and as I am a Christian I make no secret of feeling closer to God.

While understanding the drawbacks of saying something that sounds so pretentious, I believe that in the mountains I accomplish myself.

I believe that, for me, to suffer and to win through is to excel myself. This happens particularly in the case of first ascents; but I want to make it clear that even if I have the vanity to believe myself still young and therefore seek only to accomplish exploits—this is not quite accurate either, but confessions are always complicated—nevertheless I do love the mountains. I am by nature an enthusiast, and every passion demands that deliverance of the entire being that is self-surpassment. I believe that I react thus to every enthusiasm, though it is true that I sacrifice the most to mountaineering, my first love.

Climbing is also a way of working off the fatigues and frustrations of city life. Even outcrop climbing is a development of this. The mountains hold me because when I am among them I become a different person and am aware of fulfilling myself intellectually, physically, perhaps morally and even religiously, since certain happenings have brought me closer to God.

In addition to all this, I have an uncomplicated love of nature. Although I love the soft beauty of meadows, yet I prefer the savage wildness of high mountains where the structure of the land is laid bare. Another incentive to this taste for nature is that nothing can stale its infinite variety. The scene is always different, the sensations likewise. No two ascents of a given piece of rock, no two sunsets, no two bivouacs are the same.

The taste for adventure does not find its fulfilment only in exploration and first ascents, since on every climb we seek and find, and so discover. In this respect mountaineering is a school of life, since I never know what joy or ordeal the next moment will bring. Thus each moment is an adventure the outcome of which I can never subconsciously foresee in the way I can foretell the outcome of, for example, a legal case.

The last item in this confession, and perhaps the main one, is friendship. Being painfully sensitive, I need friends, and I find that true friendships are virtually only made in the mountains, since only there are the personalities of myself and others stripped to their essentials. Laid bare of our wrappings and defences we have the same passions, reflexes, complexes, reactions and even sentiments, since our common love of the mountains is of our essence. I have a certain hunger for friend-ship of this quality, which accounts for my suffering when I am robbed of it by death. In that, too, the hard realities of moun-taineering are a school of life.

Since climbing has become popularized, such friendships cut across class boundaries. This is a most important par-ticularity, since many other sports have definite social con-notations. The mountains bring people together and bring out what they have in common however dissimilar they may appear externally.

I approved of the theme of *Cordée européenne* and believe that I have demonstrated my desire to be in the mountains with friends of different nationalities. To this I would add— and this is also part of my confession—that I learn more from foreigners than from French people, whose reactions I under-stand from the outset. Thus I learn from people like Bonatti, Hiebeler and Darbellay, and learning is something I enjoy particularly when, like this, it is in a school of reality, more tangible than the lessons of Alpine literature.

Obviously, I am an incomplete being. However, without going into the realms of philosophical discussion which I leave to the psychiatrists or other doctors of the sentiments, I believe that I have borne true witness regarding myself. Let us there-fore proceed to the second panel of the diptych, that in which we seek to justify our common passion for mountaineering to the layman.

In doing this, I must begin by distinguishing amateurism from professionalism, which can be justified purely on the grounds of needing to earn a living. I am an amateur myself, but I know that many a guide has exactly the same feelings for the sport, and that his client is often a friend, the monetary aspect of the relationship being secondary.

We climbers are and must therefore seem human; if we are sometimes rough, we are always highly sensitive. In the mountains we find private joys unknown to the everyday world, and in hoarding them jealously for ourselves we are apt to appear pretentious. However, it is not true that we are beings apart, any more than sailors. Yet our fellow men judge us, and we owe them an explanation.

Let us begin with the subject of achievement. No matter how inflated by the press, a feat should always be seen in human proportions. The climb is not itself a spectacle, whatever others make out of it. The only apology we can proffer is that we are enthusiasts eager to prove the survival of certain human values in a world to which we appear socially ill-adapted. The achievement is useful not only for us but also in its own right. The proof is in the performance, just as in the case of the 10 second barrier in the 100 metres. In climbing it may seem more spectacular to the public because the ordeal is more prolonged, but let us once and for all get rid of the idea of the climber as a knight in shining armour.

Next, let us touch on the subject of what happens when things go wrong. Why should any man sacrifice his life for a pastime which has no practical utility? That is the great question which always receives silly answers on the part of the public. Is it then never justifiable to risk death climbing? At the funeral of Lionel Terray, Lucien Devies affirmed that the real justification is the human value of the man himself. It is not a question of being a conquistador of the useless, but, on the contrary, of the useful. Nothing can do so much to rescue the youth of the world from despair. In his simplicity and grandeur the climber can save many things. The mountain gives him hope, and his success gives a reason for hope to others. Thus the dead themselves are our justification. Each in his own way, they have left an example and a message. The message is on a human scale, and they know well that it is as men that we their friends judge them.

Were they heroes? With all their good and bad qualities, yes, but not the unbearable figures that the public mistakenly canonizes after their death. This sort of *a posteriori* judgement is useless and silly. No! On the contrary, it is a sign of immense hopefulness. Our fallen companions had the privilege of dying young where they wished to die. Our passion is so great that it even exceeds our love for our wives, a fact which they should know and understand. That too is part of our justification.

We who survive have to complete the message of the dead by showing its simple, human aspect. The mountaineer climbs for himself and also for others. He will never be a hero of legend; merely a real one.

This seems an appropriate juncture to consider the evolution of climbing. Because the development of information media

H

has brought it increasingly before the public, the sport would appear to have left behind the era of adventure and entered into that of performance. Henceforward the climber is submitted to the judgement of the spectator; his achievement has become public property. This state of affairs calls first of all for the evaluation of mountaineers themselves, and it seems more desirable to sum up now than at any other period in the history of mountaineering. Are present achievements commensurate with the great deeds of the past? Briefly, is it reasonable to speak of any evolution in climbing?

Certain mountaineers endowed with acute critical minds, and thus doubly more qualified to speak than myself, have expressed the view that, since all the finest climbs that can be ascended by classical means have already been done, the outlook for the younger generation is sombre. Others endowed with equally critical minds have rejoined that, on the contrary, a great deal of unbroken ground remains for coming generations provided they are prepared to use new means. While respectful of the incontestable authority of both groups of gentlemen, may I be permitted to suggest that there is nothing incompatible about their points of view and that they are both perfectly right? It would appear to me that one cannot say whether mountaineering has evolved without defining the context and the premises of the discussion.

In the majority of sports, evolution is traced by performance. In certain individual disciplines such as athletics the stopwatch remains the infallible witness. Evolution may be slow, but it is demonstrable. Thus, for example, Jesse Owens ran the 100 metres over thirty years ago in 10.2 seconds, whereas nowadays several athletes can do it in under 10 seconds. The stars of the track write their own fragments of history, and many magnificent combats have led to new records. Think of the finish of the 400 metres at the Rome Olympic Games where Davis and Kaufmann both lowered the world record to 44.9 seconds. Naturally, the evolution of athletics, like that of other sports, is not to be judged on records alone, and its spreading popularity has a place in the story too. Nevertheless, the records do show how it has evolved and will continue to do so, since there is no precisely known limit.

In mountaineering, a very much more complex discipline, a considerable number of external factors come into play.

Coefficients of difficulty such as weather conditions (too often bad), applied dietetics, and the development of new equipment and techniques mean in effect that yesterday's data no longer correspond to those of today, so that the whole debate is falsified if one applies the standards of one epoch to the results of another. Thus, to say: "Some years ago the great north faces were climbed with limited means, whereas with improved equipment we are now doing direct routes on them" really offers no possible basis of comparison. There can be no question of considering some present-day climber better than some other of earlier times, because the improvement in standards, if any, is due to external and objective causes. Mountaineers frequently argue about who was the greatest climber of all time, but the different context of each epoch is an insurmountable obstacle to the formal evaluation of the relative merits of, for example, Mummery, Preuss, Welzenbach, Cassin, Brown, Bonatti or Darbellay. Each of these masters has his own references, so that one might certainly say that each of them was the best in his own context, but the deeds of one can never be eclipsed by those of the others.

There is a scientific side to climbing, and it is here that progress takes place, making it possible to seek for ever more daring routes. Thus the direct route up the north face of the Eiger, climbed by Lehne and his companions, would not have been made until later had it not been for Heckmair's party climbing the original route many years before. As remarked by Reinhold Messner in an excellent article in the February 1968 issue of *La Montagne*, the criterion of evolution in climbing is not performance, the achievements of yesteryear having exactly the same intrinsic value as those of today in their new context. However, I disagree with this penetrating critic and excellent friend when he speaks of devaluation. After all, although it is true that the Walker spur can easily be climbed in a day in favourable circumstances such as its original conquerors, not knowing the route, could not possibly experience, it is also true that in different conditions it may take several days of desperate struggle. Certainly it is in the nature of things that repetition implies devaluation, but the argument can be turned around by saying that in the case of first ascents the effect of competition is to cause a continual rise in standards. Obviously, the choice of undertaking is dictated by what remains unclimbed, and as the choice narrows the intrinsic difficulties become greater.

Does this mean that mountaineering does not change essentially? The fact that earlier climbs caused their authors as much difficulty as modern climbs do modern climbers, each in its context, does not exclude the possibility of evolution. It is in the external elements that the development takes place. Thus the inhabitants of big cities, anxious to escape from the constraints of urban life, throng the rock outcrops in the neighbouring countryside, with the result that they attain a very high standard on difficult rock and evolve appropriate techniques, so that when they go to the mountains they again concentrate on rock, and ice-climbing technique evolves much more slowly. The big ice-faces are repeated far less often than the major rock-faces. Moreover, there is far more incentive to look for different lines on a rock wall such as the north face of the Cima Grande than on an ice slope.

Another case is the development of artificial climbing, including means of overcoming any kind of difficulty, for example expansion bolts. In Yosemite, California, these are in current use. Some people attack this technique, others defend it, just as in the battle that once raged over the use of ordinary pitons.

Again, there is the technique of fixing ropes, particularly on winter ascents. There is no doubt about its novelty, but is it a good thing? That is a different question; my point is that evolution has occurred.

It must be recognized that young climbers have no other course open to them if they are to find new routes. If they renounced the use of artificial means and relied solely on human willpower, for example, it would become impossible to climb really big overhangs. In other words, recent advances in mountaineering have very often been due to the application of outcrop techniques.

To sum up, then, we can say that the great achievements of different epochs cannot be ranked, but that the evolution of technique and equipment makes it possible nowadays to surmount difficulties which would have been insuperable by earlier means.

This brings us to the question of the future. Leaving expeditions to distant ranges out of account, what is going to happen to the competition when the Alps have been fully worked out?

So far as human performance is concerned there is of course never any fixed limit, but when, as in climbing, we deal with the sort of achievement in which the human factor is only one of several, it is possible to foresee an approximate limit being attained. So when all the great lines in the Alps have been climbed in all conditions, what will remain for new generations? Heckmair has given me an answer in a recent letter. In his view, competition is not the *primum mobile* of mountaineering. I will go further, and say that it cannot be. Mountaineering is so rich in possibilities that it cannot be assessed merely through the medium of the stop-watch like so many other sports. Each generation will discover the mountains for itself and will find outlets for human performances other than in first ascents. Apart from his own discovery, anyone who climbs the north face of the Matterhorn, for example, will always find joy in remembering the adventures of others, and by virtue of treading the stage of earlier exploits will become an actor in his own right.

Apart from his own exceptional first ascents, Walter Bonatti repeated all the routes on and around the Brenva face of Mont Blanc, often alone. The pages of his book dealing with various ascents of the Route Major, for example, are full of serenity and enthusiasm. Although he knew every detail of the climb, each occasion brought with it something unexpected and new. Armand Charlet, who climbed the Aiguille Verte a hundred times by all its faces and ridges, found the same thing. It is in this total encounter with the mountain that satisfaction lies for climbers who have something more in their heads than mere performance. The solution is subjective, and each individual will find it in his own feelings and reactions.

To achieve this state of mind can be a difficult step, but anyone who takes it can be said to have a lover's understanding of the mountains which marks him indelibly. Gaston Rébuffat once told me that he felt as much happiness on the ordinary route of the Aiguille de l'M as on the Walker. This may seem surprising to some, but is in fact normal in a mountaineer who has grown out of the spirit of competition and is sensitive to the real joys of the sport wherever they may be found.

This then is the form that our adventure will take in the future. Without going so far as to say that mountaineering needs to be rediscovered entirely, I think it is clear that the hunger for performance at all costs does the sport little good, as witness certain climbs of recent years which aroused so much controversy that the actual achievement was almost forgotten. So let us finish with a paradox: although evolution in all sports will always tend towards higher performance, it will not be so in mountaineering. Though new techniques make possible harder routes, they do not change the fact that in certain conditions a repetition may be harder than a first ascent. One day performance will be held in check for lack of an objective, so that only the climber's human qualities come into play, and these do not change. All of which amounts to saying that mountaineering is far more than just a game or a sport: it is a great and beautiful adventure.

CHAPTER XIX

In Memoriam

ONCE AGAIN THE mountains had taken away our friends, leaving us to suffer their loss. Once again it was Mont Blanc that had struck. As they fought their way over the top of the Route Major, noblest of climbs, Bernard was exhausted by the struggle against the unchained elements. Petit Claude sacrificed himself to remain beside him; then, after his death, battled on up the ridge that led to the summit and the Vallot hut, only to die in his turn. Their passing seemed not so much to perpetuate our too-frequent grief as to change something in our common enthusiasm. Memories are for those who remain behind. I wish only to salute them and the lesson they taught us.

As I watched over my brother's body in my chalet I thought of our ascent to the Vallot hut a month earlier and of the immense pain he must have felt there in the ridge, longing to reach it. The future would seem empty without him but for the lesson of his courage, so that, like Antoine, Pierre and the others, his presence will only grow with time. And so I thank him for the manner of his going. No other death could have taken him: he was destined to the mountain.

Courmayeur, 24th February 1967. Through the window of the Guides' Office I looked up past the Mont Checrouit to the Peuterey Ridge of Mont Blanc. Beside me stood a woman in tears; behind us lay the body of her husband, Gigi Panei. Like a message of faith and love of the mountains, his face still bore the smile we knew. Caught in the waves of an avalanche with a young companion, he must have fought to the end. No doubt he foresaw the outcome, since he had dedicated his life, a story of self-sacrifice and goodness. Now he lies at rest in Courmayeur, but tomorrow, when we stand on other summits, he will continue to speak to us. The voice will not sound sad but full of hope, like the voice of one who, from above, wishes only to go on giving.

From the wall of my chalet, the photographs of my dead

friends speak to me. They have become irreproachable. Is it death that confers this privilege? The solidarity that bound us together in the face of impending disaster still binds us in memory. From Jean Couzy to John Harlin, how many of my friends have been killed! They were all quite different from each other but alike in their human nobility, which, as Saint-Exupéry remarked, is also that of the saints. I who write am no author, but I dedicate these lines to them. Their message is infinite, and I hope that mine too may find some echo, my love of the mountains be shared by others, my passion be understood. Above all I would desire to convey that there is no ending; that the mountains, like life, are there to be accepted and loved and assumed into our very being.

CHAPTER XX

Chomolungma

IN FEBRUARY 1970 I received a letter from Norman Dyhrenfurth asking if I would be interested in joining an international
expedition which he would be leading to Mount Everest the
following year. It would be difficult to imagine a more fantastic proposition for any climber to receive, and I immediately
answered yes. Is there any mountaineer who has not longed to
visit the Himalayas? So far no Frenchman had stood on that
fateful, 8847 metre summit. Might I be the first?

Immediately I plunged into the abundant literature concerning previous expeditions to the mountain, learning about
Dyhrenfurth from the account of the American expedition
of 1963. I also began to prepare myself morally and physically
for this culmination of my climbing career.

One year later, in February 1971, the twenty or so members
of the expedition left Frankfurt for Katmandu. Two members
were missing: Don Whillans, held up in Manchester by a
lecture tour, and myself, with preparations to make for the
municipal elections. On 7th March I said goodbye to my
father and my wife at Orly. As I settled myself into my seat,
there was time at last to start worrying. Would I be able to
rise to the occasion? Would I prove capable of seizing the
fantastic chance that was being offered to me? Supported by
companions of the highest calibre, many of whom I knew
already, acclimatized by the approach march and determined
to go any length to achieve the goal, it seemed that I should
be able to reach the summit of the highest and most beautiful
mountain in the world.

Changing aeroplanes at Frankfurt, I met Don Whillans.
It was a meeting without warmth. Ten years earlier, the dramatic outcome of our attempt on the Pillar of Fresnay had
incited him to take the first opportunity to make the ascent,
a fact which I had never been able to forget.

At Katmandu we were met by Mike, an assistant of James
Roberts, and taken to the Hotel Shankar, the gathering point

of all expeditions. I spent the next two days alone seeing the sights of Katmandu and surroundings, my mind constantly wandering to the fabulous chain of mountains which seemed to bar the horizon. Riding around on a bicycle, I passed a number of young Europeans seated on the pavements. They had come here to pursue the hippy adventure to its source.

On 10th March a Pilatus aeroplane took us to Lukla, a magnificent flight offering views of the Himalayan range including, at last, Mount Everest, or, to give it its proper name, Chomolungma. What a mountain! My wildest ideas fell far short of the reality. It dominates the whole range, casting its spell over you immediately, so that you develop a physical need to come to grips with it which lasts all through the approach march.

After flying over some of the foot-hills, the plane landed at Lukla, where a short strip of level ground can be used by aeroplanes in fine weather. Around the airstrip clustered a few houses. This was the real Nepal, and as we clambered out of the aeroplane we were greeted with smiles and extreme kindness. Dyhrenfurth was there too with several BBC cameramen who filmed our arrival, the first shots of a film which should have finished on the top of Chomolungma but never got there and never will.

Here, then, we joined in the marvellous approach-march. Everything around was beautiful, from the 7000 metre peaks to the narrow valley into which we descended via a track which was just like an Alpine path. Although we were still in the dry season, a torrent raged through the bottom of it. The scale of everything was as unexpectedly grandiose as that of the range itself. That evening we caught up with the rest of the expedition. It was a pleasure to see Carlo Mauri and Yvette and Michael Vaucher again. I was to share good and bad times with them in the days ahead. Our enthusiasm was identical. There too were Hiebeler, Axt, Schlömmer, Surdel, Haston and all the others.

From now on nothing counted but the immediate future. Our life in Europe with all its cares faded into the background; it was not until mid-April that I learnt the result of the municipal elections. Our minds were totally set on the single goal of Chomolungma.

Carlo and I shared a tent, chatting far into the night about our common memories. I was avid to know how the expedition was working out. He reassured me that everything was in proportion to our hopes.

The approach march was long and strenuous, exactly what was needed to bring us into condition. I felt well and happy. Ahead of us trudged the porters and Sherpas, wonderful people of incredible strength. Men and women of any age could trot with a load of 30 kilos and more. Their devotion was total, and it was easy to see how no expedition could hope to succeed without them. Some of them had a few words of French, souvenirs of the expeditions to Annapurna, Makalu and Jannu. Behind them plodded those known as the sahibs, i.e. ourselves; and so the kilometres slipped by, climbing, descending, and climbing again. We reached Namche Bazar, an astonishing village set down on the mountainside. There is hardly a book on the Himalayas which does not speak of this tiny capital perched at over 4000 metres. Already one could sense the nearness of the Tibetan world. Our passing created a certain stir. The inhabitants crowded around, offering a thousand and one souvenirs for sale. Commerce was to be our last contact with civilization.

In the distance Samagartha—the Nepalese name for Everest, Chomolungma being Tibetan—lorded it over Nuptse and Lhotse. As we marched on, we passed innumerable small pyramids called "chortens" painted with Buddhist eyes, and prayer-stones inscribed with the words "om mani padme hum" as though generations of monumental masons had spent their lives carving nothing else. Then, set down in a dream landscape, we came to the quietly beautiful monastery of Thyangboche, the highest of all Buddhist shrines. The saffron-coloured robes of the monks struck a gay note in the severe landscape. On one side rose Kantega, on the other Ama Dablam, which some people say is the most beautiful mountain in the world. Behind, obsessive and fascinating, the summit of Chomolungma reared up from behind the grandiose southern walls of Nuptse and Lhotse. These walls of ice and snow are almost 4000 metres high. We stayed at Thyangboche for several days in order to acclimatize, and this also gave us time to get to know each other better. Carlo and I were allowed to attend a religious ceremony in the temple, the atmosphere of which is deeply impressive.

In due course the expedition quit this lovely knoll and moved on into a very different world. Henceforward there was no more vegetation, and we slowly climbed up towards base camp through a landscape of utter bleakness. The only signs of life were a few dwellings and the occasional herd of yaks or goats. Around us now were peaks of 7000 metres. Incessant wind and cold would seem to be the invariable lot of those who cross the Pheriche plain. The altitude was beginning to have an effect also. Cackling over some joke in the night, Carlo and I had to roll out of the tent gasping for breath. After this warning we found that each movement must be slow, each gesture measured if we wanted to avoid feelings of suffocation. The views of the west ridge of Makalu were splendid, and I wished I could be there two months later to see the French expedition climbing it.

We stopped again at the hovel called Lobuje, and once more, for the last time, at Goratchep, where the names of those who had not returned from Chomolungma were carved on an imposing slab. From there on we marched along the immense moraine of the Khumbu Glacier, and at last on the glacier itself. It was a long day, but at the end of it we were able to set up our base-camp. What with sahibs, Sherpas and porters it was a veritable village, swarming with life. Red tents sprang up everywhere. On all sides there were conversations in practically every language under the sun. Somehow, now that we were face-to-face with our objective, there was an urge to move fast. A feverish feeling superseded the thoughtful trance of the last few days.

How would we find the ice-fall, the major obstacle of the Khumbu Glacier? Eight hundred metres high and inclined at an average angle of 40 degrees, it seemed in a particularly complicated state this year. The gigantic crevasses yawned, and the multitude of ice-towers looked like an unstable forest. The fact that our mountain was still hidden, now that we were longing to see it, only made us the more restless. At sunset Pumori seemed to catch fire. Everything here was of a cold and grandiose beauty.

Carlo and I were used to each other by now, and spent much of the time in our tent. We did not speak a lot, but when we did it was of the summit.

As we prepared for the assault down at Base Camp we often

had what Dyhrenfurth called "meetings". Our leader would sit there with his deputy James Roberts at his side, explaining his point of view. He let it be understood that he would not interfere in the course of operations since our own experience was adequate to cope with all eventualities. The most he would do would be to offer bits of advice stemming from his previous knowledge of the terrain, since he had led the American expedition in 1963. The only thing he asked was that each of us should desire to reach the summit and have the conviction that he was going to do so. All this served to confirm what I had read: Dyhrenfurth never took a decision.

One thing, however, had been decided in advance, and had even formed part of the terms on which we were engaged. This was that there were to be two objectives, namely the first ascent of the south face and the repetition of the west ridge.

Each of us had made his own choice of route. Those who wanted above all to reach the summit, including the Italian Carlo Mauri, the Swiss Yvette and Michel Vaucher, the Austrian Wolfgang Axt, the Indian Harsch Bahuguna, the Norwegians Odd Eliassen and Jon Teigland, the Polish cameraman Jerzy Surdel, the American David Isles and myself, had chosen the west ridge with the approval of the expedition leader. The others, consisting of the Anglo-American team and two Japanese climbers (one of whom, Naomi Uemura, had already been to the summit by the ordinary route), led by the exceptional mountaineer Dougal Haston, had opted for the south face and the modern techniques of fixed ropes and Jumars. There was no question of competition between the two groups. Each had its own programme, and as far as Camp 2 we should all be working together to force the ice-fall. Michel Vaucher was given the job of co-ordinating this first part of the assault, which took place at the end of March.

So began our struggle with the greatest giant of them all. At this stage no one was thinking in terms of national rivalry; on the contrary, we used the climbing of the ice-fall as an opportunity to observe each others' techniques, and I had occasion to rope up with Carlo, Michel, Naomi, John Evans and Odd Eliassen.

The first day, Dougal, Carlo and the Japanese found the best place to tackle the ice-fall and worked out a route through a maze of séracs and crevasses. Next day Michel and I pushed on to over 5000 metres, but in view of the difficulties and dangers of our line Wolfgang decided to look for a better one and duly succeeded. We were thus able to set up an advanced camp which we called "the Dump". This consisted of two tents and all the equipment which the Sherpas carried daily up the cataract of ice, murmuring prayers as they did so. The trickier places were embellished with metal ladders and tree-trunks brought up from Namche Bazar, but we were remark-ably lucky to have no accidents at this stage. Tottering seracs up to 30 metres high overhung the route, but by some miracle they only seemed to fall at night. Every expedition to the Nepalese side of Mount Everest has unpleasant memories of the Khumba ice-fall, but usually they have been able to deal with it fairly fast. Perhaps because there had not been a lot of snow the winter before, 1971 seemed to be a particularly bad year, and altogether it took us almost a fortnight to com-plete this operation. From the Dump to Camp 1 the vertical height was 300 metres, every one of them delicate and danger-ous. The altitude was making itself felt, and parties relayed each other. One night at the Dump, after a hard day, I was seized with headaches and vomiting due to lack of oxygen. It was impossible to keep any food down at all. Wondering if I was going to get through the night, I dosed myself as best I could with aspirin. John Evans and Jerzy Surdel looked after me with wonderful kindness. In the morning I drove myself to follow them up, but in the end my state was such that Jon Teigland had to escort me back to Base Camp. Without realizing it, I had used up too much energy. This came as a great surprise as I was on excellent form, but I had yet to learn the extent to which one must economize one's efforts at these altitudes. It is quite different from anything we know in the Alps, where speed counts above all. In the Himalayas, on the contrary, one must go slowly in order to last out.

Back at Base Camp Carlo and Michel found me tired, and Dyhrenfurth insisted that I take two or three days' rest. Dougal, Carlo, Naomi and Reiso reached the top of the ice-fall after a lot of trouble with the final séracs. These were only to get worse as time went on. The glacier was advancing at up to two metres per day, and everything was in movement. Some of the crevasses over which we had put bridges opened so wide that the logs and ladders fell in too deeply to be recovered. Camp 1 was pitched at the edge of the Western Cwm, and we took turns to go up for several nights in order to acclimatize. Some of us fell ill, so that there were constant comings and goings between Camp 1 and Base. The Sherpas continued their infernal round, carrying 15 and 20 kilo loads which we prepared for them. Meanwhile other teams pushed farther up the Cwm, and after several kilometres Camp 2, the real Advanced Base, was established at about 6500 metres.

When my turn came to go up there with Naomi, I saw the same fabulous vision as my companions who had preceded me. Shortly after leaving Camp 1 it was necessary to traverse across under the north face of Nuptse in order to avoid some gigantic crevasses. This implied some risk of avalanche, but the face was so steep that only powder-snow avalanches were to be feared, and in the circumstances these were unlikely to be very big. In the course of this traverse the south face of Everest was suddenly revealed. There are no words which can convey the impression it created. Perfectly pyramidal in form, it rose in splendour infinitely high to where, just at the point, a small cloud trailed out towards the Cwm. Each time we see a sight of astonishing beauty we are apt to think it the finest of all, but I can say that I have never felt a stronger emotion than at that moment when I suddenly saw the summit of the world towering 3000 metres above me. At the end of the glacier rose the majestic form of Lhotse where I could pick out the ordinary route, the Geneva spur and the south col above it. Our thoughts went out to the triumph of Hillary and Tenzing, and to the struggles of those who had followed them. Naomi told me about his ascent with the Japanese expedition a year earlier; he had reached the summit on 11 May and the monsoon had broken a day later. As we walked on up we met Carlo coming the other way. He was tired, and was going down to Base for a few days' rest before the final assault on the ridge.

At Camp 2 the two teams were preparing to go their separate ways. From the group for the ridge there were Wolfgang, Harsch and Odd, and from the south-face group Dougal and Don. I wanted to help set up Camp 3 the following day, but Harsch advised against this. As he had considerable Himalayan experience, and had already been to Everest two years earlier with an Indian expedition which had failed on account of bad weather, I accepted his opinion that I should wait a day while

he and Odd set up the camp. This gave me the opportunity
to go with Dougal and Naomi to the foot of the south face, a
couple of hours from the camp. While they continued, I made
my way up to the end of the Western Cwm where I took a lot
of photographs and felt happy to be alone at 7000 metres.
Slowly, economizing my movements, I then returned to camp.
I felt fit, and it seemed that nothing more stood between us and
the realization of our dream. I felt sure of reaching the summit.

Back in camp I watched Odd and Harsch trying to climb
an ice-gully to reach the west ridge. Their progress was desperately slow, and I felt disturbed. When they got back they
stoutly defended the advantages of their line. I replied that
I thought it a mistake, and that the shoulder on the left would
offer a safer route, even if somewhat longer. Vaucher, who had
just come up with some of the others from Camp 1 carrying
a load of oxygen bottles, was of the same opinion as myself.

There was never enough to eat on that expedition, and
none of us got any meat for over two months. There were also
not enough Sherpas to carry loads from Camp 1 to Camp 2, so
finding ourselves short of food and equipment Naomi, myself
and several others went down to Base, where Carlo was waiting.
Dyhrenfurth agreed that we should go up again for the final
assault in three days' time.

It was good to be back down at 5300 metres. One felt so well.
There was post waiting for us and also copies of *Le Monde*,
sent on by the French ambassador, in which I read the results
of the municipal elections. I wrote a lot of optimistic letters
saying that we should reach the summit about 10th May. We
basked on rocks in the morning sunlight, and as it often
snowed in the afternoon we slept in our tents. After supper,
with the help of sleeping pills, we would sleep again. In the
rare intervals between sleeping, we shot a few scenes with the
BBC cameramen. Carlo, who speaks excellent French, told
me stories about his expeditions with Bonatti to Gasherbrum
IV and the Cerro Torre, and also about his maritime adventures on Thor Heyerdahl's Râ. The lack of a good square meal
made us dream of monster steaks with salads to match and—
Carlo was emphatic about this—cherries. In Italy they would
soon be in season. Thus we rested 24 hours a day, and not
surprisingly we began to get bored. As soon as we felt really
rested, therefore, we were impatient to get going.

Carlo and I set off in company with the doctor, Peter Steele. The bad pitches in the ice-fall gave us exactly the same sensations as before, and we were glad to reach Camp 1 where we spent the evening listening to Beethoven symphonies on Peter's cassette player. Next day we went on up to Camp 2, where our little Karrimor tent suddenly seemed rather cramped after all this relative luxury.

On 18th April the weather deteriorated. Through occasional gaps in the murk we could see Harsch and Wolfgang Axt on the shoulder leading to the west ridge. They had been doing a lot of work, having set up Camp 3 the day before; their intention this day had been to reconnoitre a sight for Camp 4. As the afternoon wore on a blizzard began to blow, and suddenly disaster struck. Wolfgang staggered into camp with the news that Harsch was hanging exhausted from some ropes that Michel had previously fixed across a long traverse. Fearing the worst, we immediately prepared to go to his aid. The wind was now blowing at over 100 kilometres per hour, freezing us to the bone and dashing snow into our eyes with such force that it was hard to see anything. Don, Michel and Odd nevertheless literally set off running, while Peter Steele and I followed more slowly. It was too late. Our friend was dead of exposure at nearly 7000 metres, his body attached to the rope by a karabiner which he had not had the strength to open.

The gathering darkness obliged us to descend, leaving Harsch in his sanctuary. We stumbled back to camp through the storm overcome with grief, and in the big tent where we gathered each evening there was silence and consternation as we thought of our poor comrade. The blizzard rose to still greater violence, shrieking through the Western Cwm as though to intensify the painfulness of our emotions. It was to remain thus for a week.

The following morning we were shocked and angered to be questioned by Dyhrenfurth with the BBC sound engineer working away at his side. He wanted to absolve Wolfgang of blame; as though any of us could have imagined him guilty in any way! Nevertheless, I could not agree with Don's verdict that Harsch was responsible for his own death, having exhausted himself by overwork. It is the job of an expedition leader to direct and apportion everybody's efforts.

In the course of a lull Michel, Don, Odd, Carlo and I went up with several Sherpas to bring down the body of our friend.

Thus a funeral procession began at 7000 metres which was to finish at Goratchep with one more name engraved on the slab that carries the names of those who have died on Chomolungma.

We lay long hours in our tents, with only the traditional tea to recall us to reality, while outside the snow was driven ceaselessly by the gale. Even inside several sleeping bags we remained cold. Over the walky-talky we learnt of Hiebeler's decision to return to Europe. He was the first of several victims of altitude; later Odd and some of the cameramen had to descend to Base. A few of us held on in the hell that was Camp 2 until we ran out of food and gas, after which we had to return to Camp 1 for the supplies which the Sherpas had left. Both the descent and the climb back up were exhausting, some of the gusts being so strong that they knocked us flat. We knelt in the snow with our hands raised to protect ourselves.

Dave Petterson brought up our post from Base Camp. Letters from Paris told me of the unfortunate polemics following Desmaison's winter attempt to make a new route to the left of the Walker spur on the north face of the Grandes Jorasses, in the course of which his companion died of exposure. Certain unpleasant articles went so far as to hint that the cause of the tragedy was René's thirst for publicity. These cruel suggestions at a time of grief showed how little their authors knew of the best climber in France. I had seen René at the hospital in Chamonix just before setting out for Everest, and he had begged me to be careful with tears in his eyes.

So time went by, and as the weather remained impossible and the Sherpas were paralysed by the disaster which had occurred, we came to a decision which was to have a crucial effect on the future of the expedition. In the circumstances there seemed little hope of climbing the 5 kilometre west ridge, so the west-ridge party changed its objective to the usual route via the south col. In this we were unanimous except for David Isles, who was in any case obliged by illness to go back to Thyangboche. The expedition leader regretted our decision but agreed to help, and asked Michel to direct operations. Knowing that the technical difficulties were not great we regained hope. With a little help from the weather, it should only take us a few days to realize our desire to see the Indian flag fluttering from the summit of Everest, a cherished dream of our missing friend.

On 28th April the tent was suddenly touched by the rays of the sun. We hurriedly squirmed out; the sight was fantastic. The weather was perfect, and everything was coated in white. Already the powder-snow avalanches were seaming the south face of Everest and pouring down the couloirs of Lhotse and Nuptse. Dyhrenfurth thought that we should try to set up Camp 3 the same day, so Yvette, Odd, myself and several Sherpas including Kancha—who was happy to be revisiting the south col and hoped to have a try for the summit, which he had been foiled of twice—set off rapidly. Naomi and Reiso were also setting off to resume their patient work on the south face. The knee-deep snow, the altitude and a hot sun made progress slow and halts frequent. Curiously enough, we suffered more from heat than from cold during our time in the Himalayas. Presently the Japanese turned off to cross their rimaye while we continued on to the end of the Cwm. Here we found a way through the seracs and began to climb the first slopes of the Lhotse face. A thousand metres above and to the left was the south col. Odd stopped exhausted, so I took over the tent he was carrying. Thus heavily loaded and with Yvette behind me on exceptional form, I reached the site of Camp 3 at 7150 metres. While Kancha and the other Sherpas were getting up the tents I looked up the face. It seemed certain that the major difficulties were over. We should have to fix a few ropes between here and Camp 4 higher up the Lhotse face. Then, following the route taken by other expeditions, we would traverse across to the top of the Geneva Spur and from there easily reach the south col and the site of Camp 5 at 8000 metres. Last would come the ridge and the summit. It was like a wild hope, yet we felt absolutely certain of victory. We descended happily, already envisaging setting out again next day with oxygen to go faster.

Back at Camp we received news which affected our whole group. Michel had to return to Base with a suspected phlebitis, and Yvette went with him. Odd, who was worn out, also had to go down, and Carlo and I remained alone to set up Camp 4 and reach the south col, where we hoped the others would rejoin us for the final push. Next day we prepared all the equipment for the assault. Standing in burning sunlight we discussed the remainder of the route with Dyhrenfurth, picking out all the details through binoculars as he explained where the Americans had gone in 1963. We made no secret of our enthusiasm and our will to succeed. By early afternoon everything, including the flags of our countries, was packed into our sacks.

About 4 o'clock, as we lay resting happily, the expedition leader came into our tent. He said that our companions on the south face were having a difficult time and wanted us to give up our project to support them. We could hardly believe our ears. Give up at this stage?

Nevertheless, that evening everything was confirmed. A meeting was held in the big tent. The south-face group was there almost in its entirety; Carlo and I were the only representatives of ours. There were also Dyhrenfurth and the Sherpas. The discussion which followed was scarcely believable and marked the beginning of our disillusion. Don Whillans announced that there could be no question of anyone climbing the ordinary route, which he considered unworthy of mountaineers of our calibre. We replied that it was important for the prestige of the expedition for someone to reach the summit. Supported by John Evans and Dave Petterson, Whillans then gave an account of the difficulties of the face and insisted that we should all help by carrying up loads of food and equipment so that the summit team, i.e. himself, could reach its goal. In other words, he wanted us to act as porters. This idea was unanimously approved by the others, and there was even applause when Dyhrenfurth adopted it as his decision and informed us that the second objective would now be dropped from the programme. In any case, he said, the ordinary route was now impossible—this despite the fact that a few hours before he had been urging exactly the opposite, and that we all knew in our hearts that the ordinary route was in fact the only one that now offered any chance of success, as the future was to prove. Polite discussion was soon abandoned, and we became a target for rude names on the part of the Anglo-Saxons, who considered us selfish and lacking in team spirit. Only the British were to be given a chance of reaching the summit; and when the BBC men, notably Cleare, announced that they had no intention of filming anything but a British victory, we got up and left the meeting without comment. The only one who had not contributed to the argument, no doubt out of feelings of friendship, was Dougal. Even the Sherpas were against us. No further dialogue was possible.

Disappointed, uncomprehending, almost in tears, we went back to our tent. All our hopes had vanished, all our efforts had been for nothing. The reality was unveiled in all its bitterness and disillusionment. Neither Carlo nor I had ever undergone such moral suffering. It was a pity that our Swiss and Japanese friends had not been present, but the former were at Base Camp, the latter up on the face. We both wondered what Bonatti would have done in the circumstances, but in the end we decided to go down next day. In the night I heard Carlo breathing like one in tears; my eyes were overflowing also. Sleep was impossible.

As we got ready to go down next morning, John Evans came and took away all the equipment we had carefully stacked outside the tent in preparation for the south col. Not a word from Dyhrenfurth or from any of the British or Americans. Only the Sherpas came over one by one, each repeating "I'm sorry" like a leitmotiv. Since they were being paid by the leader of the expedition, there was not much else they could do, but we were grateful for their human feelings.

As we turned back to look at Chomolungma towering 3000 metres over the Western Cwm, a fresh wave of sadness swept over us. At Camp 1 we found a card from Michel saying: "Have carried up all the kit you need. Wish you success". When we reached Base Camp that afternoon there was complete consternation. Yvette and Michel were incredulous, the Norwegians refused to accept the decision, Wolfgang decided not to go back up to Camp 2.

Worried about our attitude, Dyhrenfurth came back down to Base Camp. We had another futile discussion, but although our arguments were all aimed at the success of his expedition they fell on deaf ears. He had made up his mind to support the British point of view. Finally, recognizing that his case would not hold water, he disclosed the real grounds for his attitude: he was tied to the BBC, and was in fact without authority. It was imperative that the summit should be reached by British climbers, and if Yvette had become the first woman to climb the highest mountain in the world it would have eclipsed their success. The press and world public opinion attach little importance to the particular route followed up a mountain. To them it is the summit that counts, and the Swiss girl would have captured all the publicity. The reader can imagine the extent of our resentment and disillusion.

Seeing that we were all determined to stand or fall together, Dyhrenfurth withdrew, stating that he would think things over; then, apparently unconcerned about any reputation for cowardice he might acquire, sent his friend James Roberts to dismiss us from the expedition. The latter was only interested in the south-face project. In this way he consolidated the position of his company "Mountain Travel" as supplier of Sherpas to future expeditions.

We left Base Camp on 2nd May. A few friends turned out to say goodbye, notably some Sherpas and the TV-film director Antoine Thomas. And so we set off back along the trail up which we had marched with such high hopes a short while before. It was like a rout—a shipwreck, said Carlo—as the two Vauchers, Mauri and myself turned away from the mountain, all thinking the same thoughts. Our contest had sadly fizzled out there under Pumori, at the beginning of the long Khumbu Glacier. As we passed Lobuje we were already beginning to think of the future, consoling ourselves with the idea that we might come back. That night our little retinue of Sherpas and porters pitched camp at Pheriche, and next day, as though to put as much ground as possible between us and the scene of our disappointment, we marched all the way to Namche Bazar with only a brief halt at Thyangboche. Everything around us seemed to have lost its beauty. The high summits faded behind us; we came down into narrow valleys. After a forced march of ten hours we reached Lukla the third evening.

In the morning we said goodbye to our Sherpa friends and climbed into the aeroplane. Behind me Yvette was crying, while Michel looked out of the porthole at Chomolungma, more majestic than ever. In my seat beside the pilot I resolved to return. My heart was set on renewing the struggle. At Katmandu we were greeted by a Reuter despatch broadcast by Dyhrenfurth from Base Camp saying that the expedition would be better off without us. We were apparently so incompetent that we had been a drag on the other climbers! One wondered how he had ever come to select us. Knowing our record the local press and all the foreign correspondents, including our friend Creiser of the *Figaro*, condemned him for the communiqué.

Not so much to forget our pain as to whet our appetites to return, we toured Katmandu. The Nepalese were kindness itself, as were the French ambassador and the helicopter pilot, Bernard Seguy, who was busy shuttling supplies to the team on Makalu. Our thoughts and wishes went out to them in their attempt to make this great first ascent, inspired and steadily supported by Lucien Devies.

Finally we took off for Europe. Though it was the end of what could have been a fine adventure, not all the memories were bad. At New Delhi we separated, Carlo—with whom I had shared so much joy, pain, hope, exaltation and bitterness— heading for Bombay, while I continued on to Paris.

I learnt of the failure of the expedition on 21st May. Instantly I felt regret for Dougal, a fine climber who had deserved success, and for Naomi, who had already climbed Chomolungma and the highest summits of every continent. But the judgement was heavy on Dyhrenfurth, whose expedition had ended in double failure when we could have given him a great victory. Above all, I felt in my heart the desire to return to the highest mountain on earth and to succeed.

Index

Compiled by H. E. Crowe

Comici, climber 39, 40, 194; ledges on Civetta 193; and Prusik loops 48; route on Cima Grande 179, 180; routes 39, 40, 104
Como, lake of 32, 34
Concord, chalet 172
Contamine, André 160
Contamine route of Aiguille du Midi 82; of Aiguille du Peigne 85, 87
Cordée européenne, Cima Grande film 176–81, 224; Trento prizewinning film 187; presented at Salle Pleyel 203
Cortina 39, 46, 53, 56, 61, 66, 72, 103, 155, 176, 179
Cortina Olympic Games 40
Cosmic Research Laboratory hut (Cosmiques) 157, 158, 160
Cosmiques, *see* Cosmic Research Laboratory
Couloir des Drus 76
Coupé, Serge 40
Coutin, climber 118
Courmayeur 35, 95, 96, 120, 138, 139, 153, 154, 170, 171, 182, 186, 208, 231
Courtet, Pierre 34
Couzy, Jean, Parisian climber 31, 38, 39, 41, 68, 100; death of 45, 232; route in Cima Ovest 181
Creiser, of *Figaro*, condemns Dyhrenfurth communiqué 247
Creton 27
Cristallo 72
Crozoli, doctor at Courmayeur 139
Cuvier, mountaineer 17

Dame Jeanne 17
Darbellay, Michel, French climber 169, 170, 203, 224, 227
Dassonville, Hélène, woman climber 103
Dauphiné 13
Deck, Claude, French climber 187
Demût ridge 60, 68, 71
Denis, Edmond 208
Dent du Géant 23
Desmaison, René, French climber 38–72 *passim*; on Cima Ovest ascent 47–72; 88–94 *passim*, 118, 139, 169, 179, 189, 242–6
Devies, Lucien 73, 215, 247
Dienberger, Kurt 154
Dijon 143
Dimai brothers 40
Direttissima of north face of Cima Grande *between pages* 80 and 81
Dobbiaco 46
Doigt d'Etala 29
Dolomites 29, 39, 46, 63, 70, 71, 79, 89, 97, 102, 119, 155, 183, 185, 188, 194; guide to 62
Dômes de Miage 83
Dreux, Philippe, climber 32, 36

Dru, the 24, 29, 30, 75, 95, 118, 136, 151, 173, 182, 210; Bonatti pillar 186; north face 76; west face 75, 76, 77, 79, 161
Dubois, Robert, French climber 32–8 *passim*
Duchesne, Belgian climber 42, 75–82 *passim*
Dumont, climber 27
Dump, the 238
Duplat, climber 77
Durand, Louis 40
Durier, the 208
Dyhrenfurth, Norman, leader of Everest expedition (1971) 233–45 *passim*; communiqué criticized 246–7; decisions criticized 242, 245

Echelle 45
Eckpfeiler buttress 122
Ecole de Haute Montagne 30
Ecole Militaire de Haute Montagne 27
Ecole Nationale d'Alpinisme 88, 90
Ecrins, les 32
Eggeler, climber 73
Egger, Toni 41
Egralets 30
Eiger 47, 95, 105, 129, 173, 182, 188, 203
Eigerwand 143, 182, 190, 212; ascent 183; German winter ascent 113
El Capitan 173
Electioneering 233
El Golea oasis 204
Eliassen, Odd, Norwegian climber 237, 239, 240, 242, 243
Ender, Wino 176, 179, 180, 186, 203
Engadine 103
Entrèves 149, 186, 218
En Vau 103
Ertaud, Jacques (Jackie) and ascent of The Hoggar 204, 208, 209, 216
Etter, Paul, Swiss climber, ascends Matterhorn 142, 143, 148
Evans, John 237, 238, 244, 245
Evêque, the 16
Everest expedition (1971) 233–47; disagreement on 244–5; failure of 247

Fauteuil des Allemands 36
Fédéracion Française de la Montagne 187
Ferrata, the 201 and n.
Ferré, Leo 103
Film work 114
Flores, Lito Tajda de 182, 187, 189
Fontainebleau 17, 18, 20n., 23, 25, 26, 27, 29, 87, 104, 154
Forbes ridge of Aiguille du Chardonnet 24
Forclaz, the 32